ORDNANCE SURVEY
LEISURE GUIDE
WESSEX

Produced jointly by the Publishing Division of the
Automobile Association and the Ordnance Survey

Cover: Salisbury Cathedral
Title page: Stonehenge – an ancient mystery
Contents page: Shop window, Salisbury
Introductory page: Burrow Mump, near Athelney

Editor: Antonia Hebbert

Copy Editor: Sue Gordon

Art Editor: Dave Austin

Design Assistant: Neil Roebuck

Editorial contributors: Martyn Brown (Gazetteer, Short Features, Rural Crafts); Derrick Charles (Directory); Stan Davies (Wessex Wildlife); Dr R. Dunning (Consultant, Duke of Monmouth and Prince of Orange); Andrew Lawson (The Ancient Landscape, Saxon Kingdom, Landscape Gardens); Charles Pettit (Thomas Hardy's Wessex); Ralph Robbins (Walks)

Picture researcher: Wyn Voysey

Original photography: Rich Newton

Typeset by Avonset, Midsomer Norton, Bath.
Printed in Great Britain by Chorley & Pickersgill Ltd, Leeds

Maps extracted from the Ordnance Survey's 1:625 000 Routeplanner Map, 1:25 000 Pathfinder Series and 1:250 000 Routemaster Series enlarged to a scale of 1:200 000, with the permission of Her Majesty's Stationery Office. Crown Copyright reserved.

Additions to the maps by the Cartographic Dept of the Automobile Association and the Ordnance Survey.

Produced by the Publishing Division of the Automobile Association.

Distributed in the United Kingdom by the Ordnance Survey, Southampton, and the Publishing Division of the Automobile Association, Fanum House, Basingstoke, Hampshire RG21 2EA.

The contents of this publication are believed correct at the time of printing. Nevertheless, the Publishers cannot accept responsibility for errors or omissions, or for changes in details given.

© The Automobile Association 1988
   The Ordnance Survey 1988

All rights reserved. No part of this publication may be reproduced, stored in a retrieval system, or transmitted in any form or by any means – electronic, mechanical, photocopying, recording, or otherwise – unless the written permission of the Publishers has been given beforehand.

AA ISBN 0 86145 668 8 (hardback)
AA ISBN 0 86145 658 0 (softback)
OS ISBN 0 31900 132 6 (hardback)
OS ISBN 0 31900 131 8 (softback)

Published by the Automobile Association and the Ordnance Survey.

AA ref: 50762 (hardback)
AA ref: 50759 (softback)

WESSEX
Contents

Using this Book 4
Saxon Kingdom 6
The Ancient Landscape 8
Wessex Wildlife 14
Thomas Hardy's Wessex 18
Rural Crafts 22
A to Z Gazetteer 27
Directory 75
Atlas 81
Wessex Tours 94
Walks in Wessex 102
Index 118

Using this Book

Each entry in the A to Z Gazetteer has the atlas page number on which the place can be found and its National Grid reference included under the heading. An explanation of how to use the National Grid is given on page 82.

Beneath many of the entries in the Gazetteer are listed AA-recommended hotels, restaurants, garages, guesthouses, camping sites and self-catering accommodation in the immediate vicinity of the place described. Hotels, restaurants and camp sites are also given an AA classification.

SELECTION ONLY
For some popular resorts, not all AA-recommended establishments can be included. For full details see current editions of the relevant AA annual guide and the AA Members' Handbook.

HOTELS

1-star	Good hotels and inns, generally of small scale and with acceptable facilities and furnishing.
2-star	Hotels offering a higher standard of accommodation, with some private bathrooms/shower; lavatories on all floors; wider choice of food.
3-star	Well-appointed hotels; a good proportion of bedrooms with private bathrooms/showers.
4-star	Exceptionally well-appointed hotels offering a high standard of comfort and service, the majority of bedrooms should have private bathrooms/showers.
5-star	Luxury hotels offering the highest international standards.

Hotels often satisfy *some* of the requirements for higher classifications than that awarded.

Red-star	Red stars denote hotels which are considered to be of outstanding merit within their classification.
Country House Hotel	A hotel where a relaxed informal atmosphere prevails. Some of the facilities may differ from those at urban hotels of the same classification.

RESTAURANTS

1-fork	Modest but good restaurant.
2-fork	Restaurant offering a higher standard of comfort than above.
3-fork	Well-appointed restaurant.
4-fork	Exceptionally well-appointed restaurant.
5-fork	Luxury restaurant.
1-rosette	Hotel or restaurant where the cuisine is considered to be of a higher standard than is expected in an establishment within its classification.
2-rosette	Hotel or restaurant offering very much above average food irrespective of the classification.
3-rosette	Hotel or restaurant offering outstanding food, irrespective of classification.

GUESTHOUSES
These are different from, but not necessarily inferior to, AA-appointed hotels, and they offer an alternative for those who prefer inexpensive and not too elaborate accommodation. They all provide clean, comfortable accommodation in homely surroundings. Each establishment must usually offer at least six bedrooms and there should be a general bathroom and a general toilet for every six bedrooms without private facilities.

Parking facilities should be reasonably close.

Other requirements include:
Well maintained exterior, clean and hygienic kitchens; good standard of furnishing; friendly and courteous service; access at reasonable times; the use of a telephone and full English breakfast.

SELF CATERING
These establishments, which are all inspected on a regular basis, have to meet minimum standards.

Full details are in the AA annual guide *Holiday Homes, Cottages and Apartments in Britain*.

CAMP SITES

1-pennant	Site licence; 10% of pitches for touring units; site density not more than 30 per acre; 2 separate toilets for each sex per 30 pitches; good quality tapwater; efficient waste disposal; regular cleaning of ablutions block; fire precautions; well-drained ground.
2-pennant	All one-pennant facilities plus: 2 washbasins with hot and cold water for each sex per 30 pitches in separate washrooms; warden available at certain times of the day.
3-pennant	All two-pennant facilities plus: one shower or bath for each sex per 30 pitches, with hot and cold water; electric shaver points and mirrors; all-night lighting of toilet blocks; deep sinks for washing clothes; facilities for buying milk, bread and gas; warden in attendance by day, on call by night.
4-pennant	All three-pennant facilities plus: a higher degree of organisation than one–three-pennant sites; attention to landscaping; reception office; late-arrivals enclosure; first aid hut; shop; routes to essential facilities lit after dark; play area; bad weather shelter; hard standing for touring vans.
5-pennant	A comprehensive range of services and equipment; careful landscaping; automatic laundry; public telephone; indoor play facilities for children; extra facilities for recreation; warden in attendance 24 hours per day.

WESSEX Introduction

The ancient kingdom of King Alfred and the inspiration of Thomas Hardy, Wessex today is a region of historic towns and idyllic villages, set in beautiful countryside and fringed by glorious coasts. This book explores Dorset, Wiltshire, Avon and the greater part of Somerset, together with Winchester, King Alfred's capital city. As well as comprehensive coverage of places to visit, it includes feature articles on the region's extraordinary prehistoric sites, its wildlife and rural crafts, and on its special place in the novels and poems of Thomas Hardy. Also here are walks, drives and a Directory of practical information. Backed by the AA's research expertise and the Ordnance Survey's mapping, this guide is for those who know and love the area, and for those discovering it for the first time.

Saxon Kingdom

Winchester's Broadway is dominated by the statue of King Alfred. It is a proud reminder that following the defeat of the Vikings at Edington in AD878 the ruler of Wessex had laid the foundations for a united England, with Winchester as its capital.

In the 5th century the Romans recalled their legionary army from England. With the removal of this cornerstone of their civilisation, governmental administration collapsed, leaving the Angles, Saxons, Jutes and other groups, originally from Germanic Europe, to take control. Many of these people had been introduced by the Romans to support their troops, but others arrived in raiding and land-seeking parties. From eastern England their forces spread westwards, meeting resistance from Romanised Britons, such as Ambrosius Aurelianus and perhaps the leader called Arthur. This is poorly documented as the Germanic peoples were largely non-literate: only later accounts by men of the Church and archaeological evidence create the historical framework of the 'Dark Ages'. In the 6th century at least 15 small kingdoms were created throughout England. Following the taking of Old Sarum (Salisbury) by Cynric in AD552, the area south of the Thames headwaters, including much of modern Avon, Gloucestershire and Somerset, Dorset, all of Wiltshire and much of Hampshire and Berkshire became Wessex. During the 7th and 8th centuries, at the same time as the formerly pagan rulers of the kingdoms came to accept Christianity, three English kingdoms (Northumbria, Mercia, and

Wessex) became dominant. But in the late 8th and 9th centuries none escaped the raids and later concerted attacks of the Vikings. By the 870s these Danes controlled most of Northumbria and East Anglia. However, their westward advance into Wessex was repulsed by Alfred, who drove Gudrum back to the line of the Watling Street Roman road. Alfred's successors, Edward the Elder and then Athelstan, later restored the lost lands and by AD937 controlled all England. This sovereignty was later overcome by further Danish invasions and the Norman Conquest, but it was the dominance of Wessex that had established a cohesive national kingdom.

Unsettled times

Villages, royal palaces and cemeteries of this period have been excavated by archaeologists (for example, near Andover, at Cheddar and Clarendon Park, and near Salisbury respectively). Many fascinating finds fill museum exhibitions, but apart from a few barrows little visible trace of their sites is left in the landscape. Only from the 9th century is the evidence from towns and churches more easily discerned.

In such unsettled times the need for fortification was strong. Linear earthworks, such as the Wansdyke in Wiltshire, or Bokerley Dyke between Dorset and Hampshire, defended boundaries. Earlier Iron Age hillforts, such as those at South Cadbury and Cadbury Congresbury in Somerset, were refurbished to serve as military bases. Some surviving Roman towns, such as Bath, Dorchester, Ilchester and Winchester, already possessed defensive circuits, but under Alfred's strategy other important towns were fortified with earthen ramparts. These new defensive 'burhs' can be seen at Cricklade, Shaftesbury, Langport, or best of all at Wareham in Dorset.

The skill of building in durable stone had been lost with the demise of Roman influence. However, masonry buildings were reintroduced with the acceptance of Christianity. The See of Sherborne, for example, was established by AD704 and some fragments of an early cathedral can still be seen within the later abbey. But other minster churches, such as that at Breamore, near Fordingbridge, show better the features of Anglo-Saxon ecclesiastical architecture. However, nowhere has the zeal for church-building been more graphically demonstrated than in Winchester.

Left: the conspicuous landmark of Glastonbury Tor, linked by tradition with King Arthur.
Inset: King Alfred's statue in Winchester, capital of England in his reign. Below: the legendary Round Table of King Arthur and his knights hangs in Winchester

An archway in the transept of Glastonbury abbey church, a Saxon foundation

Here, extensive archaeological excavations have revealed the phases of enlargement and remodelling of the Old Minster from the mid-7th century, and the building, literally abutting it, of the New Minster from the early 10th century. Similar fervour is seen in other Christian centres such as Glastonbury and Wells. Much more modest, but no less enchanting, are the smaller chapels of the period at St Martin's, Wareham, or St Lawrence's, Bradford-on-Avon. By the time of the Norman Conquest, a system of parishes was long established, but only from the 12th century were built the medieval churches that form such a characteristic feature of the English landscape.

Domesday Book of AD1086, which was compiled in Winchester, records for us the structure of society and the environment within which the people lived following the Norman Conquest. Lasting reminders of the innovations brought from Europe by the Normans survive throughout Wessex. Simple motte and bailey castles such as those at Sherrington, Cranborne or West Dean, or more important examples such as those at Montacute, Marlborough or Wareham, or ringwork castles such as those at Old Sarum, Devizes or Downton were the precursors of the imposing stone castles such as Corfe Castle, Sherborne, Mere, Old Wardour and Ludgershall, to mention but a few.

If the castles displayed the power of the new baronies, the cathedrals and monasteries displayed the influence of the Church in such buildings as Malmesbury, Milton Abbas, Muchelney, Sherborne and Winchester. One of the finest of England's cathedrals is at Salisbury, to the side of the new town planned and established by Bishop Roger in AD1220. Largely based on the fertility of its hinterland, but above all on the wool industry, Salisbury became the most successful new town of the Middle Ages. Such security led to the development of more refined building styles, many examples of which survive in the houses of Salisbury and in the individual homes of wealthy landowners throughout Wessex.

The Ancient Landscape

The nature of the Wessex countryside is best known through the novels of Thomas Hardy, who immortalised a scene of verdant, flowing downland. Because this traditional scene, with its small rural villages, dependent for their livelihood on the flocks that grazed the great swathes of upland grassland, remained unchanged for centuries, the pastures have preserved a vast number of ancient monuments, and arguably some of the finest archaeological landscapes in western Europe. In such landscapes ceremonial and settlement sites with fields are preserved. Examples of this preservation are best seen on the Dorset Ridge Way, the Marlborough Downs, or on Salisbury Plain. So numerous are the monuments that many, especially the most spectacular, have public access.

Ice Age evidence
The Wessex landscape was not always as Hardy described. Dramatic climatic changes during the Ice Ages caused changes in the plant and animal

populations as far apart as today's Arctic and African plains. As the climate changed the polar icecap and more local glaciers advanced and retreated. Although the glaciers reached the Thames Valley and the Bristol Channel, Wessex was not covered by them. Instead, the soft chalk that underlies much of the region was rounded and smoothed by meltwaters, the erosive effects of repeated deep freezing and thawing, and abrasive Arctic winds. This era of extreme climatic oscillation started more than 2,000,000 years ago, but the earliest trace of people in Britain dates from about 500,000 years ago, in the middle of the Ice Ages. At Westbury-sub-Mendip a rock fissure has been found to contain stone implements with the bones of small animals long extinct in Britain and probably dating from this remote period. Although groups of Eskimo-like hunters undoubtedly roamed the Wessex downland during the Ice Ages, the erosion of the landscape has swept away virtually all traces of their camps. However, stone implements of the period are frequently found, at times in great abundance in the stoney gravels of both valley floors and uplands. Only where the archaeological deposits have been protected from erosion, such as in caves, are we able to study, from their discarded tools and rubbish, the way in which people lived. Dating from the final cold phase of the last Ice Age are the traces which have been found at the Hyaena Den, Wookey, while slightly later are the flint and bone implements from Gough's Cave, Cheddar and Aveline's Hole in the edge of the Mendip plateau.

By 10,000BC the glaciers had disappeared and the climate was improving. England was still joined to the Continent and groups of people could move to and fro exploiting the rapidly developing forests that came to occupy virtually all of southern Britain. Because the hunters and foragers of this Mesolithic period did not construct substantial houses, and only modified their environment by limited forest clearance and burning, their mode of life is difficult to reconstruct. They have left no visible mark on the landscape, but they must have been successful and adaptive, making wide use of the rich forest flora and fauna.

Massive monuments

England became separated from the Continent by 6500BC, but by 4000BC the insular population had adopted farming, and with this more sedentary life-style had begun to construct massive monuments. Because we know so little about the way of life of the Mesolithic population it is difficult to assess how the change to the new Neolithic farming life-style came about – whether it was an indigenous development through the local domestication of forest animals such as cattle and pigs; or as a result of the importation of domesticated animal breeds and cereal crops; or from colonisation by new groups of people.

Because of the need for animal grazing and for open fields in which to plant crops, the broad-leaved forest was gradually cleared. But before this was achieved on a wide scale some important monuments had already been built. Among the earliest monuments were massive tombs, or long barrows, to hold the remains of the dead together with ceremonial provisions in pottery vessels (an innovation of the time), stone tools, and personal ornaments. In areas where large blocks of building stone were easily available, massive chambers were created, usually at the eastern end of the planned long mound, while the edges of the mound may have been provided with a retaining kerb or façade. Excellent examples of the megalithic ('large stone')

Wiltshire is extraordinarily rich in the ritual monuments of early man. Of the two focal points of Avebury and Stonehenge, Avebury (main picture) is the older and the larger. The stone circles and their surrounding bank and ditch were constructed in late Neolithic times. An avenue of 200 paired stones (inset, right) leads from the south entrance to another ceremonial site 1½ miles away, known as the Sanctuary.
Inset left: The Sweet Track, laid across the bogs of the Somerset Levels in Neolithic times

technique can be seen at Stoney Littleton and West Kennett. In other areas timber was used instead of stone, but this has rotted away, and all that appears to be left is an earthen long barrow. Many of these exist, for example at Pimperne, Winterbourne Stoke or Thickthorn Down. A few examples in Dorset, such as those at Martin Down or Broadmayne, have been greatly exaggerated in length so as to form a long bank barrow.

At much the same time that the long barrows were constructed, circular camps surrounded by one or more continuous banks were built in a variety of landscapes. The material for the banks was quarried from interrupted ditches, frequently with numerous causeways between the ditch segments. Good hilltop examples are found at Knap Hill and Windmill Hill, but others have been covered by later fortifications, or have become obscured by ploughing and soil wash downhill.

Managing the wildwood

Forest clearance was necessary to establish fields, but other areas of the wildwood were carefully managed. Timbers preserved beneath the peats of the Somerset Levels show that trees were systematically coppiced (cut near the base) and pollarded (cut so that a trunk was left – both methods allow the tree to grow again). This supplied straight, thin withies and rods, which could be used for making wattle fences, houses and even track surfaces. Carpentry was already skilful in the fourth millennium BC and this was put to effective use in the construction of the Sweet Track, one of many timber trackways that were constructed in prehistoric times to cross the soggy bogs of the Levels. The waterlogged conditions and thick peat covering have preserved many of these trackways, while others have been revealed by painstaking excavation, and then reconstructed.

Age of the henge

The circular causewayed camps that had probably been constructed as communal meeting places were later replaced by 'henge' monuments, some of which were extremely large. In these the ditch from which material was dug to build the bank is normally inside the bank, suggesting that the earthworks were not for defence. Within Wessex there are remarkable examples of a number of broadly contemporary Neolithic monuments in close proximity. At Hambledon Hill and Whitesheet Hill causewayed enclosures, other enclosures and linear banks exist side by side. Both have later forts, while the former also has a long barrow. At Knowlton parts of three circular henges surrounded by later barrows survive; similarly at Priddy, three circles survive near later barrows. In the Dorchester region a causewayed enclosure lies beneath the later hillfort of Maiden Castle. This enclosure is crossed by a bank barrow. Close by are the henge monuments of Mount Pleasant and Maumbury Rings. When Mount Pleasant was excavated it was found to contain traces of massive circular buildings. Recent archaeological investigations beneath the centre of modern Dorchester have revealed further Neolithic circular monuments, barrows and settlements.

Silbury Hill as depicted in an 18th-century engraving (below) and (right) as seen today. The highest man-made prehistoric mound in Europe, it must have been constructed with baskets, antler picks and shoulder-blade shovels

THE ANCIENT LANDSCAPE

A stunning feat of prehistoric engineering, Stonehenge stands immense among the silent round barrows of the surrounding fields

One of the largest henge monuments was constructed at Avebury. Within the great circular bank stands a ring of huge stones, while in the middle of the circle formerly stood two smaller circles of stones, the northern of the two containing a central box-like arrangement or 'cove'. These colossal flat stones are natural sarsen stones and were probably collected from the nearby downland or valleys. From the circle led two avenues of paired standing stones: that to the west has long been demolished, but part of the southerly avenue survives, snaking its way for nearly 2.5km towards West Kennet and to the summit of a hill on which a circular building, 'The Sanctuary', once stood. The Sanctuary was a complex monument which included two small stone circles and six concentric circles of posts. Doubtless these elements were not all contemporary, but represented the phases of rebuilding of an important structure. Close to Avebury are the causewayed camp of Windmill Hill and the chambered tomb of West Kennett, and also other long barrows and formerly another stone circle. But the most enigmatic monument in this landscape is Silbury Hill, the largest artificial prehistoric mound in Europe. Excavation has failed to find burials, but this enormous tump was probably a funerary monument. Like Dissignac, a tomb in the Loire-Atlantique of France, it was built with a stepped profile. Only the topmost step is now left unfilled. The mound is complex in structure: at least three phases of building are known. In its final form the mound comprises 17,000,000 cubic feet of dumped chalk which had to be excavated and transported from the vast surrounding ditch without the aid of machines or metal tools. Internally the mound was stabilised by radial and concentric chalk block walls, which consolidated the growing heap of chalk rubble and allowed gangs of workers to develop a unique structure that might have seemed more at home in Old Kingdom Egypt than Neolithic Wessex.

Silbury Hill is unique, but other complexes of stone circles and avenues survive at Stanton Drew and at Stonehenge, without doubt the most famous prehistoric monument in Wessex.

Stonehenge

Like many ancient monuments, Stonehenge is a complicated monument set in a rich and varied landscape. In its first phase, at about 2800BC, Stonehenge was a henge monument with a simple bank and ditch, modest in size compared with Avebury, for example.

This phase was abandoned and the grassy downland in which the monument sat reverted to scrub. At this time other henge monuments at Durrington Walls and Coneybury Hill were built. In about 2100BC Stonehenge was refurbished: a new axis pointing towards the midsummer sunrise was established for a repositioned entrance, an avenue, axial and peripheral sarsen stones, and a central setting of Welsh bluestones. It appears that this arrangement was never completed and immediately a third phase followed. In this, large, shaped sarsen stones were erected both in a circle surmounted by carefully fitted lintels, and also in five massive free-standing 'trilithons' (two stones with a stone lintel). Subsequently, the bluestones were re-erected and re-arranged, and other minor modifications including the lengthening of the avenue took place.

Stonehenge developed over a period of more than a thousand years. In this time the use of the surrounding area changed and different monuments were placed in it. Not only were there the huge henge monuments with their massive timber post circles both inside and out (as with Durrington Walls and Woodhenge), but also there were curious, long, parallel-sided earthwork enclosures called 'cursuses'. There are two of these near Stonehenge, but also others in Wessex, such as the Dorset Cursus near Cranborne, which is nearly 10km long. In the thousand years over which

The hillfort of Maiden Castle as it might have looked when occupied. The site was used by Stone Age, then by Iron Age people and finally by the Romans. Inset: a Roman coin, part of the Maiden Castle hoard, now in the County Museum, Dorchester

Stonehenge was built, burial practice changed, so that at 2000BC, for example, burial beneath round mounds became commonplace. At times, groups or cemeteries of these round barrows were established. Accompanying the inhumation or cremation burials that were covered by the mounds were new pottery types and the first metal objects of the Bronze Age. A wide variety in the form and size of barrows existed, as can be seen in the groups on Normanton Down, Winterbourne Stoke, or the King Barrows near Stonehenge. Thousands of barrows are known in Wessex – there are other fine groups at Oakley Down, Poor Lot, Bincombe and Martin Down, to name a few.

The funerary monuments of the Bronze Age, the round barrows, dominate many skylines in Wessex, but the settlements of the communities to which they belonged are not as obvious. A few have been recognised on Shearplace Hill, South Lodge and on the Marlborough Downs, where small groups of round houses were surrounded by banks, while others had no form of defence. Associated with these settlements are extensive systems of small fields. It appears that by 1000BC much of the Wessex landscape was divided into blocks by long 'ranch boundaries', while the blocks contained patchworks of fields. Where subsequent ploughing has not obliterated the boundaries of these fields, they can still be seen in areas of long-established pasture: on Pertwood Down, Fyfield Down, or on the Dorset Ridge Way. On Quarley Hill, the later Iron Age hillfort sits over the 'ranch boundaries' which radiate from the summit.

How hillforts were used

The introduction of iron around 800BC brought the use of bronze for tools and weapons to an abrupt end. Although there was a gradual change in the traditions of other basic manufactured products, such as pottery, there appears to have been little change in the basic farming economy of the people. However, stress within the orderly framework of farming communities is obvious from the construction of massive hilltop forts, often surrounded by several ditches and huge earthen banks. Warfare and defence were not new phenomena, as evidence of battles, of killing, and of efficient weapons are clear from Neolithic times. Indeed, during the second millennium, the bronze smiths had produced increasingly sophisticated weapons, including spears, knives, axes, swords and shields. But the appearance of hillforts suggests new pressures, and with the first use of the horse at this time as a cavalry mount, highly mobile and well-armed warriors must have been at the disposal of many rulers.

Modern excavations at hillforts such as Danebury and Maiden Castle have shown that one of the principal functions of the hillfort was as a centralised grain store. Because grain was a fundamental element of diet and of the farming economy, its safety was paramount. Those who controlled the grain controlled the well-being of society, and if raiding by mobile bands occurred, there was a need to defend the community's wealth in hillforts. Within the interior of the fort the grain was stored in deep pits or in small granaries built with substantial posts at each of their four corners to carry a strong raised floor and roof. Circular houses of the inhabitants were also set about the fort, although the majority of the community seem to have lived on farmsteads in the surrounding countryside. The ramparts of the forts were frequently revetted with and surmounted by wooden palisades, while the entrances were strengthened by additional obstructing banks and substantial gateways. To meet demands, hillforts were frequently rebuilt and enlarged, and the entrances remodelled. Such a sequence is perhaps best seen at Maiden Castle. Here, an Early Iron Age hillfort occupied the eastern knoll of the hill, covering the earlier Neolithic camp. Later, the fort was enlarged to encompass the western knoll. Finally additional ramparts were added and the entrances, one at each end, given extra defensive banks. By the time it was complete the fort covered 47 acres. The need for defence is stressed by the number of hillforts in Wessex. The construction of each would have required a massive investment of labour, so it can be deduced that a large population was available to aid construction, perhaps by forced labour. The territory that each hillfort served was not massive: they are frequently in close proximity. For example, in the area between Salisbury and Warminster we find the forts of Figsbury, Old Sarum, Ogbury, Middle Woodford, Grovely, Yarnbury, Bilbury, Scratchbury and Battlesbury, all within a distance of 30km as the crow flies. In the same area are smaller defended settlements typical of the period such as Hamshill ditches or at Hanging Langford, Knook Camp, or Codford Circle. There are many other fine examples of these hillforts in Wessex, at Badbury Rings, Buzbury, Eggardon, Hambledon Hill, Poundbury, Dolebury, Worlebury, Barbury, Bratton, Rybury, and so on.

Armies of Rome
Hillforts served as an adequate defence against Iron Age raiding parties, but were little obstacle to the invading armies of Rome. In AD43 the Emperor Claudius landed in Kent with four legions of troops, together with auxiliaries, amounting in all to about 40,000 men. Britain had for some time had links with the Roman civilisation, importing luxury goods such as wine, and adopting the basics of a written language and coinage. From the coinage and early accounts we know that Wessex was occupied by organised tribes: the Durotriges in the west, the Dobunni in Avon and Gloucestershire, and the Atrebates in north-east Wiltshire and eastwards. The Roman historian Suetonius tells us that, under their legate Vespasian, the Second Legion of the Roman army fought thirty battles, overcame two powerful tribes, over twenty hillforts and the Isle of Wight in a single campaign. Natural harbours, for example Poole harbour, would have facilitated naval support for the suppression of the Wessex tribes. Dramatic evidence for the might of Rome was found at Spettisbury hillfort: when the railway line cut through the fort's ditch in the middle of the last century, mass burials, presumed to be the slain defenders of the Durotrigian stronghold, were found. At Hod Hill, only a few miles west of Spettisbury, the army overran the hilltop and established their own fort within the circuit of the hillfort. Although both camps are now merely earthworks the change in style is obvious.

Roman life
Under Roman rule many changes occurred. For the first time towns with regular street patterns, covered markets, bath-houses, shops and houses were established. Major towns became regional administrative centres replacing the earlier tribal capitals: Dorchester (Durnovaria) and Ilchester (Lindinis) in the territory of the Durotriges, Winchester (Venta Belgarum) in the territory of the Atrebates. Later, these important towns were surrounded by walls, as was the smaller town at Mildenhall, but lesser towns such as Wanborough or Sandy Lane remained open.

Movement between the towns was aided by well-constructed roads. The road system both within the towns and between them remained in use for centuries, and in some instances still forms the foundations of modern streets and highways. The raised carriageway of the roads can be seen at the Ackling Dyke on the Dorset/Hampshire border, or passing the Oakley Down barrow group; or at the road east of Salisbury (Sorviodunum), where the modern A30 veers towards Figsbury Rings; or that to the east of the A361 near Beckhampton. The roads would have facilitated the movement not only of troops but of farm produce and industrial wares. Country estates were centred on new villas built in the rectangular style of the new civilisation. These luxurious buildings frequently contained elaborate mosaic floors, heating systems and painted plaster walls, all beneath substantial tiled roofs. The nature of these villas can be seen at Rockbourne, Littlecote, or at King's Weston and Sea Mills in Bristol, as the foundations and floors have been exposed by excavation. Not everyone lived in a villa and many continued to live in a very similar way to that prevailing before the Conquest. It is probable that some complicated earthworks, for example those at Ebbsbury and Stockton, close to the Roman road which runs westwards along the ridgetop from Old Sarum (Sorviodunum), are the remains of such farming communities.

Baths and temples
An essential part of the Roman way of life was bathing, and consequently for all towns and prestigious villas bath suites were built. In order to ensure a water supply to Dorchester and its public baths, an elaborate aqueduct was built. This took water from the River Frome at Notton Mill and carried it on a tortuous route for 30km to the town. Part of its route used the redundant defences of Poundbury hillfort. However, the greatest development of Roman baths was at Bath (Aquae Sulis), where natural hot springs were harnessed to serve convalescing troops and visitors. In the late Roman period a walled area enclosed three massive public buildings – a huge vaulted chamber enclosing the central sacred spring, the temple of Sulis Minerva to the west of it, and the main baths to the south.

The Romans had many gods so, as in Bath, towns and country areas were adorned with temples, such as those on Maiden Castle overlooking Dorchester, or at Jordan Hill overlooking Weymouth Bay.

Under Roman authority an orderly way of life existed in Wessex for 400 years. With such stability the towns and industries used natural resources such as the lead of the Mendips, the clays and shale of the Isle of Purbeck, or salt from the sea, and society prospered. But 'all good things come to an end' and because Rome had overstretched its ability to control a vast empire, by the 3rd century uncivilised barbarians began to attack the vulnerable province. Mercenaries were brought in, but these were not sufficient to maintain and further develop the civilisation, and by the 5th century collapse was inevitable. So began a new chapter for Wessex, the era of invasions, of Arthur and of King Alfred, ruler of the kingdom which retains a distinct identity within the larger domain of England today.

Wessex Wildlife

The male silver-studded blue butterfly, most often seen flying on chalk or limestone downland. It lives mainly on heaths and is distinguished by the blue-studded 'eyes' on its silver underwings

The sheer variety of special places for wildlife in Wessex means the area is able to support a vast range of birds, animals, plants and insects. From the flat grazing marshes of the Somerset Levels in the west to the rolling slopes of Salisbury Plain in the east, from the mudflats of the Severn Estuary in the north to the limestone cliffs of Dorset in the south, the region has widely differing wildlife habitats, some of which are becoming very scarce nationally.

Heathlands

A good example is Dorset heathland which is now one of Britain's most threatened wildlife habitats. These fragmented heaths support a whole community of scarce animals and plants, many of which can no longer be found elsewhere in Britain.

Summer is the time when the heaths of Dorset are at their best, the purple of the heathers providing a colourful backdrop for a host of spectacular insects. Dragonflies and damselflies are among the most evident with the sparkling blue of the emperor dragonfly and the delicate shades of the azure damselfly likely to be seen on any sunny day.

The wet heaths are special places for flowers, with the yellow bog asphodel and the white tufts of cottongrass showing up well in early summer. Hidden amongst the vegetation there might be such plants as marsh gentian and heath spotted orchid. Then there are the butterflies. Some, like the silver studded blue, are restricted almost entirely to heathland as is the grayling, whilst the silver washed fritillary can be found elsewhere but is commoner on the larger heaths.

The birdlife includes several species that are rare nationally: for instance, the shy and elusive Dartford warbler and the hobby, a falcon which migrates from Africa to spend the summer hunting dragonflies and even swallows and house martins. One bird seen and heard only at dusk is the nightjar, its churring song echoing across the heathland just as darkness falls. It is well worth making a special visit to hear and even perhaps to see it hawking for moths as the light fades.

You are unlikely to see the reptiles which live on the heaths, but all six British species can be found, including the two rarest – the smooth snake and the sand lizard.

Dorset heathland is much reduced from former times but some of the largest remaining blocks have now been made nature reserves. In the Purbeck area, both the RSPB's Arne reserve and the Studland National Nature Reserve are well worth visiting.

The smooth snake, one of Britain's rarest reptiles, is mostly found in Dorset, on open heath

Sea coast

The sea coast of Wessex is that of south Dorset, from Hengistbury Head in the east to Lyme Regis in the west. Away from the built-up areas much of this coastline is protected and undeveloped, with beaches, cliffs and clifftops supporting a surprising variety of birds, plants and insects.

The limestone cliffs between Durlston Head and Lulworth are outstanding, with many rare and interesting plants such as bee and pyramid orchids. Certain plants are important as the food source for the caterpillars of butterflies such as the adonis blue and a local speciality, the Lulworth skipper.

Shelduck, seen here sunbathing in spring, breed in the estuaries of Wessex before migrating

Seabird colonies occur at Durlston and on Portland Bill – mainly gulls (including kittiwakes) but also guillemots and a few razorbills, with even the occasional puffin. Portland Bill, extending six miles out into the English Channel, is a major bird migration point with a permanent bird observatory. In spring and autumn, concentrations of numerous migrant birds are found here, often including extreme rarities. Nearby the long coastal lagoon of the Fleet is enclosed by the 16-mile shingle ridge of Chesil Beach. Partly tidal, it boasts a large nesting colony of mute swans at Abbotsbury, which can be visited in summer.

Estuaries

Wessex possesses some outstanding estuaries. The Severn estuary is the third largest in the country, forming the shoreline of both Avon and Somerset. The estuaries of Dorset, Christchurch harbour and Poole harbour, are much smaller but are also superb wildlife sites.

At low tide the open mudflats may seem empty but on closer inspection birds will be seen scattered right across them. The tidal flats are feeding grounds for a vast number of wading birds and wildfowl: the Severn supports almost 100,000 in midwinter and thousands more pass through on migration. Most numerous are the small dunlins, but larger wading birds like redshanks, curlews and oystercatchers are present in good numbers. High tide brings the waders much closer to the shoreline and this is the best time to visit for a close view.

Among the wildfowl, the black and white shelduck remains to breed during the summer in both the Severn and Poole harbour. The birds which are most obvious in the summer are gulls, with a large breeding colony of black-headed gulls on the saltmarshes of Poole harbour.

This is also the best place to see terns in summer. These elegant white seabirds breed on Brownsea Island, and both common and Sandwich terns can be seen between May and August.

Farmland

There are considerable contrasts in the types of farmland in Wessex. The open chalkland of Wiltshire and Dorset is mainly cereal-growing country and in early spring the wide vistas provide the chance to see brown hares going through their courtship rituals. While the ground is not covered by growing crops, other mammals can be seen – especially rabbits, but also foxes and roe deer. Game birds are widely managed in these areas, and pheasants and partridges are often found in the open fields. One bird to profit from the increase in cereal crops has been the corn bunting, a dumpy brown bird with a song which resembles the jangling of keys. Elsewhere in Wessex the farmland has more hedgerows and scattered woodland. It is still possible to find sheltered valleys and lanes with wild flowers and butterflies in summer, especially in Blackmoor Vale and west Dorset.

West of the Mendip hills lies the wide expanse of

A corn bunting perches characteristically on fencing wire. It is often seen in downland Dorset

Above: an aerial view of the Somerset Levels, showing the water-filled ditches or 'rhynes' and the winter flooding that attracts huge numbers of Bewick's swans from Siberia (right)

the Somerset Levels. These low-lying grazing meadows are criss-crossed with waterfilled ditches known locally as 'rhynes'. In winter, flood waters attract many thousands of wildfowl and waders, including wild Bewick's swans, whilst in spring and summer the meadows are superb places for flowers, insects and birds. The rhynes have a host of aquatic plants, like arrowhead with its characteristic upright leaves and frogbit with floating white flowers. Beneath the surface are aquatic insects such as great diving beetles and the larvae of dragonflies. Traditional grazing meadows have a wealth of wild flowers, with cowslips, marsh orchids and yellow rattle as just a few examples. Then there are the birds: curlew and lapwing fill the air with their evocative calls and on calm evenings the drumming of snipe echoes across the moors. At Swell Wood near West Sedgemoor is a large nesting colony of grey herons overlooked by a hide which can be visited in spring and summer. The Somerset Levels are one of the largest wetlands of their type in Britain and have been designated as an 'environmentally sensitive area', where farmers are to be financed to assist conservation.

Limestone and chalk
In the past, the grazing of animals on limestone and chalk areas created a short grassland turf with a range of specialised plants. Certain scarce wildflowers will only grow in such places, and although modern farming methods have destroyed many of these areas, a few have survived, either because of difficult terrain or as nature reserves.

The hard limestone of the Mendips has been formed into a landscape of rugged gorges and caves, with Cheddar Gorge a prime example. Here there are many specialised plants – the ox-eye daisy is a common example and rarer ones include the Cheddar pink and the superb blue gromwell. The downland of Dorset and Wiltshire is a very small remnant of what once existed but two good examples can still be found at Maiden Castle and Hod Hill in Dorset. The variety of wild plants to

be found in the short turf includes several orchids, horseshoe vetch and harebell. A selection of butterflies rely on these downland plants as the food for their caterpillars, and a warm summer day when they are on the wing is the best time to visit downland sites.

Rivers and inland waters
Many of the rivers and streams of Wessex run off the high ground of Salisbury Plain or the Mendip hills and through chalk soils which make them rich in fish such as the brown trout. Chalk streams have a vast aquatic insect population which in its turn provides the food for waterside birds like the dipper and grey wagtail. Where the river valleys widen, the flow has been used to create watermeadows which are often wonderful places for wetland plants. In spring the flowers of marsh marigold are mixed with the swaying heads of ladies' smock to create a superb sight. The breeding birds found here include redshank and snipe as well as the colourful yellow wagtail. Most of the lakes in Wessex occur where valleys have been dammed to provide water supply reservoirs such as Sutton Bingham in Dorset and Blagdon and Chew Valley lakes in Avon. Chew Valley lake is the largest of these reservoirs and is well worth visiting (several roads cross the lake margins). Although wildfowl are most numerous in winter, there are many birds to be seen in spring and summer. Great crested grebes going through their breeding display are a delight to watch and other water birds include the diminutive ruddy duck, originally from North America but now established here.

Gravel pits provide one of the other major areas of open water and the Cotswold Water Park in north Wiltshire is a good area with many waterbirds. The reedbeds which grow around the edge of most of the large lakes are important habitats for birds. One of the largest is at Radipole Lake in Weymouth, an RSPB reserve with a series of hides where both the bearded reedling and Cetti's warbler breed, and many migrants occur in spring and autumn.

Woodlands
There was once dense woodland at the heart of Wessex in Cranborne Chase, but now the remaining woods here, as in much of the rest of the region, are very fragmented. Just a few large blocks of woodland remain, such as Savernake Forest in Wiltshire. In the Mendips, the underlying limestone rocks favour ash woods, of which Ebbor Gorge, a National Nature Reserve, provides a classic example. Beech woods on the chalkland of Dorset and Wiltshire include some of the country's best bluebell woods. Some coppice woodlands – managed by cutting young shoots which grow again – are also good for bluebells. The practice of hazel coppicing to make sheep hurdles is still found in a few Wessex woods, and makes a suitable habitat for nightingales and migrant warblers. Garston Wood in North Dorset is a typical coppice woodland and well worth a visit in May or June just to hear the melodic notes of the nightingale.

Mature broadleaved woodland can be found in parts of Savernake Forest and here as elsewhere it supports good populations of butterflies, especially the early flying brimstone but also the white admiral and purple hairstreak. These older woodlands have the greatest range of wildlife. They support three species of woodpecker and several birds of prey, and they are also rich in fungi and lichens. Among the more obvious mammals, the grey squirrel is widespread, but the once common red squirrel can now only be found in Wessex among the pines on Brownsea Island in Poole Harbour.

Modern conifer plantations lack the wide range of wildlife found in our native woodlands but nevertheless should not be entirely ignored. In the early years after planting, before they become dense and impenetrable, they are worth exploring for both butterflies and birds. Some of the largest blocks of conifers occur in south Dorset in areas which were once heathland.

The future
Despite the wealth of wildlife in Wessex, the loss of heaths, downlands, hedgerows and other habitats make it far less rich in wildlife than it used to be. Positive steps need to be taken to conserve what remains and to begin the task of recreating some of the special wildlife habitats lost in the last few years. This is a major task for the future which can only be helped by more appreciation of the wonderful heritage of wildlife in the region.

Below and inset: the hard limestone Mendips support a profusion of ox-eye daisy in summer and the rocky ledges of the gorges, notably Cheddar Gorge, bear many rare and localised plants such as Cheddar Pink

Thomas Hardy's Wessex

In an age when we can take out a mortgage with the Wessex Building Society, pay water rates to the Wessex Water Authority and go to a concert at the Wessex Hall, when, in short, the term 'Wessex' is widely used and almost universally understood as the name of a region of modern Britain, it is hard to believe that not much more than a century ago the term was used only by historians and archaeologists who were referring to the ancient kingdom of the West Saxons. If it is surprising that 'Wessex' has become part of the language without ever having been given any official status, it is little less than astonishing that the term owes its revival chiefly to one man, Thomas Hardy, and that he intended it only as a unifying setting for his fictional writings.

Hardy's basic plan was to use real names for landscape features while using fictional names for towns and villages, so that he could draw largely on his extensive local knowledge and yet have the freedom to alter the details as he needed. Many readers find Hardy's Wessex world so vital that they forget that it is fiction. To avoid disappointment, we must not lose sight of the fact that it never existed as such outside his works, while modern development has altered many of the places which were originally drawn from reality. However, it is still possible to recapture the flavour of Hardy's works and to add to our appreciation of them by a visit to modern Wessex.

Hardy's Wessex covers a vast area of southern Britain, stretching from Oxford (Hardy's *Christminster*) in the north-east to Cornwall and even the Scilly Isles in the south-west. However, as the map on p. 20 makes clear, the centre of Wessex is in Dorset, and its heart is in Dorchester and its immediate vicinity where Hardy spent so much of his long life.

Early days at Higher Bockhampton

Hardy was born on 2 June 1840 in a large thatched cottage at Higher Bockhampton near Dorchester. The cottage had been built by Hardy's great-grandfather, a builder like Hardy's own father. Now maintained by the National Trust, it has interior furnishings of Hardy's day and a charming garden. Upstairs you can see the bedroom where Hardy was born, only to be thrown aside as stillborn until rescued by the monthly nurse who exclaimed: 'Dead! Stop a minute: he's alive enough, sure!'

The raw materials of his novels were all about him: the country folk with their vivid folktales and superstitions, the contrasting landscapes of lush fields in front of the cottage and untamed heath immediately behind, and only a few miles away the bustling market town of Dorchester, connected to London by railway during Hardy's childhood.

From the cottage Hardy attended school and in due course started work, as an architect's apprentice in Dorchester. At the age of 21 he left for more prestigious architectural training in

Dorchester's West Street as Thomas Hardy (inset) knew it. The modern town still retains much of the atmosphere captured in The Mayor of Casterbridge

THOMAS HARDY'S WESSEX

Hardy was married twice, to Emma (left) in 1874 and, after her death in 1912, to Florence (right) in 1914.

London but returned after five years and then continued to live for much of the time at Higher Bockhampton. It was from here that he set out on the momentous morning of 7 March 1870 to undertake what he expected to be a routine assignment, drawing plans of St Juliot Church in Cornwall in preparation for its restoration. However, it was here that he met Emma Lavinia Gifford whom he was later to marry and it was Emma who played a crucial role in his decision to abandon architecture and devote himself to his real vocation as a writer. By the time that he left the cottage to get married in 1874 he had already published four novels, the latest of which, *Far from the Madding Crowd*, had really made his name.

There are abundant literary associations at Higher Bockhampton, particularly with the charming early novel *Under the Greenwood Tree*, for the home of the Dewy family is clearly modelled on the Hardys' cottage and one can imagine the boisterous Christmas party taking place in its main room. Immediately behind the cottage is the edge of Hardy's *Egdon Heath* which forms the sombre but magnificent setting of *The Return of the Native*. The land is now used by the Forestry Commission, but periodic fellings give some idea of the expanse of bracken, heather and gorse which used to stretch from here to Bournemouth.

A short walk across the heath will take you to the bracken-covered tumulus called Rainbarrow which is featured in *The Return of the Native* and from which there is a magnificent view over the wide Frome Valley, the *Valley of the Great Dairies* in *Tess of the d'Urbervilles*, where Tess works as a milkmaid and enjoys her happiest days.

The Dorchester years

After a restless first nine years of marriage, in which Hardy and Emma lived in many different towns, it was to Dorchester (Hardy's *Casterbridge*) that they chose to come in 1883 to settle down. It was here at Max Gate, a house built to Hardy's own designs on the edge of the town, that they spent the remainder of their lives. Here Emma was to die in 1912 and here Hardy was to bring his second wife Florence Emily in 1914.

The effect on Hardy's writing of this return to the sources of his inspiration was dramatic and immediate. The years of wandering had produced only one major novel, *The Return of the Native*, and four minor works. The first 12 years in Dorchester were to produce four major novels, of which three, *The Mayor of Casterbridge*, *Tess of the d'Urbervilles*

Right: a scene from the dramatised version of Far from the Madding Crowd *performed in Dorchester, 1909*
Below: Hardy's birthplace at Higher Bockhampton

Thomas Hardy's study at Max Gate, evocatively reconstructed at the County Museum, Dorchester

and *Jude the Obscure* rank among the greatest novels in English. There were also some marvellous short stories, and then in 1898 *Wessex Poems*, the first of the eight volumes of poetry with which Hardy was to build up a second reputation as one of the greatest poets of the 20th century. Add to this the epic-drama *The Dynasts* and you have some idea of the magnitude of his achievement in these years.

Max Gate is not open to the public, but fortunately Hardy's study there has been painstakingly reconstructed in the Dorset County Museum in Dorchester. You can look through a window and see its contents just as if Hardy had that moment left the room: the calendar shows January 1928 (the month he died), his books are on the shelves, his walking stick is to hand and his pens are on the desk, each carefully inscribed by him with the name of the work he had written with it. The Museum also houses many of Hardy's manuscripts and personal items, including his watch and shaving mug. The Rural Craft Collection is also fascinating to anyone interested in the rural world so vividly evoked by Hardy.

Next door to the Museum is St Peter's Church, one of the many Dorset churches which Hardy helped to restore in his days as an architect (the plan he drew hangs inside), while the site of the architect's office in South Street is marked by a plaque at first-floor level. At Top o' Town there is a fine statue of Hardy.

Literary associations abound in Dorchester, particularly with *The Mayor of Casterbridge*. Most notable sites are the King's Arms Hotel whose splendid bow-window still juts out over the pavement as it did during Henchard's banquet, and the fine 18th-century house in South Street, now occupied by Barclays Bank but imagined by Hardy as Henchard's house. The delightful Walks, on the site of the old town walls, bring memories of Farfrae's dance, when shelter was provided by rick-cloths hung from tree to tree, while bleak Poundbury Camp was the site of Henchard's ill-fated competing entertainment. Maumbury Rings is where Susan arranges to meet Henchard after her return, and just outside the town is Maiden Castle, mentioned in *The Mayor of Casterbridge* and vividly described in the short story *A Tryst at an Ancient Earthwork*. Near Fordington (*Durnover*) the Frome flows under Grey's Bridge, prominent in more than one novel. Under the prison is the disarmingly attractive Hangman's Cottage, featured in the short story *The Withered Arm*.

Stinsford

The last of the three key places in Hardy's life is Stinsford, the *Mellstock* of *Under the Greenwood Tree* and many poems. This was the church which Hardy attended as a boy and later came to from Max Gate, for he remained (as he put it) 'churchy' in his feelings even though he was unable to accept conventional Christianity. In the graveyard his heart lies buried, though his ashes are in Poet's Corner in Westminster Abbey; nearby is the

A map of Wessex drawn by Hardy. He distinguishes between fictitious and real placenames

tombstone of the former poet laureate C. Day Lewis. Inside the church you can see a memorial window to Hardy.

The instrumental choir of Stinsford Church had been disbanded when Hardy was very young but he immortalised their activities in *Under the Greenwood Tree*. The gallery where the choir sat has now been removed, but an impression of what it was like can be gained by visiting the church of nearby Puddletown (the *Weatherbury* of *Far from the Madding Crowd*) where a splendid 17th-century gallery is still in place.

Along an attractive riverside path from Stinsford is Lower Bockhampton where Hardy first went to school; the building is now a private house.

Further afield

Away from the heartland of Wessex one can pick out only a few of the literally hundreds of places which have some association with Hardy.

Just over Ridgeway Hill from Dorchester is Weymouth (*Budmouth*) where Hardy lodged at various times before his marriage, at 3 Wooperton Street. A number of poems and some scenes in *Desperate Remedies* describe the fashionable Victorian seaside resort with its bands on the Esplanade and rowing boats on the bay. *The Trumpet-Major* shows the town at the height of its fame when George III had his summer residence on the Esplanade. Beyond the causeway is Portland (*Isle of Slingers*); virtually an island, its grey rock, stone-built houses and lack of trees form a unique landscape, memorably encapsulated in Hardy's minor but fascinating novel *The Well-Beloved*.

In north-west Dorset is the attractive village of Evershot (*Evershead*) where Tess stops for breakfast on her long walk to Beaminster (*Emminster*) in the cottage by the church now named Tess Cottage. Nearby is Melbury Osmond, Hardy's mother's home village; in this church Hardy's parents were married. This is *Woodlanders* country as Hardy originally imagined it, so the churchyard is the scene of Marty South's moving lament at the end of that novel. In Sherborne the magnificent Abbey Church is described in *The Woodlanders* and the Old Castle is the scene of the short story *Anna, Lady Baxby*.

In the delightful north Dorset market town of Sturminster Newton (*Stourcastle*) one can still see Riverside Villa, the house overlooking the River Stour in which Hardy lived from 1876 to 1878 and wrote *The Return of the Native*. A few miles north in the Blackmoor Vale is Marnhull, *Marlott* in *Tess of the d'Urbervilles*, where Tess spends her childhood. The most likely contender for the original of her house is now inevitably named Tess Cottage, and one can also see The Crown Hotel, described in the novel as *The Pure Drop*. Looking over the Vale from the north is the ancient hilltop town of Shaftesbury (*Shaston*) where Sue and Phillotson (*Jude the Obscure*) lived in *Old Groves Place*, the house now called The Ox House in Bimport.

Cranborne Chase, which features memorably in *Tess of the d'Urbervilles*, straddles the Dorset/Wiltshire border, and within its precincts are Cranborne itself (*Chaseborough*) and Pentridge which is the original of *Trantridge*, the nearest village to *The Slopes*, the house of the Stoke d'Urbervilles. It is at Stonehenge that Tess is captured by the police, while nearby Salisbury (*Melchester*) contains Hardy's favourite cathedral. In the cathedral close is the former Teachers' Training College which both of Hardy's sisters attended and which served as the model for the one attended by Sue Bridehead in *Jude the Obscure*.

Woolbridge Manor, down the River Frome from Dorchester, has a photogenic grouping of Manor, Elizabethan bridge and peaceful river. Now a hotel, the Manor will be remembered by readers of *Tess of the d'Urbervilles* as the scene of Tess's traumatic honeymoon. A few miles to the north, over a part of Egdon Heath now used for tank training is Bere Regis (*Kingsbere*) where Tess and her family camped under the d'Urberville window of the church; the holes in the wall where the memorial brass has been removed are just as Hardy describes and there is the bonus of a magnificent roof. Further down the Frome from Wool is Wareham, *Anglebury* in *The Hand of Ethelberta* and guarding the pass through the nearby Purbeck Hills are the famous ruins of Corfe Castle (*Corvesgate Castle*), the scene of a memorable excursion in the same novel.

One of the delights of touring Wessex is that you do not really need an itinerary, for you can find some Hardy association in almost every town, village, hill and valley. Leaving aside specific associations it is still possible in the remoter areas of Dorset like the Marshwood Vale to recapture the very atmosphere of that 'partly real, partly dream country' which was Hardy's Wessex.

Other Wessex Writers

Although usually associated with the Lake District, Wordsworth and Coleridge first met, when both were in their twenties, in Wessex. So well did the two poets get on that Coleridge persuaded Wordsworth and his sister Dorothy to move from Racedown to Alfoxden, only a couple of miles from his own cottage at Nether Stowey on the edge of the Quantocks. Here it was that they collaborated in the writing of *Lyrical Ballads* (1798), a volume which changed the course of English poetry.

Jane Austen was a frequent visitor to Bath in her youth and lived there for five years after her father's retirement in 1801. Both the early *Northanger Abbey* and her last completed novel *Persuasion* have extensive scenes set in Bath which brilliantly describe the social round of the day. The elegant Palladian architecture which was so familiar to Jane Austen can still be seen, as can many places mentioned specifically in her novels, like the Pump Room and the Assembly Rooms. It was at Winchester that she spent the last few weeks of her short life, being nursed by her sister Cassandra at 8 College Street. It was here that she died on 18 July 1817, and her tomb lies in the famous Cathedral nearby. Jane Austen enjoyed two happy holidays at Lyme Regis and recalled the town with evident affection in *Persuasion* where it is the scene of Louisa Musgrove's dramatic fall from the Cobb, the harbour wall.

Lyme Regis and its Cobb are also prominent in *The French Lieutenant's Woman* by the contemporary novelist John Fowles. Victorian Lyme Regis is vividly evoked in the novel, and a few years ago the town was temporarily transformed back to its Victorian past for the shooting of the award-winning film based on the novel.

The 19th-century Dorset poet William Barnes was born near Sturminster Newton but spent most of his adult life in the Dorchester area. Dorset County Museum contains a number of Barnes items, and his statue looks over the town centre from outside nearby St Peter's Church. A plaque marks the site of the school he ran in South Street, and the beautiful thatched Rectory of Winterborne Came in which he spent his last 24 years can be seen just outside the town. Barnes is buried in the tree-shaded churchyard of Winterborne Came.

Rural Crafts

The countryside of Wessex, ranging from the southern Cotswolds to the English Channel and from Salisbury Plain to the Quantock ridge, is richly diverse; the variety of its geology has structured the landscape, and determined both its economic uses and its patterns of settlement. The massive expanse of chalk downland which dominates Wiltshire was traditionally the area of sheep and corn farming, where the fertility of the corn lands was maintained by the dung of the sheep as they were folded at night after grazing over the rolling downs all day.

The clay vales of north Wiltshire, north and west Dorset and central Somerset were dairy districts.

A willow figure stands in Somerset's willow growing area

Areas like the Vale of Taunton Deane were outstandingly fertile: this 'paradise of England' supported a whole range of crafts and it was particularly in these regions that the cloth making industry flourished.

The hilly country of the Mendips and south Avon and the southern border of Somerset were notable for their mixed dairy and arable farming as well as for cloth making.

The region also includes Dorset's heathland stretching from Dorchester through to Hampshire and including the Isle of Purbeck – the area Hardy vividly described in *The Return of the Native* and which he called *Egdon Heath*.

Woollen cloth making
The principal rural industry from 1500 to 1900 was the woollen cloth industry – although, paradoxically, it was not found in the sheep-grazing areas of chalk downlands. In the early Middle Ages it was confined to the towns, for example Bristol, Salisbury, Devizes and Marlborough; and not until the introduction of the fulling mill did the industry spread to the countryside and particularly to the banks of fast running streams. It was in the fertile clay vales that the rural communities had the time to invest in secondary employments, in the spinning, weaving, fulling and dyeing processes of the cloth industry.

Towards the end of the 18th century new machines, like the Spinning Jenny, were being introduced to replace old hand methods; later, cheap imported cloth and mass-produced cloth from the north of England competed successfully with the traditional high quality West Country cloth, and the industry, in Wessex, went into decline. Ghosts of the industry survive in the gracious wool merchants' houses, pokey lanes of mill-workers' cottages and woollen mills of towns like Trowbridge, Frome and Bradford-on-Avon.

The cheeses of Wessex
The clay vales were also areas of pastoral farming with relatively little arable land, where the small dairy farmers produced butter and cheese for sale in local markets and fairs. In north Wiltshire a full-

Spinning is demonstrated at the Great Barn Museum of Wiltshire Folk Life at Avebury

Cheddar cheese being made by traditional methods at the Chewton Cheese Dairy, Chewton Mendip, Somerset

milk cheese was made, known as 'Marlborough', 'North Wilts' or 'Gloucester', as it resembled cheese from the nearby Vale of Berkeley. In Dorset several skim-milk cheeses were produced, including the renowned 'Blue Vinney'. Milk from the Somerset Levels was used to produce a cheese that was destined to become a household name throughout the world – 'Cheddar'. The quality of cheese from the Cheddar area was recognised as early as 1625 when cheeses were said to be held 'in such high esteem at Court that they are bespoken before they are made'.

Daniel Defoe, on his tour through Britain in 1724, reckoned Somerset cheese to be the best in the country; he noted that it sold for 6d (2½p) to 8d (3p) per pound, compared with Cheshire cheese at 2d to 2½d (1p). He also described the co-operative system that was practised:

The milk of all the town cows is brought together every day in a common room, where the persons appointed measure every man's quantity, and set it down in a book; when the quantities are adjusted, the milk is all put together, and every meal's milk makes one cheese, and no more; so that the cheese is bigger, or less, as the cows yield more, or less, milk.

In fact until the mid-19th century the making of cheese was a pretty haphazard business. Joseph Harding, of Marksbury near Bath, is credited with standardising the process of making Cheddar; he stressed the need for cleanliness, encouraged the training of dairymaids and improved the design of cheesemaking equipment.

Most cheese is now made on an industrial scale and produced in easily packaged rectangles, but there are a handful of farms where it is still made basically following Harding's recipe. The Chewton Cheese Dairy at Chewton Mendip, near Wells, is open to the public, but even here the scale of production, about 11,000 litres of milk per day, is far greater than on a small farm. You must go in the morning – cheesemaking won't wait until the afternoon.

The process is fascinating to watch. Rennet is added to warm milk in a huge stainless steel tub and stirred, the blancmange-like curd is broken up using rotating knives, and the whey is drained off; the remaining curd consolidates to a consistency like foam rubber. It is sliced into slabs, milled, and packed into moulds which are laid out and pressed by tightening a massive screw.

Towards the end of the 19th century Wessex

cheese makers had to face competition from imported factory-made cheeses from America and New Zealand. At the same time the growing demand for fresh milk from the rapidly expanding urban and industrial centres encouraged Wessex farmers to cease cheese production and to sell their milk fresh. The Great Western Railway, which collected and transported so much of that milk, became known as 'The Milky Way'.

Peat digging

The marshes and moors of central Somerset were 'much neglected, being destitute of gentlemen's houses, probably on account of the stagnant waters and unwholesome air'. Much of the area is below sea level and only prevented from flooding by constant pumping and careful water management. High tides and fierce winds in the winter still threaten the sea defences; within living memory the sea has burst the banks and spread far enough inland to lap the foot of Glastonbury Tor. The main roads and settlements follow the ridges of higher ground, the 'burtles', with side lanes down to the moors proper, often grinding to a halt where the ground is too soft to continue. Locals remember when every cottage had a flat-bottomed boat moored by the back door in case of emergency, and most winters, as the flood waters rose, the boat became their essential means of transport.

North of the Polden ridge, on either side of the River Brue, there are 6,000 acres of peat moor, around the villages of Meare, Shapwick, Westhay and Catcott: between 4500BC and AD400 up to seven metres of peat accumulated, the product of rotting vegetation. Since then it has been excavated, initially for use as fuel and now, at the rate of more than half a million tons per year, to be packed into plastic bags and distributed to garden centres to nourish the soil in gardens throughout Britain. Until quite recently all peat cutting was done by hand, a tough, arm-aching task as each block of water-sodden peat has to be cut out and heaved onto dry ground from a trench as much as two metres deep. The blocks are laid out to dry, then sliced neatly into three bricks. The aim is to dry out the peat as thoroughly as possible, so the bricks are built into airy card-houses, then into great domes, called 'ruckles', about two and a half metres high. It is these bricks that are sold for fuel. Before the coming of the railway, peat-laden carts delivered to every cottage in the district. In 1845 a hundredweight of peat bricks cost 8d (3p). The railway brought cheaper coal and peat excavation declined until the 1950s.

Our enthusiasm for gardening and the success of container-grown plants has created a demand that was never imagined by the ague-ridden peat diggers of a hundred years ago. Peat land that fetched just £5 an acre before the war can now be sold for £10,000. Huge machines dig out the peat effortlessly and deposit cleanly sliced blocks at the side of the trench in neat little walls. The dried peat is stacked in great black mountains to be packed automatically in the vast sheds that fringe the digging areas. The innovations have created new problems: the machines tear out all peat, to a depth of six or seven metres, right down to the clay beds beneath, and constant pumping is required while digging is in progress to remove water. As soon as the excavation is complete and the pumps are turned off, the trenches become grim black scars of murky water. It was peat digging that created the Norfolk Broads in the Middle Ages, and it has been suggested that the Levels could be developed into a similar area.

One unexpected treasure arising from the peat has been a wealth of archaeological information. Peat is acid and poor in oxygen, so organic materials, like wood, fibre and pollen, are preserved within it. This has meant the survival of a unique archaeological record of life on the Levels from the fifth millennium BC to about AD100 including timber trackways that lead from one area of higher

Women working on the peat moors near Glastonbury in the 1930s. Peat bricks are being built into 'hiles' before being stacked into domes called 'ruckles'

RURAL CRAFTS

The complete process of willow growing and basket making can be seen at Stoke St Gregory, near Taunton.
Left: turning the willow.
Below: a basket maker at work and the tools of his trade

ground to another or provide access into the bog itself. Museum displays of the trackways and associated finds can be seen at the Somerset County Museum, Taunton, and the Tribunal Museum, Glastonbury.

Willows and baskets

Avenues of pollarded willow trees line the zig-zag lanes of the Moors of central Somerset – but these are more likely to be used for making cricket bats than baskets. The basket makers' willows are cultivated as a field crop, the willow 'rods' being harvested from 'stools' or 'stumps' growing in the willow or 'withy' beds.

Basket making is one of the oldest and most widespread crafts. The oldest surviving fragment of basket work in Britain was found in the Iron Age 'lake village' at Meare, near Glastonbury.

Willow furniture was in the height of fashion at the end of the 19th century; and willow baskets in many shapes and sizes were in demand from every delivery boy and packer before the days of plastic bags and polystyrene. Originally willow sticks were foraged from thickets, but as the industry expanded a regular and plentiful supply was required. Willows were grown commercially throughout Britain, especially in the wet lowlands of the West Country, East Anglia, and Yorkshire. Today the only place to see the growing and processing of willows is the area of Sedgemoor between the rivers Parrett, Tone and Isle in Somerset.

In summer the willow shoots form a tall and dense spiky forest. Cutting begins in November after the first frost. The willows are bound into bundles, called 'bolts', tied with a willow knot. Twenty or so bolts are stacked upright together to make a 'heap'.

The bolts are transported back to the grower's yard for processing. First each bundle is dropped into a barrel sunk in the ground and the willows are sorted into sizes by length. Some are then selected to be stripped of their bark for 'white' willows. These are then left to stand in water until the sap begins to rise. Beside the A361 near Athelney the 'rhynes' or drainage ditches are often used for this purpose. Stripping the willows begins in May and June and is another labour-intensive task: a revolving drum with sharp iron flags fixed to it tears the bark off a bundle at a time.

Other willows are destined to become 'buffs'. They are laid in a large brick-built, coal-fired boiler and cooked for several hours, the tannin in the bark staining the rods a rich chestnut. The buff willows are stripped when still wet. Both whites and buffs must then be spread out to dry: they can often be seen along the roadside propped against fences and railings.

'Brown' willow is dried with the bark still on. It is steamed for two hours before the basket maker uses it and this makes it dark and shiny.

Although so closely associated, willow growers and basket makers seldom combine; however, many basket makers have chosen to set up their workshops in the county, and generally they are pleased to have visitors and to talk about their craft. Most sit on a low box or cushion with a board in front of them, between their legs. They make the basket on this 'lapboard', using the simplest of tools – a bodkin, a sharp knife, secateurs and a beater, for hammering down the willows to firm-up the basket as it takes shape. It is a highly skilled process to watch and the sturdy products of the basket maker's hands provide ideal souvenirs, from babies' rattles to laundry baskets.

At Stoke St Gregory, near Taunton, the Willow and Wetlands Visitor Centre explains the story of the Levels. Here can be seen the complete process of willow growing and basket making.

Traditional cider making on the farm. The beam of the press is screwed down by hand to compress the apples

Cider making and cider folklore

Until quite recently cider was the drink most commonly consumed throughout Wessex, and especially in the apple growing areas of Avon, Somerset and west Dorset. Visitors will find locally made cider for sale direct from many farms and in many of the pubs. Much is now manufactured on an industrial scale by the Taunton Cider Company, at Norton Fitzwarren, and by Showerings at Shepton Mallet, but farmhouse cider is something different and something special.

Apple orchards dot the countryside with gnarled trunks and in the spring shower the ground with pink and white blossom. By full summer trees have been known to be bent to the ground by the weight of fruit hanging from the branches; but do not be tempted to eat cider apple fruit – it is revoltingly bitter. Each farm uses its own particular blend of apples from the rich variety available. Those commonly used are the Kingston Black, Redstreak, Court of Wick Pippin, Yarlington Mill, Cackagee and White Sour.

Cider has been made in the region for at least 700 years. In the 17th century John Evelyn described Somerset cider as 'generous, strong and sufficiently heady' and he compared the best cider favourably with French wines.

The method of making cider has not changed significantly since then, although more modern machinery makes the task easier. It is surprising how many small-scale cider makers still use the apple mills and presses which their grandfathers bought a hundred years or so ago.

When ripe, usually in October or November, the apples are shaken from the trees (not too much care is taken as a little bit of rot, it is said, only adds to the flavour), packed into sacks and carted back to the cider house. An apple mill is used to break up the fruit to the consistency of very lumpy porridge, called 'pomace'. In north Avon, the mill was sometimes a circular stone trough, with a circular stone in it, which was dragged around by a horse, but more commonly a hand-turned mill is used with the fruit passing through spiked rollers.

No metal implements are allowed to come into contact with the fruit or juice, for fear of tainting the cider, so a wooden shovel is used to transfer the dripping pomace on to the bed of the press. Traditionally, clean straw was used to hold the pomace in place until a cube of alternate layers of pomace and straw had been built up about 4ft high; nowadays, however, horse-hair cloths are more commonly used.

Next the top beam of the press is screwed down to compress the 'cheese', the local word for the cube of pomace, using a massive bar, like a giant's spanner, to squeeze out the juice. One 'cheese' can yield as much as 120 gallons. The juice flows into a wooden tub and is ladled into barrels.

After three or four weeks' fermentation in a cool cellar the cider is ready to drink, but it improves if left rather longer. Stories tell of all sorts of things being added to the cider, from parsnips to rusty nails, and there may be some truth in the theory that a piece of meat helped 'to feed the yeast'.

Cider has played a central part in many events of the folklore calendar; on Twelfth Night it was the custom to 'wassail', or drink the health of the apple orchards.

> *Old apple tree we wassail thee*
> *And happily thou will bear*
> *For the Lord doth know where we shall be*
> *Till apples another year*
> *To bloom well, to bear well,*
> *So merry let us be.*

The ceremony has been revived at the Pike and Musket, Walton, near Street.

Burning the 'ashen faggot' on Christmas Eve or New Year's Eve provided a good excuse for more intense drinking; the faggot was bound with willow bonds and as each one burnt and broke, a fresh jug of cider was passed around the company. The King William at Curry Rivel, near Langport, has kept this tradition going. Sixty or seventy years ago cider making was becoming a dying craft: as beer drinking became more popular the large breweries began to take over the old local pubs and cider was relegated to the 'cider bar' or the 'jug and bottle'. However, the skills of the cider maker were kept alive, particularly through the efforts of the National Fruit and Cider Institute at Long Ashton, near Bristol.

In recent years cider has regained its former popularity and lost its rustic stigma. Some producers, like Sheppy's at Taunton and Perry's at Dowlish Wake, have developed their production and marketing to vie with the major companies.

A transportable cider press in use in 1934

WESSEX
Gazetteer

Each entry in this Gazetteer has the atlas page number on which the place can be found and its National Grid reference included under the heading. An explanation of how to use the National Grid is given on page 82.

Above: Weymouth Harbour

Abbotsbury, Dorset

Map Ref: 91SY5785

Early in the 11th century a Benedictine monastery was founded here by Orc, a follower of King Canute, but little remains except the huge 14th-century abbey barn. The thatched part is only half of the original building which was 270ft long. In the churchyard there is a gable wall of another monastic building and, isolated on a bare hilltop south-west, St Catherine's Chapel stands as a landmark. Its 14th-century roof is barrel-vaulted.

St Nicholas Church, in the pretty, thatched village, is mostly 15th-century; the shot holes in the pulpit are said to be the result of a skirmish during the Civil War. In the north porch notice the carved effigy of an abbot of about 1200.

The Abbotsbury Swannery was established by the monks in the 14th century. It is at the western end of the brackish waters of the Fleet, behind the high bank of Chesil Beach. Between 400 and 800 mute swans make their home here in the breeding season and feed on the eel grass which grows abundantly. Reeds are harvested for thatching and there is a 17th-century duck decoy.

West of the village, the Sub-Tropical Gardens are protected from the prevailing wind by a curtain of trees. The gardens were started in 1760, and have a walled garden in the centre which is a mass of azaleas, camellias and rhododendrons.

AA recommends:
Hotel: Ilchester Arms, 9 Market St, 2-star, tel. (0305) 871243

Amesbury, Wiltshire

Map Ref: 89SU1541

According to Thomas Malory, Queen Guinevere came to Amesbury Abbey when she heard of Arthur's death. The abbey was succeeded in 979 by a nunnery which eventually became one of the richest in England. It achieved fame as the retreat of Mary, daughter of Edward I and her grandmother Queen Eleanor, Henry III's widow.

The property was granted to the Duke of Somerset in 1540. He and his son, the Earl of Hertford, built a house on this site. This was replaced in 1661 by a new mansion, designed by John Webb in the style of Inigo Jones, his father-in-law. Here the handsome and hospitable Duchess of Queensberry inspired John Gay to write *The Beggar's Opera*. The present Amesbury Abbey was rebuilt in 1840, but a cave in the grounds,

St Catherine's Chapel, Abbotsbury, was built entirely of stone, roof and all, with heavy buttresses and 4ft walls

where Gay is said to have worked, still remains.

Amesbury is a pleasant market town, set in a bend of the River Avon, which is crossed by a five-arched bridge built in Palladian style. Today the neighbourhood is dominated by military and RAF camps and their personnel.

Antrobus House, the Queen Anne-style building in Salisbury Road, was built in 1925 from funds provided by the estate of the late Lady Antrobus; it is a social centre and a museum, housing her personal effects.

West of the Avon, on the border of Amesbury Park, are the outlines of the prehistoric site known as Vespasian's Camp, an Iron Age refuge held by the Romans.

About a mile north of the town, Woodhenge, the site of a large Neolithic wooden structure, was recognised in 1925 when Squadron Leader Install flew over in a Sopwith Snipe and noticed marks in the chalk where posts had stood.

AA recommends:
Hotel: Antrobus Arms, Church St, 2-star, tel. (0980) 23168

Woodhenge Neolithic monument, Amesbury. Small concrete pillars mark where timber posts stood

Athelney, Somerset

Map Ref: 90ST3429

In a field beside the A361 at Athelney, an obelisk marks the spot where King Alfred built an abbey to give thanks for his salvation from the Danes. The 'island' of slightly higher ground, surrounded by dank marshes and bogs, proved a safe retreat for him in the winter of AD 877–8. Somewhere near here, the legend persists, Alfred burnt the cakes. He also built two forts, one on the edge of the 'island', the other at East Lyng. Burrow Mump, a mile east, may also be the site of an early fortification; it was replaced by a church in the 15th century. Changes were made in about 1793 but it was never quite finished. The Mump is now owned by the National Trust and serves as a memorial to Somerset's dead in World War I.

The village of Athelney has brick cottages with pantiled roofs and colourful gardens stretching down onto the moor. Roadside stalls offer fruit, vegetables and baskets: this is willow country, where 'withies' are grown as a field crop, and processed in the growers' yard. Stubby brick chimneys identify the boilers, most now redundant.

In winter the moors around Athelney and Burrowbridge are intentionally flooded partly to save the river banks from damage, but partly to fertilise and protect the early spring grass. It is worth climbing the Mump to get an impression of how the Levels must have looked in the past.

Avebury, Wiltshire

Map Ref: 89SU1069

In 1663 John Aubrey wrote that Avebury 'does as much exceed Stonehenge in greatness as a cathedral does a parish church'. Only recently has it begun to reveal

King Alfred's monument at Athelney commemorates his campaign here, in 878, against the Danish invaders

its mysteries. Unlike bleakly isolated Stonehenge, this megalithic circle, built 4–5,000 years ago, encloses the village, the pub, the chapel and the cross roads, an odd juxtaposition which enhances the magic.

From the south an avenue of sarsen stones forms a processional way from the Sanctuary on Overton Hill to the southern entrance of the massive circular embankment – a site of 28½ acres is enclosed by the bank and ditch. Around the inner edge of the ditch was originally a ring of 98 large upright sarsens set at intervals of 36ft. Within the enclosure are two smaller stone circle complexes, the 'Northern Circle' with a group of three sarsens called the 'Cove' at its centre, and the 'Southern Circle', still largely unexcavated but with The Obelisk, a monolith, at its centre.

The first archaeologist to analyse the site in a modern way was Alexander Keiller (1889–1955), heir to the wealth of the Dundee marmalade empire. The museum of his name, in the converted stables of the Manor House, includes finds from Windmill Hill, Silbury Hill, the Sanctuary and the Avebury circles.

For all this, the village of Avebury is remarkably unaffected. The pretty stone Church of St James, its Saxon font embellished with Norman carving, is set in a large churchyard bounded by a thatched wall; the adjacent charming Manor House is Elizabethan. The Manor's estates were broken up earlier this century, but local people saved its 17th-century 'Great Barn' and it is now the Great Barn Museum of Wiltshire Folk Life.

Avonmouth, Avon

Map Ref: 87ST5178

Mud flats and marshes at the mouth of the River Avon were transformed into an industrial dockland in the Port of Bristol's response to competition from other ports. Previously all vessels had to negotiate the narrow and twisting Avon through the Gorge to reach the docks at the very heart of the city centre. Ships constantly ran aground, stuck in the mud or simply missed the tide, and as ships grew in size so the problems increased. It was vital to the economic health of the community to improve the docks, and the natural place to do that was at Avonmouth. Private enterprise led the way with the first dock opened in 1877. In 1908 the Royal Edward Dock was completed, and it was more than doubled in size by extensions in 1921 and 1928. The Royal Portbury Dock, which has the largest lock in the country, opened in 1978.

From the M5 Avonmouth appears as a smoke-laden jungle of pipelines, steaming chimneys and power cables, but the dockland is a fascinating world of international trade and activity. It is the largest municipally owned port in the country, handling 3½ million tons of cargo per year. Timber from British Columbia, cocoa and coffee from Africa, ores from South America, animal feed from India and China and motor vehicles from Spain and Japan arrive daily in exotically named cargo vessels.

The dock is a police controlled area where only bona fide visitors are permitted entrance. The dockside is dominated by towering cranes, huge warehouses and giant processing works. Here are the CWS flour mill (now disused), almost classical in style; a 30,000-ton granary, built in 1966; and huge oil storage areas for Shell and Esso. Developments continue. Back in Gloucester Road, the rich, if faded, ornamentation of the Royal Hotel and its adjoining rank of shops illustrates the anticipation of prosperity that followed the first development of the docks.

AA recommends:
Garage: Avon Filling Station (AFS Garages), St Andrews Rd, *tel* (0272) 821211

Axbridge, Somerset

Map Ref: 86ST4254

Lying at the south-west end of the Mendip Hills, just a stone's throw from the A38 and not far from the M5, Axbridge has retained its charm and interest thanks to a bypass along the line of the redundant Cheddar Valley railway.

The twisting and narrow High Street, flanked by medieval buildings, many disguised by Georgian façades, leads to the Market Square, now a central car park. Some of the buildings are jettied and timber-framed, unusual in Somerset. The best example is King John's Hunting Lodge, a house which was nothing to do with King John or hunting, at the corner of the High Street and the Square. It has been beautifully restored by the National Trust and is open to the public as a museum of local history. A painting in the museum shows the buzz of activity around the covered market cross which stood in the Square until the mid-18th century when it was demolished to improve the traffic flow for stage coaches.

Up a dented flight of steps from the Square and dominating the town is the Parish Church of St John the Baptist, rebuilt in the 15th century at the height of the town's prosperity. The moulded plasterwork ceiling of the nave was done in 1636 for ten guineas by George Drayton, a local craftsman. There is an interesting brass to Roger Harper and his wife (late 15th century).

The old workhouse is an impressive, if austere, building and the old railway station has become a youth club.

AA recommends:
Hotel: Oak House, The Square, 2-star, tel. (0934) 732444
Guesthouse: Lamb, The Square (Inn), tel. (0934) 732253
Garage: Rooksbridge, Rooksbridge, tel. (093472) 229

King John surveys the scene from 'King John's Hunting Lodge', Axbridge, built about 300 years after his reign

Badminton, Avon

Map Ref: 88ST8082

The pretty village of Badminton has a fine collection of cottages and houses for the estate workers from Badminton House. The range of almshouses for retired servants, built in about 1714, bears the Beaufort badge in triplicate; others are in rustic style with verandas and diamond window panes.

About a mile north, at Little Badminton, thatched cottages and farm buildings cluster round the pleasant village green with a circular dovecote at its centre. The Cotswold stone-tiled church, which is the private ducal chapel, is Norman in origin, and the earliest feature is the 12th-century arcade, which still has traces of wall painting.

The Beaufort coat of arms, displayed on almshouses built for retired workers on the Badminton House estate

Badminton House has been the home of the Beaufort family for 300 years. The central block dates from the original building of 1682, as do the Grinling Gibbons limewood carvings in the dining-room. The rest is mainly late 18th century, the work of William Kent.

Kent also planned the great park to provide a visual setting and pleasing vistas from the house. It is dotted with buildings and follies, notably Worcester Lodge, at the end of a three-mile ride from the north entrance of the house. In the park, the Badminton Hunt is said to have started the fashion for fox-hunting, in about 1760, and to have bred special hounds from staghounds and harriers. Today the Park is famed for the annual Horse Trials, a three-day event held in April.

The game of badminton was another innovation, first played about a century ago in the great hall, where it is said that the duke played tennis, found he was damaging his pictures and substituted a shuttlecock for the ball.

About a mile to the south, near Acton Turville, is Badminton Railway Station, now closed. It was opened in 1903 when the GWR constructed its last major line to connect the Severn Tunnel direct with London without having to go via Bristol. This was achieved by the construction of the Badminton Tunnel under the Southwold ridge, 2½ miles long and ventilated with a line of castellated towers, such as the one at Old Sodbury.

Bath, Avon

Map Ref: 88ST7564

Georgian Bath remains magnificent, with its splendid array of crescents and squares, mansions and terraced town houses, a picturesque backdrop of warm-coloured stone.

Strangely enough Bath stone is not an outstandingly good building material. Its use was the result of high pressure salesmanship by the postmaster-come-quarry owner, Ralph Allen, who successfully displayed the stone's superficial quality on his magnificent house, Prior Park, at Combe Down. The house was designed by John Wood, one of the city's principal architects in its mid-18th-century heyday.

Georgian Bath was created by builders aiming to cash in on the demand for fashionable residences to be hired for the season by society 'taking the waters'. People came to recuperate from the excesses of London and to participate in the social round led by Beau Nash, and later so exquisitely described by Jane Austen.

The waters which made Bath popular in the 18th century had attracted the Romans 1,700 years earlier. They created the town of Aquae Sulis (Sulis was the local Celtic goddess of hot springs), and for four centuries enjoyed the pleasures of bathing and lounging around the warm water. The Great Bath of the Roman city can still be visited and the extraordinary, torrential hot spring can be seen.

The Saxon church of the Monastery of St Peter and St Paul was chosen by Archbishop Dunstan in AD973 for the coronation of Edgar as King of All England. The medieval market town developed around the monastery as a flourishing woollen manufacturing centre. The present Abbey church, which overlooks the Roman baths, was begun in 1499 by Bishop Oliver King; he dreamt that angels ascending and descending a ladder from heaven had instructed him to restore the church. The dream is represented by a unique carving of ladders and angels on the buttresses at the west end.

The city has a wealth of museums and places to visit, including the Pump Rooms where spa water or tea can be taken; Pulteney Bridge built in 1770 to Robert Adam's design; the Theatre Royal, now expertly restored; the Assembly Rooms with the Museum of Costume in the basement; the Circus; and the Royal Crescent overlooking Victoria Park. Number 1 Royal Crescent has been rescued from time and is a museum piece of a Georgian house with carefully arranged ornaments on thin-stalked Hepplewhite furniture. The National Centre for Photography houses an important museum and exhibition galleries. Victoria Park has botanical gardens and a children's play area.

Bath's diverse cultural life is enriched by the annual festival, in May, of music and arts together with colourful fringe events.

In the village of Bathampton, 2 miles east of Bath, the church has an Australia Chapel and the tomb of Admiral Arthur Phillip, who led the first fleet of settlers to Sydney in 1787/8 and became the first Governor of New South Wales. He retired to Bath in 1806 and lived here until his death in 1814.

At Claverton Manor, 2 miles east of the centre, is the American Museum. Eighteen rooms depict American life from 250 years ago and there is a collection of quilts.

AA recommends:
Hotels: Francis, Queen Sq, 4-star, *tel.* (0225) 24257
Royal Crescent, 16 Royal Crescent, 4-red-star, *tel.* (0225) 319090
Lansdown Grove, Lansdown Rd, 3-star, *tel.* (0225) 315891
The Priory, Weston Rd, 3-red-star, *tel.* (0225) 331922
Restaurants: Popjoys, Beau Nash House, 3-forks, *tel.* (0225) 60494
The Hole in the Wall, George St, 2-forks, *tel.* (0225) 25242
Rajpoot Tandoori, Argyle St. 2-forks, *tel.* (0225) 66833
Clos du Roy, Edgar Buildings. 1-fork, *tel.* (0225) 64356
Guesthouses: Brompton House, St Johns Rd, *tel.* (0225) 20972
Eagle House, Church St, Batnford, *tel.* (0225) 859946

Two of Bath's treasures: the Baths and the Abbey, dating from 1499

Orchard House, Warminster Rd, Bathampton, *tel.* (0225) 66115
Paradise House, Holloway, *tel.* (0225) 317723
Garages: Hinton, Albion Pl, Upper Bristol Rd, *tel.* (0225) 22131
Lansdowne Auto Svcs, 59 High St, *tel.* (0225) 25784
A. Richardson & Sons, Bathwick Hill, *tel.* (0225) 66286

Selection only: see page 4

Kennet and Avon Canal

One of the most exciting and ambitious restoration projects in Wessex is that undertaken by the Kennet and Avon Canal Trust to recreate the navigable waterway between Bristol and London. The Trust, which was established in 1962, has its headquarters at the Canal Centre in Devizes where there is a comprehensive exhibition explaining the development and demise of the canal.

The Trust has relied heavily on volunteers, who have cleared the canal bottom and repaired its sides; but recognising the complexity of the scheme, and its long-term value, the British Waterways Board is responsible for engineering maintenance and supervises employees, with financial support from County and District authorities.

The first meeting to discuss the idea of linking the Kennet, which flows into the Thames at Reading, with the Avon, at Bath, was held in 1788 in Hungerford. The navigation of the two rivers had been improved earlier in the 18th century, by John Hore, a local engineer. The artificial waterway between the rivers had to rise to 450ft above sea level; 104 locks were needed, two aqueducts and, at the summit, a tunnel over 500 yards long.

Only 22 years later the complete navigation, executed by the canal engineer John Rennie, was open to traffic.

The Claverton Pumping Station, near Bath, raises water from the River Avon to the canal, 47ft above, by a unique waterwheel-powered pump built in 1813; and the Crofton Beam Engines, near Marlborough, are the oldest 'in steam' in the world. One was built by Boulton and Watt in 1812 and the other in 1845 by Harveys of Hale.

Rennie was also a first-class architect and the Dundas and Avoncliff aqueducts, between Claverton and Bradford-on-Avon, are in splendid classical style.

The canal was used to carry vast quantities of coal, iron, stone and slate, local agricultural products and timber, and to bring luxuries like tobacco and spirits from London. While canal transport was popular, the Kennet and Avon was extremely successful, but only 40 years after its completion railways took over bulk transport.

Thanks to the work of the Trust and the Waterways Board, the canal banks and towpath are accessible throughout its length.

The original seal used by the Kennet and Avon Canal Company

The tower of Beaminster church is elaborately decorated with friezes, pinnacles and sculptured figures

Beaminster, Dorset

Map Ref: 90ST4701

The town grew up as a market and a centre for the woollen cloth trade, especially high quality broadcloth. Later, linen and sailcloth manufacture increased, using flax and hemp grown in the area. It has not changed very much in the last 100 years largely because it was never on a railway.

In 1644 during the siege of Lyme Regis, some of the royal forces were garrisoned at Beaminster; on Palm Sunday a dispute amongst the soldiers led to a fire being started and a contemporary account records that 'the whole towne was all destroyed in Two Hours; and those goods for the most part which were carried out of the fire, were carried away by the soldiers'. There were further fires in 1684, 1781, 1786 and 1842.

The roads radiate from the covered market cross in the middle of the attractive Market Square. Hogshill Street, to the west, is lined with a mixture of cottages and shops all in the local creamy golden limestone: notice the very individual shop sign over Gibbs the butchers', opposite Robin's Real Bread Shop. The Pines grocery shop in Fleet Street is the best of several 18th-century shop fronts.

The church is particularly fine, with an ornamented tower.

Nearby Parnham house, a fine Tudor mansion, has become a mecca for wood craftsmen, where John Makepeace runs courses in furniture-making and design.

AA recommends:
Restaurants: Bridge House Country, 1-fork, *tel.* (0308) 862200
Nevitt's Eating House, 57 Hogshill St, 1-fork, *tel.* (0308) 862600
Guesthouse: Hams Plot, Bridport Rd, *tel.* (0308) 862979

Bere Regis, Dorset

Map Ref: 92SY8494

This pretty little village was once a thriving market town. In the 14th century the population was decimated by the plague, which may well have arrived in England through the port of Melcombe Regis (Weymouth).

The neat church, of Saxon foundation, is the burial place of the Turberville family on which Hardy based his *Tess of the d'Urbervilles*; in the novel, Bere Regis is called 'Kingsbere-sub-Greenhill'. The family vault is beneath the south aisle, but the feature of this church that justifies its claim to be the most visited village church in the county is the fabulously carved and painted roof. Here life-size, brightly coloured figures of the Apostles hang out dizzily from the arched braces. Also noteworthy are the ancient altar slab, the carved pew ends, and the grappling hooks, in the south porch, used to tear the thatch from the roofs of burning cottages.

AA recommends:
Campsite: Rowlands Wait Touring Park, Rye Hill, 2-pennants, *tel.* (0929) 471958

Blaise Hamlet, Avon

Map Ref: 87ST5678

Tucked away in the northern suburbs of Bristol, Blaise Hamlet was planned as a village for estate workers and old retainers from the Blaise Castle estate. The entrance to the central green, complete with village pump and weather vane, is through a little wicket-gate off the road. There are ten cottages, each quaintly different, with thatched or stone-slated roofs, leaded windows and curlicue chimneys. The hamlet was designed by John Nash and completed in 1812, for the Quaker banker, John Scandrett Harford, who lived at Blaise Castle House. The house, now the City of Bristol's Museum of Social History, was built in 1796 by William Paty; its plain style, appropriate for the Quaker banker, was embellished with an orangery and thatched dairy, both by Nash. The grounds were laid out by Humphry Repton and sweeping grass slopes lead to the natural gorge of the Hazel Brook. A mill was brought here in 1952 from West Harptree (Avon).

Blaise Castle itself, a gothic fantasy, was erected in 1766 for a Bristol merchant, Tom Farr.

Blandford Forum, Dorset

Map Ref: 92ST8806

Despite its name, this was never a Roman town, but it was an important market for agricultural produce at the crossing point of the River Stour. Lace was manufactured here in the early 18th century, of which Defoe said, 'I think I never saw better in Flanders, France or Italy'.

In 1731 the town centre was gutted by fire and almost wholly rebuilt between 1732 and 1760, creating one of the most attractive and complete small Georgian towns in England. The rebuilding was planned and partially executed by two brothers, local builders and architects, William and John Bastard. At the east end of the market place is the 'Fire Monument', a miniature classical temple. The church has box pews and a gallery, with great round pillars supporting the roof.

The side streets are worth exploring: the museum is in Bere's Yard, and the Old House in the Close is one of the few that pre-dates the fire.

Over the bridge to the south is Blandford St Mary and the home of 'Badger' beer at Hall and Woodhouse's brewery. The impressive gateway nearby is the entrance to Bryanston House, now a school.

AA recommends:
Hotel: Crown Hotel, 1 West St, 3-star, *tel.* (0258) 56626
Restaurant. La Belle Alliance, Portman Lodge, Whitecliff Mill St, 2-fork, *tel.* (0258) 52842

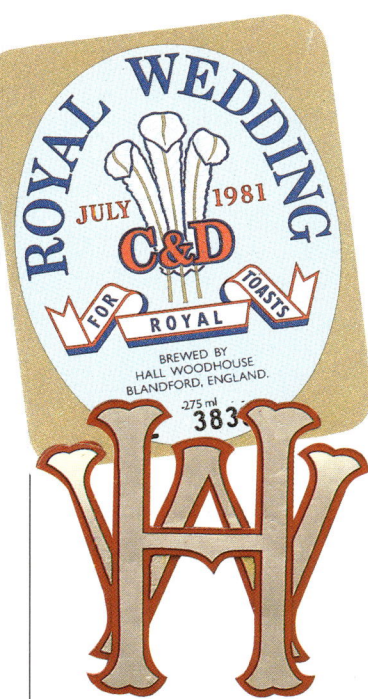

Hall and Woodhouse brew Badger Beer in Blandford. Their bottles display a special label for a special occasion

Bournemouth, Dorset

Map Ref: 93SZ0891

In a peaceful valley where the little River Bourne meets the sea, Lewis Tregonwell, 'a Dorset gentleman', built a house in 1810. By 1851 the population was still only 695, but with the arrival of the railway in 1870, the town mushroomed overnight, and in 1901 the population had rocketed to over 47,000. In *Tess of the d'Urbervilles* Hardy described it, under the name of Sandbourne, as it appeared to Angel Clare:

a fashionable watering place, with its eastern and western stations, its piers, its groves of pines, its promenades and its covered garden.

He added that it was

a Mediterranean lounging-place on the English Channel.

Today the built-up area of Poole, Bournemouth and Christchurch combined forms the largest non-industrial conurbation in Europe. Bournemouth has an international clientele, attracting the elderly to its balmy climate, and the young to its language schools and night-life.

The pine trees (planted from the early 19th century) and heather of the heathland over which Bournemouth now sprawls have been saved wherever possible, and the valley which attracted Tregonwell remains a delight to modern visitors: right through the commercial heart of the borough, the Bourne is fringed by lush and colourful pleasure gardens, leading past the bandstand and Pavilion Theatre to the promenade, pier and beach. Other valleys, or 'chines', remain as tree-lined, pine-scented paths to the beaches – such as Durley Chine, Alum Chine and Boscombe Chine.

Around the Square, in the centre of town, a few of the original Victorian buildings remain: but there has been much rebuilding to make way for modern hotels, shops and restaurants. Entertainments of every sort abound, from the Bournemouth Symphony Orchestra at the Winter Gardens, to the one-armed bandits of the pier amusement arcade, and from the Ferndown Golf Club to the table-tennis in Central Park.

The two Victorian town centre churches have survived. Of the interior of St Stephen's Sir John Betjeman wrote: 'worth travelling 200 miles and being sick in the coach'. St Peter's is now overwhelmed by towering buildings around it, but the poet Shelley's heart is buried in the churchyard, together with his wife, Mary Wolstonecraft Shelley, author of *Frankenstein* (1818).

The Russell-Cotes Art Gallery and Museum at East Cliff is a fascinating treasure-house of the weird and wonderful. Outside on the Geological Terrace are displayed blocks of over 200 different rocks.

Young and old come to Bournemouth to enjoy its promenade, beaches and pier, its pine-scented chines, its pleasure gardens and bandstand

AA recommends:
Hotels: Heathlands, Grove Rd, Eastcliff, 3-star, *tel.* (0202) 23336
Pavilion, 22 Bath Rd, 3-star, *tel.* (0202) 291266
White Hermitage, Exeter Rd, 3-star, *tel.* (0202) 27363
Belvedere, Bath Rd, 2-star, *tel.* (0202) 21080
Restaurants: Sophisticats, 43 Charminster Rd, 2-fork, *tel.* (0202) 291019
La Taverna (Palace Court Hotel), Westover Rd, 2-fork, *tel.* (0202) 27681
Crusts, The Square, 1-fork, *tel.* (0202) 21430
Provence, 91 Belle Vue Rd, Southbourne, 1-fork, rosette, *tel.* (0202) 424421
Raj Khana, 43 Seamoor, Westbourne, 1-fork, *tel.* (0202) 767142
Guesthouses: Alumcliff Hotel, 121 Alumhurst Rd, *tel.* (0202) 764777
Naseby Nye Hotel, Byron Rd, Boscombe, *tel.* (0202) 34079
Ravenstone Hotel, 36 Burnaby Rd, *tel.* (0202) 761047
Silver Trees Hotel, 57 Wimborne Rd, *tel.* (0202) 26040
Garages: Iford Bridge Motor Co, 1374 Christchurch Rd, *tel.* (0202) 479751
St Pauls, 14 Carbery Row, Southbourne, *tel.* (0202) 423243
Westover Mtrs, Castle Ln, *tel.* (0202) 510201
Winton, 41-7 Alma Rd, Winton, *tel.* (0202) 526501

Selection only: see page 4

Bradford-on-Avon, Wiltshire

Map Ref: 88ST8260

The steep slopes of the north bank of the River Avon here are lined with mellow stone cottages, fine clothiers' houses, narrow lanes and flag-stone steps. Below, along the river, the old woollen mills look empty and derelict; but the town is prosperous once again with tourists and new residents, many of them commuters to Bath, Bristol and even London.

For the best view of the town and surroundings head for Top Rank Tory. The road runs along the crest of the hill, past 18th-century houses and terraces to a superb row of 17th-century weavers' houses and, at the town's highest point, the hospice chapel of St Mary, Tory.

Down by the river, the tiny, bare Saxon Church of St Lawrence is the jewel in Bradford's crown. It was founded by St Aldhelm in about AD700 and this building dates from the 10th century. For generations it was forgotten: the chancel became a house, the nave a school, and the west wall formed part of a factory. In 1858 the vicar of Bradford rediscovered it and set about clearing up the mess. Notice particularly the sculptured 'floating' angels, wonderful examples of Saxon craftsmanship.

Bradford-on-Avon was recorded as a borough in Domesday Book; the broad ford was the natural crossing point of the river, now spanned by a 14th-century bridge which was widened in the 17th century by the addition of the lock-up in which, it is said, John Wesley spent some time. Its clothiers thrived – according to Daniel Defoe in 1724 'worth from ten thousand to forty thousand pounds a man' – and provided employment for spinners, weavers, dyers and fullers, until the end of the 18th century.

Off the Frome Road (B3109) and down Pound Lane to Barton Farm, the magnificent 14th-century barn illustrates the wealth and power of the nunnery of Shaftesbury, which used it to store the produce from its vast local estates. The huge building has four entrance porches and fourteen bays; at over 55yds long, it is the second largest such barn in the country.

Two miles east of Bradford, at the village of Holt, disputes among the weavers were dealt with at a house known as The Courts, now owned by the National Trust. Only the topiary garden, arboretum and lily pond are open to the public. About a mile north of Holt, Great Chalfield Manor is a beautifully restored 15th-century moated house, well worth seeing.

Bridgwater, Somerset

Map Ref: 86ST2937

The town developed as a major transhipment point where goods were unloaded from sea-going vessels and transferred into barges to continue their journey down the river; Bridgwater merchants thus controlled much of the county's trade. In the 19th century, the opening of the Bridgwater to Taunton canal reinforced its economic status and in 1841 the Bristol and Exeter Railway Company opened an impressive new docks and warehouse complex.

The town's medieval buildings have all but disappeared, but the Church of St Mary, with its soaring medieval spire, clearly demonstrates the wealth of Bridgwater merchants at that time.

In 1795 an iron bridge spanned the muddy banks of the Parrett, one of the earliest iron bridges in Britain. Made by Abraham Darby of Coalbrookdale, it was removed in 1883 because it was too hump-backed, and the present bridge was installed. On the east side lie most of the factories, the railway station and the market. Here were the Barham's Brick and Tile Works, which supplied much of the country with bricks, pantiles and decorated roof finials. 'Bath' bricks, for scouring, were made here, from the riverside mud, and the remains of one surviving 'bottle' kiln can be seen.

On the west bank the principal shopping streets radiate from the Cornhill, where Admiral Blake's statue commands Fore Street. The finest street in town is without doubt Castle Street, built by the Duke of Chandos in the 1720s. The Duke set up a glass manufacturing business nearby, and the remains of the kiln are in a car park.

Number 11 Castle Street has the Arts Centre, opened in 1946; it once welcomed Picasso as a visitor, and houses a theatre and gallery.

AA recommends:
Hotel: Walnut Tree Inn, North Petherton, 2-star, *tel.* (0278) 662255 (3m S A38).
Restaurant: Old Vicarage, 45-9 St Mary Street, 1-fork, *tel.* (0278) 458891
Garages: Harry Ball, Market St, *tel.* (0278) 422125
Bridgwater Motor Company, Eastover, *tel.* (0278) 422218
Motorcraft, Polden St, *tel.* (0278) 457240
New Westway Service Station, Taunton Rd, *tel.* (0278) 458300

Great Chalfield Manor, near Bradford-on-Avon, a beautifully mellow, moated house built during the Wars of the Roses

Bridport, Dorset

Map Ref: 90SY4692

Bridport is surrounded by the rich soils of the Marshwood Vale, which were found to be suitable for the growing of hemp and flax. A thriving rope and sailcloth industry grew up. In 1213 King John ordered the Sheriff to

cause to be made at Bridport, night and day, as many ropes for ships both large and small as they could, and twisted yarns for cordage.

The ropewalks of Bridport helped to supply the Royal Navy and nets made here equipped the fishing fleet. Now the old industry has successfully transferred to the use of new materials and man-made fibres.

At the centre of the town is the Georgian town hall and market house, where the roads swell to make room for the market, and where (in South Street) the nets were made. The back streets and alleyways are worth exploring.

Lee Lane, a track off the Dorchester Road out of town, was where King Charles II hid from the Roundheads in 1651. A stone monument on the wall bears the inscription:

King Charles II escaped capture through this lane Sept XXIII. MDCLI.
When midst your fiercest foes on every side
for your escape God did a lane provide.

West Bay, the former 'port' for Bridport, struggled and failed to become a fashionable resort. The little harbour is oddly isolated, with a handful of buildings round about, and the beach, popular with holiday-makers, backed to the east by vertical cliffs. At the harbour are shrimp and cockle stalls.

AA recommends:
Hotels: Haddon House, West Bay, 3-star, *tel.* (0308) 23626
Bull, 34 East St, 2-star, *tel.* (0308) 22878
Roundham House, Roundham Grids, West Bay Rd, 2-star, *tel.* (0308) 22753
Bridport Arms, West Bay, 1-star, *tel.* (0308) 22994
Little Wych Country House, Burton Rd, 1-star country house, *tel.* (0308) 23490
Self Catering: Coniston Holiday Apartments, Coniston House, 69 Victoria Grove, *tel.* (0308) 24049
Guesthouses: Bridge House, East St, *tel.* (0308) 23371
Britmead House, 154 West Bay Rd, *tel.* (0308) 22941
King Charles Tavern, 114 St Andrews Rd (Inn), *tel.* (0308) 22911
Campsite: Highland End Farm Caravan Park, Eype, 3-pennants, *tel.* (0308) 22139 (1m W of A35)
Garages: G Bonfield & Son, 66 West St, *tel.* (0308) 22297
Greens Motors, East Rd, *tel.* (0308) 22922
Harbour, 1 West Bay, *tel.* (0308) 22207
West Road, West Rd, *tel.* (0308) 22611

Selection only: see page 4.

Burton Cliffs, West Bay near Bridport, where Chesil Beach begins

Mud Horse Fishing

The coastline of Avon and Somerset, from Birnbeck Island off Weston-super-Mare to the looming power station at Hinkley Point, is fringed with mud flats extending, at low tide, some three or four miles out into the Severn Estuary. Low water fishing, especially eel glatting, has long been practised:

There was an old fellow of Steart,
Who went catching eels in the dirt.
When they asked 'Any luck?'
'Up to eyes in the muck!'
Said that rueful old fellow of Steart.

About a mile west of Steart Point and the mouth of the River Parrett, at the cul-de-sac village of Stolford, two fishermen, Tony Brewer and Brendon Sellick use sledges, called 'mud horses', to slither over the grey mud to set up and fish their nets. A hundred years ago there were a dozen or so fishermen sliding about on the mud.

As the tide turns the fishermen follow it out, leaning on their sledges and pushing into the ooze with their feet. Once they reach the nets, they have two or three hours to sort the catch and pack it in baskets and nets, ready to slide back to the shore with the incoming tide lapping at their heels.

The fishing season extends from April to December. They must aim to visit the nets daily or the catch will rot between the tides or be ripped to shreds by the gulls. Two types of nets are used: 'trammel' nets, set up on posts about two metres high, for catching grey mullet, Dover sole, whiting, skate and salmon bass; and shrimp nets, with gaping mouths facing upstream, tapering to a net trap where the shrimps are caught. A couple of hundredweight of fish is not uncommon for a day's catch.

Back over the mud at the shingle ridge that marks the shore, the mud horse is left below the high-water mark, moored with a heavy stone. The day's catch is carried home in a basket, slung on the back and held with a chest strap, to be cleaned as quickly as possible. The shrimps are washed and picked over in great flat baskets, called 'reaps', then boiled in an old washing 'copper'.

At one time most of the catch was sold locally in the markets at Bridgwater and Taunton, but now it is sent off by rail to London. Some is kept for sale direct and it is well worth the detour to Stolford, off the A39, to meet the fishermen, to see their strange transport across the mud and to buy some shrimps fresh from the boiler.

Tony Brewer and his 'mud horse'

Bristol, Avon

Map Ref: 87ST5873

A cosmopolitan city of international stature, Bristol is rich in culture and history, thriving as an established engineering and high technology centre.

It is the town's role as a port that has provided the key to its growth since Saxon and Norman times. In the Middle Ages Bristol was the wealthiest provincial town in England, with a flourishing overseas trade with the Continent and Ireland. This stimulated adventurous voyages further west, and culminated in the discoveries of John Cabot, Martin Pring and John Guy in the New World.

Merchants displayed their prosperity through generous gifts to the churches which still enhance the city; most notable of these is St Mary Redcliffe, described by Queen Elizabeth I as 'The fairest, goodliest and most famous parish church in England'. It was rebuilt in the 15th century by the pre-eminent merchant family of Canynge.

Thousands emigrated from the port of Bristol – some in pursuit of religious freedom. The city was a prominent centre of Nonconformity, with an Independent congregation from 1640 (later the Baptist Church in Broadmead) and Quakers from 1655. Wesley's New Room in Broadmead is the earliest Methodist Church in the world.

Trade remained the driving force behind Bristol's later development, leading to the establishment in the 18th century of new industries such as chocolate, sugar, rum, slaves and tobacco.

The Bristol 'Nails', standing on the pavement outside the Corn Exchange in Corn Street, served as trading tables on which merchants completed their money transactions: hence the saying 'to pay on the nail'.

Later, Bristol was to encourage Brunel to use the city's docks to build his *Great Western* and his *Great Britain*. The construction of

Above: Brunel's Clifton Suspension Bridge high above the Avon. Below: a maze, one of St Mary Redcliffe's innumerable carved roof bosses. Detail of SS Great Britain, fully restored

new docks at Avonmouth from 1877 enabled Bristol to cater more efficiently with larger trading ships and helped to re-establish it as a centre of international trade.

Bristol's principal shopping centre, Broadmead, adjoining Castle Park and the commercial centre, is a post-war development in an area that was devastated by bombing: the ruins of St Peter's Church in the Park have been preserved as a poignant reminder of the destruction.

Park Street rises steeply from the Cathedral and College Green towards the tower of the Wills Memorial building of Bristol University and Queens Road. This is the area of smart specialist shops, restaurants and the City Museum and Art Gallery. Just off Park Street one Georgian house has been preserved as a typical late 18th-century town house. The Cathedral itself has a Norman chapter house and a magnificent chancel of the 13th to 14th centuries. Parts of the cloisters also survive from the former abbey. The nave is 19th-century.

In recent years Bristol's dockland has been revitalised by new housing, refurbishment of old buildings and the conversion of warehouses to exciting new uses. The Arnolfini Gallery offers a full range of contemporary arts. On the opposite quay is the Watershed complex, a media centre with two cinemas, a gallery and tourist information office. Nearby are the Industrial Museum, Maritime Heritage Centre and SS *Great Britain*, which came back to be restored in the dry dock in which she was built in 1843.

Brunel's other major contribution to Bristol's landscape is the magnificent Clifton Suspension Bridge, 245ft above high water of the River Avon and with a span of 702ft.

AA recommends:
Hotels: Holiday Inn, Castle St, 4-star, *tel.* (0272) 294281
Ladbroke Dragonara, Redcliffe Way, 4-star, *tel.* (0272) 20044
Crest Hotel, Filton Lane, 3-star, *tel.* (0272) 564242
Redwood Lodge, Beggar Bush Lane, 3-star, *tel.* (0272) 393901
Restaurants: Barbizon, Corn St, 2-fork, *tel.* (0272) 22658
Restaurant Du Gourmet, Whiteladies Rd, 2-fork, *tel.* (0272) 73623
Bouboulina's, Portland St, 1-fork, *tel.* (0272) 731192
Edwards, Alma Vale Rd, 1-fork, *tel.* (0272) 741533

Guesthouses: Alandale Hotel, Tyndalls Park Rd, *tel.* (0272) 735407
Alcove, 508/10 Fishponds Rd, *tel.* (0272) 653886
Downlands, 33 Henleaze Gardens, *tel.* (0272) 621639
Glenroy Hotel, 30 Victoria St, *tel.* (0272) 39058
Garages: Clarkes of Muller Road, 175-85 Muller Road, Horfield, *tel.* (0272) 513333
Langdon Mtrs, School Rd, Totterdown, *tel.* (0272) 665740
Patchway Car Centre, Gloucester Rd, Gypsy Patch Ln, Patchway, *tel.* (0272) 694331
St Marks, 22-8 St Marks Rd, Easton, *tel.* (0272) 510763

Selection only: see page 4

Bruton, Somerset

Map Ref: 87ST6834

A picturesque and unspoilt little town on the River Brue, where the quality of the ancient stone buildings lining the main streets and the atmosphere of genteel decay suggest past splendour. This was one of the royal boroughs created by the Saxon kings of Wessex. At the time of Canute there was even a royal mint here.

Downstream from the road bridge over the river is a beautifully arched packhorse bridge, the 'Little Bow'. It was built in the 15th century when pony trains laden with woollen cloth tramped from the Mendips down to the south coast ports.

On the churchyard wall, notice the flood mark. The church is unusual in having two towers: the shorter one was built in the 14th century, the other about 100 years later. Inside, the chancel retains the original decoration and furnishings of the 1740s when it was rebuilt; the tomb of Sir Maurice Berkeley with his two wives Elizabeth Sandys and Katherine Blount is particularly fine.

The High Street is narrow, and on the south side even narrower 'bartons', or alleys, slip between the buildings down to the river. There are a handful of shops, a number of Georgian-fronted town houses and a host of antique shops. The Bruton Gallery arranges sculpture exhibitions.

On the hill south of the town, the strange tower was the dovecote of Bruton Priory. Another remnant of the monastic buildings is the great buttressed wall in the street mysteriously named 'Plox', west of the church, built apparently to hide the monks from public view.

Sexey's Hospital is a charming enclave of Jacobean almshouses with an Elizabethan hall and chapel.

AA recommends:
Restaurant: Truffles, 95 High St, 1-fork, *tel.* (0749) 812255
Guesthouse: Fryerning, Frome Rd, Burrowfield, *tel.* (0749) 812343

The tiny packhorse bridge at Bruton was for centuries the only river crossing

Burnham-on-Sea, Somerset

Map Ref: 86ST3049

Burnham is only a small town, but the holiday camps, caravan parks, apartments, camp sites and amusement areas extend some six miles, bordering the sand dunes.

Before 1830 there was nothing here save a scattering of farms and cottages. Then an enterprising curate, the Reverend David Davies, attempted to create a spa, Daviesville, and an esplanade, some terraces and a hotel were built. In 1858 a line of the Great Western Railway reached Burnham Pier and further development was assured.

There are few traces of the original village at Burnham, but the 14th-century church marks its historic centre. The tower leans, being built on sandy soil too close to the shore. The exquisitely carved altarpiece is by Grinling Gibbons.

Above the modern shop fronts in High Street there are glimpses of classic late Victorian façades, and on the Esplanade some fine hotels. Burnham manages to retain its period charm while offering a full range of modern facilities. Summer crowds are quickly dispersed in the marram grass-covered dunes.

AA recommends:
Hotels: Dunstan House, 8/10 Love Ln, 2-star, *tel.* (0278) 784343

Calne, Wiltshire

Map Ref: 89ST9970

The home of Wiltshire bacon, Calne was a resting place on the Bath road, not only for coaches and merchants, but also for drovers and their charges, flocks of sheep and herds of cattle heading from the West Country to Smithfield Market. There was a considerable traffic in Irish pigs, which landed at Bristol and hoofed it the rest of the way; and the Harris family, butchers in Calne, took their pick from the grunting mass, established their factory (recently closed) here, and in 1864 patented their bacon-curing process. Meat-processing had been a major employer in the town from the early 19th century, however.

At the centre of town, St Mary's Church owes its splendour to the generous donations of the rich clothiers and wool merchants in the 15th century. Unfortunately their public spirit was not matched in the 17th century when, despite a warning that one of the pillars was faulty, the steeple of the church was left to collapse.

Around the Green are the finest of Calne's Georgian houses, especially Adam House, and nearby the White Hart Hotel.

Bowood House, off the A4 west of Calne, has been the Shelburne family home for 230 years. The original house was built in 1625 for the Bradfords, and expanded in the 18th century by Robert Adam, whose extensive work can still be admired. Bowood's chief glory, however, lies in its grounds, which were landscaped by Capability Brown between 1762 and 1768. Today the collection of trees and shrubs is a gardener's paradise, including 153 species and 891 varieties. The lawns roll gently down to a long tranquil lake, and there are cascades, caves and grottoes. Separate from the main gardens, 50 acres of rhododendron walks are open from mid-May to mid-June.

AA recommends:
Hotel: Lansdowne Strand, The Strand, 2-star, *tel.* (0249) 812488
Campsite: Blackland Lakes Holiday & Leisure Centre, Knights Marsh Farm, Stockley Ln, 2-pennants, *tel.* (0249) 813672
Garages: Castle Car Care Centre, Unit 7, Maundrells Yd, Horsebrook, *tel.* (0249) 816765
Heddington Coachworks (M A Fenwick), Heddington, *tel.* (0380) 850198
Soho (TR Cars), New Rd, Studley, *tel.* (0249) 812337

Castle Combe, its cloth trade days over, enjoys peace and tranquillity in a beautiful setting: it is one of the more photographed villages

Castle Cary, Somerset

Map Ref: 87ST6332

A quiet and traditional country town of mellow, yellow stone, where the shops close for lunch and the pace of life seems pleasantly slow. Set in the gentle countryside of south-east Somerset, the town is surrounded by green pastures and wooded hedgerows.

The castle, built by the Lovel family in the late 11th century, was stormed by King Stephen in 1138 and now only slight traces remain at Manor Farm. The Manor House is claimed to have given shelter to Charles II, fleeing after the battle of Worcester.

In the middle of the town the Market Hall, rebuilt in the 19th century, retains the pillars of the earlier 17th-century market house; it incorporates two cells which were used by the local constable for drunkards. The ground floor houses an agricultural merchant, whilst upstairs there is a small rural museum.

Behind the Hall, on Bailey Hill, is another lock-up, the 'Pepper Pot'. Built in 1779 for £23, it is 7ft in diameter and 10ft high, with two iron grills for ventilation.

In 1797 T S Donne established a rope, twine and webbing factory here and since 1828 there has been a horsehair workshop, now the only one in the whole of Britain. The bookshop in Fore Street is well stocked and good for browsing, and down near the old horse pond there is an excellent cheese shop.

AA recommends:
Garage: Moff Motors, *tel.* (0963) 50310

Castle Combe, Wiltshire

Map Ref: 88ST8477

An exceptionally picturesque, honey-coloured, former weavers' village. There are slight remains of a castle, a fine church and a brook. The village is set in a deep hollow.

AA recommends:
Hotel: Manor House Hotel, 3-star, *tel.* (0249) 782206

The head of the huge naked giant carved in the hill behind Cerne Abbas. His origin is a mystery

Cerne Abbas, Dorset

Map Ref: 91ST6601

No one knows the origin of the great naked giant, carved in the chalk hillside overlooking the village. It is possible that he dates from the Roman period, as similarities with representations of Hercules have been noted, but it is odd that there is no documentary evidence of his existence until the 18th century, particularly when considerable labour is needed every few years to keep the outline clear.

A Benedictine monastery was founded here in about AD987 by Aethelmaer, a Wessex nobleman. The remains of the great abbey buildings can be seen behind Abbey Farm, at the top of Abbey Street. The house was mainly rebuilt after a fire but contains some abbey masonry.

St Augustine's well in the churchyard is believed to possess healing qualities: the sick used to lie on the stones hoping for a cure. It is a magical spot, surrounded by decrepit medieval walls.

From the duck pond, at the top of Abbey Street, an overflow stream washes down beside the pavement to disappear under some iron grills in the main street. The old village stocks are outside the church, opposite a row of jettied timber-framed cottages. The Pitchmarket is particularly well preserved, with a stone-tiled roof and elaborately carved door lintel.

An early 17th-century survey of Cerne for the Prince of Wales, who was Lord of the Manor, reported that 'the towne is moste unorderlie governed and as unruiellie as if there were noe magistrates, for the officers are weake men'. The Guildhall was in such a state that 'none dare sitt in it'. Cerne is now one of the prettiest villages in Dorset. Flint and brick cottages fringe the main street; the New Inn, of flint and stone, is a fine 17th-century coaching inn; Long Reach has a delicate Georgian bow front; and altogether it feels cared for.

A private drive off the Folly leads to the superb 14th-century tithe barn. One end was converted into a house in the 18th century.

AA recommends:
Self Catering: Giant's Head, 1 & 2 The Annexe (flats) and The Cottage, *tel.* (03003) 242
Campsites: Bagwell Farm, Chickerell, 3-pennants, *tel.* (0305) 782575
Golden Cap, Chideock, 3-pennants, *tel.* (0297) 89341
Newlands Caravan & Camping Park, Charmouth, 3-pennants, *tel.* (0297) 60257
Wood Farm, Charmouth, 3-pennants, *tel.* (0297) 60431/60697

Chard, Somerset

Map Ref: 90ST3208

A bustling town on the A30, Chard was founded as a 'new town' in 1234 by Bishop Jocelyn of Wells. Its economy thrived on the woollen industry and by the 16th century Chard cloth was being exported to France. The High Street has retained several buildings of historic interest, many showing an attractive use of flint and Ham stone, including the Choughs Hotel, Court House and old Grammar School. Rich clothiers' houses and 18th-century weavers' cottages also survive there and in Holyrood Street.

Potholing

Gashed with gullies and gorges, pockmarked with potholes, the Mendips offer unsurpassed delights to cavers; but beware, some of the caves are so dangerous that even the local specialist clubs only allow their members to enter with an approved leader.

This mysterious underground wonderland was created by the action of water percolating through the cracks and fissures of the 'mountain' limestone mass that forms the hills. Swirling water loaded with pebbles and boulders carved great caverns in the rock, and the dissolved limestone in the water, dripping for millennia, built stalagmite castles and stalactite curtains.

As you amble over Priddy Down or wander through Ebbor Gorge, you may be tempted by the black holes that mark the cave entrances, but you should never enter a cave without an experienced leader, without advice from the host of caving clubs and, most important of all, without notifying the cave authorities of your intentions.

Many of the caves were first discovered by miners – lead, for example, has been mined in the Mendips since Roman times. Lamb Leer (or Lair) is one such cave, first mined in the 17th century; in 1681, John Beaumont, a surgeon from Ston Easton, published an account of his exploration of this cave, describing how he was lowered at the end of a rope down the 76ft Main Shaft.

In the early years of this century Herbert Balch, one of the pioneers of British caving, delved into numerous caves on the Mendips with genuine scientific interest. Many of his finds, both geological and archaeological, are now in Wells Museum.

For those who prefer to enjoy the experience of underground chambers in relative comfort, the caves systems at Cheddar and Wookey Hole are open to the public with guided tours. Cox's Cave in Cheddar was discovered in 1837 by George Cox; it contains some awe-inspiring stalagmite pillars and stalactite curtains, now colourfully named – Peal of Bells, Home of the Rainbow, Marble Curtain. Gough's Cave boasts a tunnel penetrating a quarter of a mile into the rock; and in the Boulder Chamber a man broke the world record, in 1966, for surviving alone underground for 130 days. At Wookey Hole the caves have attracted visitors for several hundred years. Since 1973 the Wookey Hole complex has been run by Madame Tussaud's.

Wookey Hole Caves, a fascinating complex with stalagmites and stalactites, weird in shape

---

In the 19th century Chard recovered from the declining woollen industry by turning to lace-making, net-making and agricultural engineering; Denings of Chard, one of the foundries, manufactured an impressive array of horse-drawn farm machines. Two of the early 19th-century mills have particularly fine ironwork.

Unexpectedly, Chard had a canal, but it was short-lived. The canal company was founded in 1834 and built a canal from the town northwards to Creech St Michael, where it joined the Taunton and Bridgwater canal. It was bought out in 1866 by the Bristol and Exeter Railway Company. The railway was only a little more successful: Chard was at a junction on a branch which joined the Great Western Railway's broad gauge and the London and South Western's standard gauge. It was not until 1891 that all lines were converted to a standard gauge. Beeching's axe of the 1960s cut Chard off the modern railway map altogether.

Chard Museum in Godworthy House, towards the west end of the High Street, has a macabre section containing relics from the workshop of John Gillingham, a 19th-century artificial-limb maker. There are also collections associated with John Stringfellow, the aviation pioneer, who is credited with inventing the first power-driven aircraft.

AA recommends:
Guesthouse: Watermead, 83 High St, *tel.* (04606) 2834
Garage: Premier Motors (F J Hole), Crewkerne Rd, *tel.* (04606) 3146

Cheddar, Somerset

Map Ref: 86ST4553

The great gash in the limestone mass of the Mendips that creates the Cheddar Gorge has attracted huge numbers of visitors. The road, the B3135, winds its way down the high plateau of the hills, until it is walled in by the towering cliffs of bare rock which rise almost vertically on either side. Such a landscape is both dramatic and awe-inspiring.

As the Gorge widens at its southern end, so commercialisation begins; apart from the Caves, which offer another fascinating view of this natural extravaganza, there are all manner of other amusements, designed to attract visitors, and souvenir shops and cafés.

In a modern, factory-style building, demonstrations of Cheddar cheese-making are given daily, but these are a far cry from the living farm tradition.

The village straggles southwards towards the A371, and it was here by the church and the River Yeo that the original Saxon settlement developed; the outlines of the Saxon royal palace of Cheddar, associated with King Alfred, can be seen in the grounds of the Kings of Wessex School. The market cross at the road junction was a preachers' cross around which the hexagonal colonnade was built in the 16th century, converting it into a market centre where travelling merchants paid rent to sit under a cover.

Hannah More, a philanthropist, writer and teacher, opened her first school in Cheddar towards the end of the 18th century in a cottage in Venn's Close. She went on to open a number of village schools on the Mendips and devoted her life to the improvement of housing and poor relief among the region's leadminers, colliers and glassworkers, working particularly for children.

AA recommends:
Hotel: Gordons, Cliff St, 1-star, *tel.* (0934) 742497
Campsites: Broadway House Caravan & Camping Park, 4-pennants, *tel.* (0934) 742610
Church Farm Camping Site, Church St, 3-pennants, *tel.* (0934) 743048
Froglands Farm, 3-pennants, *tel.* (0934) 742058
Self Catering: Market Cross Apartments, Market Cross Hotel, Church St, *tel.* (0934) 742264
Stable & Orchard Cottages, Fairlands House, *tel.* (0934) 742629

Chippenham, Wiltshire

Map Ref: 88ST9173

The commercial hub of surrounding North Wiltshire, Chippenham has expanded enormously in recent years, but the old town centre, on a spur bounded by the River Avon, has remained.

The Market Place, or 'Ceaping', has been the focus of civic life for over 1,000 years. The old town hall, the 'Yelde Hall', an impressive timber-framed building beside the Shambles, was used by the Bailiff and Burgesses and as a court. It is now the museum. The gallows, pillory, stocks and whipping post once stood in the open space between the parish church, St Andrew's, and the Hall.

At the corner of Langley Road a little plaque commemorates an enduring glimpse of life in medieval Chippenham:

> *Hither extendeth Maud Heath's gift for where I stand is Chippenham clift.*
>
> *Erected in 1698, but given in 1474.*

Maud Heath was a market woman who trudged through mud and puddles to Chippenham from her home at Langley Burrell each week, laden with heavy baskets of butter and eggs. When she died in 1474 she left her savings for the construction and maintenance of a raised path. It is still there and offers a delightful 4½-mile walk from the town to Wick Hill, where a statue of Maud, basket on her arm, has been erected.

AA recommends:
Hotel: The Bear, 12 Market Pl, 1-star, *tel.* (0249) 653272
Guesthouse: Oxford Hotel, 32/36 Langley Rd, *tel.* (0249) 652542
Garages: Causeway, London Rd, *tel.* (0249) 655871/2
Hewitt, Cocklebury Rd, *tel.* (0249) 653255
M R G Chippenham Ltd, 127 Malmesbury Rd, *tel.* (0249) 652016
Stanton St Quinton Ltd, M4 Junc 17, *tel.* (06663) 223

Chipping Sodbury, Avon

Map Ref: 88ST7282

A medieval 'new town', it was created in the 12th century by William Crassus, 'William the fat', Lord of Sodbury. A market was granted in 1227, hence 'Chipping' which derives from the word for 'market'. Trading took place in the wide High Street.

The main street is lined with attractive gabled and stone-mullioned 17th-century houses with occasional Victorian Gothic (for example, the Police Station) and a pleasantly piebald effect comes from a mixture of sandstone and lias limestone. 'Tudor House' in Hatter's Lane is a restored 15th-century building, plastered, with an oversailing storey.

The little clock tower was erected in 1871 as a memorial to Colonel Blathwayte of Dyrham Park who served in the Waterloo campaign.

Dyrham is a splendid William-and-Mary house, with a 265-acre park, built for the Blathwaytes. The west front looks on to the medieval parish church and the garden with old ilex trees and limes. There are fine collections of Dutch pictures, and blue and white delftware.

AA recommends:
Hotel: Petty France Hotel, Petty France, Badminton, 3-star, *tel.* (045423) 361
Restaurant: The Restaurant, Bodkin House, Badminton, 2-forks, *tel.* (045423) 310
Sultan, 29 Horse St, 2-forks, *tel.* (0454) 323510
Guesthouse: Moda Hotel, 1 High St, *tel.* (0454) 312135
Garage: TT Motors, Hatters Ln, *tel.* (0454) 313181

Christchurch, Dorset

Map Ref: 93SZ1592

The town was known by the Saxons as Twynham, 'between the waters', because of its position between the Avon and the Stour.

The town is dominated by the vast Priory Church, once part of the monastery after which the town was named, a magnificent blend of Norman, Early English and Perpendicular styles.

Just north of the church the ruins of the Norman castle sit on an artificial mound; it was built in the 12th century by Richard de Redvers, Earl of Devon. All that is left are the east and west walls of the keep. More interesting are the remains of the Castle Hall, known as the Constable's House, in the grounds of the King's Arms Hotel.

Christchurch: the Priory Church, vast but dignified. Below: a rare example of a Norman house, the Constable's House has one of England's first chimneys

It is a rare example of Norman domestic architecture and has one of the first chimneys to be built in England.

Place Mill on Christchurch Quay dates back to Saxon times and the Red House Museum has local exhibits.

Stanpit Marshes, a saltmarsh haven for migrating birds, have been designated a nature reserve. The Tuckton ferry from the town to Mudeford and Hengistbury Head provides good cover for viewing.

AA recommends:
Hotels: Avonmouth, Mudeford, 3-star, *tel.* (0202) 483434
Waterford Lodge, 87 Bure Lane, Friars Cliff, Mudeford, 3-star, *tel.* (04252) 72948
Fishermans Haunt, Salisbury Rd, Winkton, 2-star, *tel.* (0202) 484071
Restaurant: Splinters, Church St, 1-fork, *tel.* (0202) 483454
Guesthouse: The Pines, 39 Mudeford, *tel.* (0202) 475121
Campsites: Hoburne Farm Caravan Park, 5-pennants, *tel.* (04252) 3379
Grove Farm Meadow Holiday Caravan Park, 4-pennants, *tel.* (0202) 483597
Tall Trees Chalet & Caravan Park, Matcham Lane, Hurn, 3-pennants, *tel.* (0202) 477144
Haven Caravan Park, 2-pennants, *tel.* (04252) 4662 & 5353
Garage: F W Jesty (Mtr Eng), Airfield Rd, *tel.* (0202) 477468

Selection only: see page 4

Clevedon, Avon

Map Ref: 86ST4071

Clevedon has the faded elegance of a thoroughly traditional seaside resort – bandstand and pier, clock tower and Royal Hotel.

The pier was built in the 1860s using rails that Brunel had intended for the South Wales Railway. In 1970 it collapsed while being tested for safety, but a local preservation trust took on the worthwhile task of reconstruction.

Between 1850 and 1880 the population of the town doubled. Sir Arthur Hallam Elton of Clevedon Court designed villas, planned streets, sponsored coffee houses, and built a lending library and a hospital.

The Eltons, a Bristol merchant family, acquired Clevedon Court in 1709. Originally medieval, it now has all the comfort of an Edwardian country house. It is owned by the National Trust and regularly open to the public.

Coleridge honeymooned in Clevedon, in a little cottage owned by the Eltons in Old Church Road, and Thackeray was also a regular visitor to the Court.

From the 1880s Sir Edmund Harry Elton ran his Sunflower Pottery from the Court; his designs can be described as weird and colourful, but they were successfully marketed especially by Tiffany's in the USA. He also invented an automatic gas lighter and a device for keeping women's skirts out of bicycle wheels.

AA recommends:
Hotel: Walton Park, Wellington Ter, 3-star, *tel.* (0272) 874253
Self Catering: Newhouse Farm, Moor Ln (cottage), *tel.* (0305) 67545
Guesthouse: Amberley, 146 Old Church Rd, *tel.* (0272) 874402
Garages: Binding & Payne, Old Church Rd, *tel.* (0272) 872201
Clevedon, Bristol Rd, *tel.* (0272) 873701
Wayside, Kenn, *tel.* (0272) 874119

Corfe Castle, Dorset

Map Ref: 93SY9682

Corfe, with its grey stone slab roofs, mullion windows and picturesque Square is a delightful town to visit.

It is dominated by the ruins of the castle. Soon after the Norman Conquest the great wall, four yards thick in places, was built; in the 12th century the massive King's Tower was added, and about 100 years later further improvements were made by King John. The castle became a favoured royal residence and a formidable prison.

At the start of the Civil War, the castle was in the hands of Sir John Bankes, the Attorney General. A royalist, he went to join the king at York in 1642, leaving his wife in charge of the castle. After a stout resistance lasting several years Lady Bankes finally surrendered in 1646, only when defeat was certain, due to the treachery of one of the garrison officers. Once the castle had been taken, its demolition was ordered by Parliament.

Throughout the Middle Ages Purbeck marble was quarried around Corfe, and the town was the centre of the industry for cutting, dressing and finishing the stone; it was used at Corfe for the village houses and throughout Britain for church building and monuments, and notably at Salisbury Cathedral. The town church, above West Street, has one of the finest towers in the county, with ferocious gargoyles and an elaborately carved west doorway.

A minor road leads south-west to Kimmeridge and Kimmeridge Bay, overlooked by a folly, Clavell's Tower. Fossils can easily be found in the oil shale here.

AA recommends:
Hotel: Mortons House, East St, 2-star, *tel.* (0929) 480988
Campsite: Woodland Camping Park, Glebe Farm, Bucknowle, 2-pennants, *tel.* (0929) 480280

Corfe Castle: the ruins of the castle tower over the town. That so much survives today is testament to the strength of the building

Corsham, Wiltshire

Map Ref: 88ST8770

A typical west Wiltshire weaving town, Corsham was tastefully built of Bath stone. A number of military establishments in the neighbourhood led to some development but the town centre has remained little-changed, and is enhanced by some fine Georgian houses, Porch House, Alexander House and the Grove. Near the Grove are the Hungerford Almshouses and School, founded in 1668. The schoolroom has its original seating and the master's pulpit chair.

The finest of the houses is Corsham Court, built in 1582. It was bought by the Methuens in the 18th century to house the family's collection of Flemish paintings and statues. Capability Brown worked on the house and laid out the park. Architects John Nash and Thomas Bellamy in turn further extended and altered the house. John Methuen is chiefly remembered as the ambassador who negotiated the treaty of 1703 with Portugal, Britain's 'oldest ally'; he also promoted port wine and brought about a major change in English drinking habits.

Near Corsham is the 17th-century Pickwick Manor. Dickens is supposed to have taken the name for his most popular character from the signwriting on a coach run by Moses Pickwick between Bath and London.

AA recommends:
Hotels: Rudloe Park, Leafy Ln, 3-star, *tel.* (0225) 810555
Methuen Arms, High St, 2-star, *tel.* (0249) 714867
Restaurant: Weavers Loft, High St, 2-fork, *tel.* (0249) 713982

CREWKERNE–DORCHESTER

Crewkerne, Somerset

Map Ref: 90ST4409

Crewkerne's church was a Saxon minster, although the present building dates from the 15th century. Set up and apart from the town it is a peaceful haven above the busy traffic of the A30.

The main road has contributed to the town's history: Catherine of Aragon stayed the night on her way from Plymouth to marry Prince Arthur in 1501. The town was a regular post stage, and a local postmaster, Thomas Hutchins, ran the first profitable postal system between London and Plymouth, in the 17th century.

The elegant proportions of the houses, inns and shop fronts in the town centre, most in honey-coloured Ham stone, are evidence of the prosperous activity generated by these comings and goings.

Crewkerne developed a number of trades connected with the cloth-making industry, including webbing, sailcloth, hair-seating and shirts. The Royal Navy stipulated Crewkerne and Coker cloth for sails in the early 19th century. Today Crewkerne Textiles manufacture webbing for the services, nylon twine and sailcloth.

Just over the railway bridge south of the town is the little village of Misterton. Helen Matthews, author of the Victorian classic *Coming through the Rye*, was born here. Youngs of Misterton act as agents for all manner of hunting and trapping devices; many of their traps were invented and first made in the workshop on the edge of the village.

AA recommends:
Hotel: Old Parsonage, Barn St, 2-star, *tel.* (0460) 73516
Garage: Haslebury Firs (K Staddon Body Repair Centre), Yeovil Rd, *tel.* (0460) 72530

Cricket St Thomas, Somerset

Map Ref: 90ST3708

On the A30 between Chard and Crewkerne, Cricket House, better known as 'Grantleigh Manor' in the television series *To the Manor Born*, is the hub of a working estate owned and run by the Taylor family and an idyllic setting for the popular Wildlife Park.

The house of honey-coloured stone was designed by John Soane in the 1780s for Rear Admiral Alexander Hood, and replaced an earlier manor house. The nearby church is similarly a replacement of an earlier building; in the 17th century, Cricket was a favourite choice for couples wishing to get married without the publicity and expense of a ceremony at their own parish church.

Right: carved double-faced head of Celtic workmanship, in Devizes Museum
Above: Wadworths' Brewery, Devizes

Today, elephants, camels, llamas, wapitis and other exotic creatures amble about the old walled garden and grounds, the noisy parrot aviary is in the Orangery, and grunting sea lions splash about in the landscaped lake. The Wildlife Park has been cleverly planned to blend in, as far as possible, with the character of the estate; and the success of its breeding programme, particularly of the Australian Black Swans which have become the estate's emblem, indicate the contentment and well-being of all the birds and animals.

The National Heavy Horse Centre, at the Home Farm, is one of the places in Britain where magnificent shire horses are bred and cared for.

There is a collection of Victorian milking and dairy equipment in the Country Life Museum and the milking of the modern dairy herd can be seen every afternoon.

Devizes, Wiltshire

Map Ref: 89SU0061

Devizes grew up around a Norman castle, built on a strategic spur to the west of the present Market Place. The first castle, built by Bishop Osmund of Salisbury, in 1080, burnt down and was rebuilt in 1138 by Bishop Roger of Salisbury, famed for his short sermons. It served occasionally as a royal residence and as a prison, but gradually fell into disrepair and was eventually demolished by Cromwell's forces in 1645. The present-day Victorian fantasy castle is a private residence.

'Between the chalk and the cheese' (Salisbury Plain and the dairy-farming Vale of Pewsey), the market, protected by the castle, prospered on the wool trade and dairy produce.

The wool trade's prosperity is mirrored in the wool merchants' 18th-century town houses of St John's and Long Street. Earlier timber-framed houses survive in St John's Alley, and in Monday Market Street where Great Porch House is probably the oldest

surviving building in town.

As a resting point on an old coaching road, Devizes has a number of historic inns. The Bear was established in the 16th century; its most famous landlord was the father of Sir Thomas Lawrence, the portrait painter, who lived here in 1772-81. He also liked poetry, and at the age of five, was put on to the bar with his father shouting, 'Gentlemen, here is my son; will you have him recite the poets or take your portraits'. The Elm Tree was once a pilgrim's rest called the Salutation.

The Market Cross was built in 1814 by Henry Addington, who was Recorder for 30 years, MP for 20 and Prime Minister. An inscription recounts the moral tale of a market woman from Potterne, Ruth Pierce, who dropped dead after telling a lie.

One delight of the town is the regular delivery of the local brew, Wadworths', to the various pubs and hotels, by a brewer's dray, pulled by magnificent paired Shire horses. The red brick brewery is on the site of the old Northgate, the beer's trademark.

AA recommends:
Hotel: Bear, Market Pl, 2-star, *tel.* (0380) 2444
Guesthouse: Castle Hotel, New Park St (Inn), *tel.* (0380) 2902
Campsite: Lake, Rowde, 3-pennants, *tel.* (0380) 2767, (2m NW A342)
Garages: Cannings Hill, London Rd, *tel.* (0380) 2569
Devizes Motor Company, 91 New Park St, *tel.* (0380) 3456

Dorchester, Dorset

Map Ref: 91SY6890

An old and typically English country town, Dorchester is full of charm and rich in history. At the top of High West Street, the bronze figure of Thomas Hardy quietly surveys the modern activity of his 'Casterbridge'. It is a small county town, little changed in many ways from the town Hardy knew.

Durnovaria was created by the Romans to supersede the great pre-Roman settlement at Maiden Castle; it was the only Roman town in Dorset, at the cross roads of two major routes, from London to Exeter and from Weymouth to Yeovil. The present-day Walks make a delightful tree-lined, traffic-free footpath, circling the town centre and following the lines of the old Roman walls. Behind the County Hall the remains of a sophisticated Roman town house have been excavated, complete with underfloor hot-air ducts, mosaics, a bathroom and a little covered verandah. In the southern outskirts, Maumbury Rings, a Neolithic henge monument, was used by the Romans as an amphitheatre.

A particularly fine example of Norman sculpture is the famous tympanum over the porch door at St George's Church, Fordington, on the east side of town. It depicts St George supporting the crusading Christians against the Saracens at the battle of Antioch in 1097.

St Peter's is the only surviving medieval church in the town. It was much restored in the 1850s by the local architect, John Hicks, who had just taken on the youthful Thomas Hardy as an assistant and a plan of the church drawn by Hardy is displayed.

Outside St Peter's, against the tower, is a statue of William Barnes, the Dorset dialect poet.

Judge Jeffreys came to the town on the 'Bloody Assize' following the Duke of Monmouth's Rebellion and the Battle of Sedgemoor. In the Oak Room of the Antelope Hotel, in South Street, between 5 and 10 September 1685, 340 prisoners were tried for treasonable sedition; 74 were hanged, drawn and quartered, 175 had their death sentences commuted to transportation, and the rest were remanded in custody or set free for lack of evidence. Across the road is the old Crown Court, where the Tolpuddle Martyrs were sentenced in 1834.

Although fires have destroyed many of Dorchester's other old buildings, the town presents an attractive mixture of Georgian and Victorian styles. At the 'Top O' Town' is the impressive Victorian keep of the Dorset Regiment, now the Military Museum.

South-west of Dorchester, the Iron Age fort, Maiden Castle, is unsurpassed in Britain for the magnitude and complexity of its defences. It was excavated in the 1930s by Sir Mortimer Wheeler who found the remains of the cemetery of the defenders massacred at the eastern entrance when the castle was stormed and taken by invading Roman troops in AD43.

For a wider understanding of local and regional archaeology and history, the County Museum is a must for any visitor.

Dorchester's history stretches back long before its most famous novelist and poet Thomas Hardy (above: his statue in Dorchester). The Romans established the town of Durnovaria *here (this mosaic is in the County Museum). They had met with fierce resistance, however, from the local Durotriges in the Iron Age hillfort at Maiden Castle (below)*

AA recommends:
Hotel: Whitefriars, Winterbourne Abbas, 2-star, *tel.* (030588) 206
Garages: Cambridge Road Service Station, Cambridge Rd, *tel.* (0305) 64245
Harris Bodyworks, 14 Casterbridge Ind Est, London Rd, *tel.* (0305) 63628
Hewitt, Unit 10, Grt Western Ind Est, Maumbury Rd, *tel.* (0305) 62211
Loders, The Grove, *tel.* (0305) 67881

Frome, Somerset

Map Ref: 88ST7747

Like many Mendip towns, Frome suffered from nearly two centuries of decline following the prosperity of its woollen industry. The town is closely packed on a steep hillside, with narrow streets, tight lanes and high pavements wending up and down the slopes.

The mass of 18th-century merchants' houses and weavers' cottages illustrates the success of the place at that time, when its population rivalled that of Bath and Salisbury. By 1826, when William Cobbett rode into the town, the industry had gone:

I saw between two and three hundred weavers, men and boys, cracking stones . . . these poor creatures at Frome have pawned all their things . . . their blankets and sheets, their looms.

The market is near the bridge over the River Frome. Cross the bridge and turn left by the sharp-nosed Victorian Literary and Scientific Institute, now the Museum. Beside the bridge, the 18th-century Bluecoat School has figures of a schoolboy and girl.

Cheap Street is the most picturesque of Frome's lanes, with a rushing conduit down the middle, small shops and cafés. On the other side of the main road the maze of narrow streets continues up Catherine Hill. There are numerous antique and junk shops, second-hand bookshops and small craft workshops. Sheppard's Barton, through an arch off the Hill, is a rare survival of a complete street of 18th-century weavers' cottages, with the Manse at one end so that Sheppard, the clothier, could keep an eye on his employees. The 'Trinity' area on the north-west of the town has been preserved after it was found to be an even older 'estate' of artisan housing.

St John's Church was heavily restored in the last century but traces of Saxon masonry from the church possibly built by St Aldhelm are incorporated in one of the walls and underneath the tower – here the fragments may be from the shaft of a cross, one of several erected to mark the resting places of Aldhelm and his bearers on his way to die at Doulting. In the 18th and 19th centuries Frome was a centre for Nonconformist sects. The former Rook Lane Chapel in Bath Street is notable for its huge Classical front of 1707.

AA recommends:
Hotels: Mendip Lodge, Bath Rd, 3-star, *tel.* (0373) 63223
George, 4 Market Pl, 2-star, *tel.* (0373) 62584
Restaurant: Halligan's, 6 Vicarage St, 2-fork, *tel.* (0373) 64238
Garage: Keyford (Linwood Motors), Keyford, *tel.* (0373) 63433

Gillingham, Dorset

Map Ref: 92ST8026

Situated at the extreme north of Dorset on the borders of Somerset and Wiltshire, Gillingham was at the centre of a Royal Forest. It developed into a prosperous market town for the agricultural produce of the lush Blackmoor Vale. The

Arthur

Arthur is an enigmatic figure whose story is shrouded in such a tangle of history and folklore that the truth will probably never be known.

The period of history immediately after the withdrawal of the Roman armies early in the 5th century is known as the Dark Ages because very little is known about it. About 200 years were to elapse before the Saxon invasions seriously affected much of Wessex, and it is suggested that a powerful leader or chieftain, or a series of powerful leaders, took command of the Celtic troops of the West Country and held the invaders at bay.

Archaeological excavations at South Cadbury show that the Iron Age hillfort was reoccupied in the late 5th or early 6th century, with massive wooden fortifications on the ramparts of the 18-acre site. Foundations of a large hall were discovered, and the site was large enough to accommodate a 1,000-strong army. So it is possible that in this western frontier zone there was a great military leader who gathered about him a large band and fought the Saxons.

The Easter Annals record 12

'Edyrn travels to Arthur's court . . .' the romantic view of a shadowy figure

great victories against the Saxons at this time, the final one at Mount Badon in about 516. The whereabouts of this battle are unknown – possibly it was near Bath, or Badbury Rings (Dorset) or somewhere on the north Wiltshire Downs. It is assumed that it was Arthur who defeated the invaders.

The 12th-century writer, Geoffrey of Monmouth, recounts that at the battle of Camlan, Arthur was mortally wounded and his body borne away to the Isle of Avalon – Glastonbury. Before he died, it is said, Arthur threw his sword, Excalibur, into the water; the town of Street claims this happened at the little bridge over the River Brue on the west side of the town, between Street and Glastonbury. Queen Guinevere fled to Amesbury where she took the veil and became abbess of the great abbey; after her death, her body was likewise taken to Glastonbury, by Sir Lancelot, to be buried beside her husband.

In 1184 Glastonbury Abbey suffered a disastrous fire; just seven years later, digging on the instructions of the late King Henry II, the monks found a tomb; on it was a lead cross, inscribed, according to Camden's *Britannia* (1610), with the words:

Here lies buried the famous king Arthur in the isle of Avalon.

Was this simply a clever device to revive the abbey as a place of pilgrimage? Or is it clear evidence of the existence of a historical figure, King Arthur?

arrival of the railway in 1859 secured its future as a principal outlet for fresh milk.

Gillingham, pronounced with a hard 'g' in conformity with the traditional Dorset dialect, gets a bad press from most guide-books. However, it is a pleasant town, not pretty, but certainly not unattractive. The town is well situated, sheltered from the north by the bulk of Salisbury Plain and from the east by the high chalk downs around Shaftesbury. The picturesque bridge over the Shreen Water, at the heart of the town, was depicted in a painting by John Constable, now in the Tate Gallery.

In the Middle Ages Gillingham was a major cloth manufacturing town. Later, silk spinning was introduced, and one of the 19th-century silk mills can be seen with its Mill House, set in charming waterside gardens. The little museum, next to the church, is packed with archaeology, bygones and documents of local interest.

A church was recorded at Gillingham in Domesday Book, but nothing remains. Of the present Church of St Mary, only the chancel is 14th-century. The rest was rebuilt in the mid-19th century.

AA recommends:
Hotel: Stock Hill House, Wyke, 2-star, country house, 1 rosette, tel. (07476) 3626
Garage: Vincents, Station Rd, tel. (07476) 3204

Glastonbury, Somerset
Map Ref: 87ST5038

The landmark of Glastonbury Tor is visible from every direction, and it is easy to see why the place has been imbued with such mystical significance. On a misty morning, when the surrounding moors are covered by a white haze, the summit of the Tor and the tower of St Michael's Chapel appear to be floating, as if on a lake.

Perhaps that is how it seemed to earlier inhabitants when the moors were frequently inundated by the sea. The town has grown up at the foot of the Tor, just above the area liable to flooding and around the ancient site of the Abbey.

The earliest origins of the Abbey are confused by a myriad myths and legends associating Christ and Joseph of Arimathea with, perhaps, the first Christian shrine in the country. Archaeological evidence so far has revealed nothing earlier than a 7th-century boundary ditch. The present ruins of the Abbey all date from after the fire of 1184, and mostly from the 14th and 15th centuries.

In the town, the George and Pilgrims Hotel has provided hospitality to pilgrims for over 500 years. The stone frontage is richly decorated with the arms of the Abbey and of Edward IV over the entrance. The Tribunal, or court house, further up the High Street has finds from the Iron Age 'lake village' at Meare — wooden artefacts preserved in the acid peat soil, the hub of a cart wheel and the remains of a dug-out canoe.

In the 18th century Glastonbury enjoyed a short-lived tourist boom as a spa town. The former pump rooms, built in 1754, survive as a private house next to the Copper Beech Hotel in Magdalene Street. The natural spring water emerges in the gardens of the Chalice Well in Chilkwell Street.

The market has been revived in recent years and is now held in the car park beside the glorious tower of St John's Church.

The 14th-century Abbey Barn, facing Bere Lane mid-way between the Tor and the town, has become the centre-piece of the Somerset Rural Life Museum. Exhibitions in the Abbey Farmhouse illustrate the life of a farm worker in Victorian Somerset; in the old farmyard, geese and hens squabble beside the cow stalls and robust farm wagons.

AA recommends:
Hotel: George & Pilgrims Hotel & Restaurant, High St, 2-star, tel. (0458) 31146
Restaurant: No 3, Magdalene St, 2-fork, tel. (0458) 32129
Guesthouses: Berewall Farm Country Guest House, Cinnamon Ln, (farmhouse), tel. (0458) 31451
Cradlebridge (farmhouse), tel. (0458) 31827
Campsite: Isle of Avalon Touring Caravan Park, Godney Rd, 3-pennants, tel. (0458) 33618
Garages: Jayem Motorcycles, 71 High St, tel. (0458) 32358
Tor View, Edgarley, tel. (0458) 31124

Glastonbury Tor (main picture), the ruins of the Abbey (below left) and (below right) the magnificent tithe barn

Ilchester, Somerset

Map Ref: 91ST5222

An important Roman town, founded where the great Foss Way, from Axmouth to Lincoln, was joined by a road from the Bristol Channel to Dorchester. Archaeological excavations have revealed that this was a walled town, a centre of administration for the district and the headquarters of a garrison.

From the 12th century, the county gaol was located in the town and until the mid-19th century it seems to have dominated the town's affairs. The site of the gaol is now largely occupied by a petrol station, although part of its laundry and bakehouse survive as cottages.

Once several churches stood here, as well as a friary and a priory, but by 1500 only one church remained. A handful of gracious Georgian houses and the Town Hall face the market place but the town is only a shadow of its former self.

The roar of jets from the Royal Naval Air Station at Yeovilton, about a mile east of Ilchester, jolts this peaceful and historic town into the 20th century. Within the aerodrome is the Fleet Air Arm Museum, which portrays the history and achievements of the Royal Naval Air Service with examples from the early days of kites and airships to the present day. Concorde 002, the first prototype to be built in England, completed its development flying career in 1974, and was ferried here from Fairford by Brian Trubshaw and his original crew on 4 March 1976.

AA recommends:
Self Catering: Flats 3 & 4, Bos House, Limington Rd, tel. (0935) 840507
Garage: Ilchester (A Capozzoli & Sons), Northover, tel. (0935) 840425

Ilminster, Somerset

Map Ref: 90ST3614

This is an unspoilt, truly rural town, the old 'minster' on the River Isle. The main road takes all the through-traffic so the charming market place, with the stone-pillared, open-sided market hall, is left in peace. The honey-coloured Ham stone glows with warmth where the locals pause to chat on the cobbles.

The Minster, the Parish Church of St Mary, is a permanent memorial to the town's prosperity in the 14th and 15th centuries. The tower, said to be a copy of the central tower of Wells Cathedral, is glorious, with 24 pierced stone windows to let out the sound of the bells, and 22 pinnacles at the top.

In the 18th century, Ilminster was at the centre of a network of turnpike roads linking it with surrounding towns. In the 19th century, the Chard Canal passed just west of the town and brought a short-lived flurry of activity, before the railway arrived in 1866.

Dillington House, off the main road on the east side of town, is a delightful small country house set in parkland, now Somerset County Council's Residential College.

About 2 miles north is Barrington Court (National Trust). The walls of mellow Ham stone are covered in lichen, and each elevation is decorated with fancy twisted finials on the gables. The ground plan is E-shaped and almost perfectly symmetrical. Its position is superb, surrounded by flat meadows skirted by gentle wooded hills. The house was restored by Colonel A Lyle, of Tate and Lyle, who lived here in the 1920s. He also created the gardens, with the help of Gertrude Jekyll. The Court is now leased to Stuart Interiors who display and sell their period and reproduction furniture here.

AA recommends:
Garages: J. Brake & Son, Station Rd, tel. (04605) 2400
Mynster Motors, Slape Ind Est, Sutton Rd, tel. (04605) 2141

Kingston Lacy: the ceiling of the Spanish Room (left) is said to have been brought here from Venice. The Saloon (above) looks out over the gardens to the north

Kingston Lacy, Dorset

Map Ref: 93ST9701

This fabulous house, which now belongs to the National Trust, is set in formal gardens surrounded by woodland walks and a park stocked with Red Devon cattle. The whole estate of some 8,795 acres includes 14 farms and chunks of two villages, Shapwick and Pamphill. It was the home of the Bankes family for over 300 years. The original brick house was designed by Sir Roger Pratt for Sir Ralph Bankes, son of Sir John of Corfe Castle fame, the Attorney General to Charles I, and built between 1663 and 1665. It was later altered and encased in stone by Sir Charles Barry, the architect of the Houses of Parliament, for W J Bankes, the traveller and collector of the family, in the 1830s.

W J's eclectic taste is reflected both inside the house and in the grounds. He brought the grand marble staircase back from Italy, the Spanish room is packed with gilded treasures he sent from Spain, and outside are an Egyptian obelisk and a sarcophagus. The superb collection of paintings includes works by Titian, Rubens and Velasquez, and two series of family portraits by Van Dyck and Lely.

The house and 1,500 acres were bequeathed to the National Trust by H J R Bankes, who lived in the house until his death in 1981. It was opened to the public in 1986.

ILCHESTER–LANGPORT 47

Father of photography Fox Talbot lived and worked at Lacock Abbey 1827–77

chimney stacks and the large courtyard.
In 1753 Sanderson Miller added a Gothick hall, and further changes were made in the 19th century.
William Henry Fox Talbot inherited Lacock Abbey when he was only a baby and he did not live here until 1827, when he was 27. Here he conducted his first photographic experiments, and naturally it was his home that provided the subjects. His first, or rather the first, successful photograph was of one of the oriel windows in the south front.
Just outside the gates of Lacock Abbey, the National Trust has opened the Fox Talbot Gallery of Photography, in a beautifully converted 16th-century barn.
The village of Lacock is a pleasant mixture of architecture, with cottages and shops with mellow roofs of tile and stone. There is an 18th-century domed lock-up, a 14th-century tithe barn, a 15th-century inn (At the Sign of The Angel), and an interesting church, St Cyriac's.

AA recommends:
Campsite: Piccadilly Caravan Site, Folly Ln, 2-pennants, *tel.* (024973) 260

A Roman road slices through the parkland just north of the house; and about a mile north-west it meets another at the impressive Iron Age hillfort of Badbury Rings.

Lacock, Wiltshire

Map Ref: 88ST9168

Lacock Abbey was founded in 1232 by Ela, Countess of Salisbury, the wife of William Longespee, illegitimate son of Henry II. Some 13th-century building work survives, including the cloisters, sacristy, chapter house, and nuns' parlour. After the Reformation, Sir William Sharington converted the monastic remains into a country mansion. Its chief features are the octagonal tower overlooking the River Avon, decorative twisted

Langport, Somerset

Map Ref: 90ST4226

The town is at the tidal limit of the River Parrett and was for centuries a small but important centre for traffic sailing upstream into the heart of Somerset and down to Bridgwater. The market that developed here specialised in the products of the surrounding moors.
Thomas Gerard wrote in 1633 that it was:
well furnished with fowle in the winter time, and full of pect eeles as they call them, because they take them in those waters by pecking an eele speare on them where they lye in their beds.
Down and feathers were also sold,

Below: Tudor stone chimney stacks as seen from the courtyard at Lacock Abbey

plucked from flocks of geese that grazed the marshy fields.
The oldest part of the town is up on the hill where there were extensive fortifications and embankments. The barrel-vaulted Eastern Gate still remains, with the 'Hanging Chapel' above. All Saints Church was rebuilt in the 15th century, but retains stone relief over the south door of Norman design.
In the Civil War there were skirmishes around Langport culminating in the war's last major battle in the region, when, in 1645, the Parliamentary army under Sir Thomas Fairfax defeated a much stronger contingent of George Goring's royalist forces. This was one of the New Model Army's most impressive achievements.
The town is built almost entirely of grey-blue Lias stone, rather drab and cold; but there are distinctive houses in Bow Street and Cheapside. Langport's most famous son, Walter Bagehot (1826-77), economist, banker and author of *The English Constitution*, was born in Bow Street, adjacent to the Bank which was founded by his family, the Stuckeys, in about 1770. When the bank was taken over by the National Westminster in 1909, its banknote circulation was second only to that of the Bank of England.
Kelway's Nursery, on the edge of town, is a profusion of blooms and colour in the spring.

Peony, Kelway's Nursery, Langport

Longleat, Wiltshire

Map Ref: 88ST8043

The playground of the Marquess of Bath, Longleat is a conglomeration of attractions focusing on the great house. Lord Bath was the first peer to open his house regularly to visitors and has set a pattern which others have followed.

The grand Elizabethan house, in a glorious, wooded, lakeside setting, was built in golden stone Renaissance style. It was completed in 1580 by Sir John Thynne, a great traveller, acting as his own architect. His idea, revolutionary in the 16th century, was that the rooms should look out over the park rather than on to inner courtyards.

The contents and furnishings represent the diverse tastes and interests of the unbroken line of Thynnes to the present Marquess, from a 16th-century shuffle-board and a 17th-century gilt steeplechase cup to a portrait of the present Lord Bath painted in 1971 by Graham Sutherland and a library table

The lions of Longleat. Inset: inside the house, the Lower Dining Room has 19th-century Italian ceilings

commissioned from John Makepeace (see Beaminster). The Victorian kitchens have been completely restored and give an interesting picture of life below stairs.

The landscaped park of dense woods on the hillside and specimen trees in the foreground was created by Capability Brown in 1757; the formal flower gardens have been developed since Brown's day.

Fossils

Late in the 18th century, a young surveyor and engineer, William Smith, was mapping and plotting the course of a canal in north Somerset (now Avon), when he noted that the rock layers or strata lay on top of each other like 'so many superimposed slices of bread and butter'. For several years he walked the hills and valleys of Gloucestershire, Somerset and what is now Avon, collecting fossils and observing geological outcrops. Just collecting fossils was not enough, however, for he began to compare known fossils with certain rock beds, then to trace the beds themselves from one locality to another. Through this meticulous study he eventually worked out the sequence and relationships of strata, published in 1816 as *Strata identified by Organised Fossils*. For this and subsequent contributions to the science, Smith has come to be called the 'Father of English Geology'.

Palaeontologists on the Dorset coast have discovered the fossil remains of flying reptiles, elephants, crocodiles and dinosaur footprints. It would be most unusual for a casual visitor to unearth anything

Mary Anning (1799–1847) who, at the age of 11, found the first complete ichthyosaur skeleton in the Dorset Lias

quite so exciting, but the cliffs between Lyme Regis and West Bay, and further east towards Abbotsbury, are a rewarding hunting ground. It is extremely dangerous to hammer specimens from the cliffs which are unstable at the best of times. The beaches below are littered with recent rock falls and it is here that a search is most likely to be fruitful. Ammonites, belemnites and bivalves are the most common, and some of them can be fine and large.

Elsewhere in Dorset, ammonites and echinoids can be found at Kimmeridge Bay, Bincombe and Lulworth Cove; at Southwell, near Portland, Pleistocene shells and snails are plentiful; inland good localities for various Jurassic fossils occur around Sherborne and Beaminster.

In Wiltshire, quarries and recent cuttings at Bradford-on-Avon, Calne, Malmesbury and Swindon yield Jurassic ammonites and brachiopods. Chalk faunas can be found in pits at Downton, Marlborough and Woodford.

Following Smith's footsteps in Somerset and Avon, you may find good Palaeozoic and Mesozoic fossils; there is a spectacular skeleton of an Ichthyosaurus from the Lower Lias near Street, exhibited in the town's library. In the fossils at Kilve Beach may lie the origins of a legend about a saint who turned local snakes to stone – 'St Keyna's Serpents' is the name once given to the conger eels that still lurk on the shore here. Quarries at Burrington, Binegar and Dulcote are good sources for limestone faunas. Displays in local museums are a good starting point for studies of the subject.

The lions of Longleat wander about a huge enclosure through which runs a road: visitors are carefully warned not to get out of their cars. Elsewhere, elephants, rhinos, giraffes, zebras and many other animals roam the valley, cleverly confined by water, ditches and planting to give an impression of natural freedom.

AA recommends:
Guesthouse: Stalls Farm, *tel.* (09853) 323

Lulworth, Dorset

Map Ref: 92SY8279

There are two villages, East and West Lulworth, a castle and the Cove. East Lulworth is a charming cluster of stone and thatched cottages surviving despite the proximity of active army artillery ranges. The castle dates from about 1600; it was built as the home of Lord Howard of Bindon, using stone from Bindon Abbey. In 1641 the property was acquired by the Weld family. Ever since a disastrous fire, the castle has remained a roofless, bird-haunted ruin.

Near by, the strange domed building, a 'Pantheon in miniature', is a Roman Catholic chapel, built by Thomas Weld in 1786, with the permission of George III, so long as it did not look like a church. At the opposite end of the castle is the Parish Church of St Andrew, all but the tower largely rebuilt in the 19th century.

West Lulworth lies back from the coast in a valley sheltered from the winter storms, a collection of cob and whitewashed stone and thatched cottages lining the narrow street, with the 19th-century church above.

The Cove and neighbouring Stair Hole are textbook examples of geological coastal scenery illustrating the effects of the sea on rocks of various hardness. In Stair Hole the sea has broken through the ramparts of Portland stone and is hollowing out the folded Purbeck beds behind. Lulworth Cove shows a further development where erosion has reached the chalk ridge and been temporarily checked.

AA recommends:
Hotel: Bishop's Cottage, 1-star, *tel.* (092941) 261
Guesthouses: Gatton House Hotel, *tel.* (092941) 252
Lulworth Hotel, Main Rd, *tel.* (092941) 230
Shirley Hotel, *tel.* (092941) 358
Garage: Lulworth (Wold Enterprises), East Lulworth, *tel.* (092941) 283

Lyme Regis, Dorset

Map Ref: 90SY3492

The port owes its importance entirely to the construction of the

The calm, blue waters of Lulworth Cove, a textbook example of erosion

dog-leg breakwater, known as the Cobb. It was built in the 13th century and provided a welcome haven for ships along an otherwise inhospitable and dangerous coast. More recently the Cobb, lashed by stormy seas, has left an everlasting impression on film-goers through John Fowles' classic novel, *The French Lieutenant's Woman*.

When Leland visited in about 1540 he described the place as:

A praty market town, set in the rootes of an high rokky hille down to the hard shore. This town hath good shippes and usith fisshing and merchauntice.

There was ship-building on the beach, and a considerable export trade, mainly of cloth.

Lyme began its career as a fashionable seaside resort in the early 18th century; Daniel Defoe stayed here in 1724 and commented enthusiastically on the society he found. It became a favourite summer resort for visitors from Bath, as the popularity of sea-bathing and seaside holidays increased. The best-known visitor from Bath was Jane Austen who recorded her impression of the town in *Persuasion*.

There are many gorgeous examples of seaside architecture of the 18th and 19th centuries, painted in the pastel colours of Neopolitan ice-cream. There are good small family-run shops and tea rooms. Country and cliff walks and excellent beaches are to hand.

The rubble-strewn beach is a fossil hunter's delight, but beware the dangerous cliffs, constantly liable to subsidence, and never, but never, attempt to excavate fossils from the cliff-face. For inspiration, an enviable display of local fossils can be seen in the museum, together with photographs.

AA recommends:
Hotels: Alexandra, Pound St, 3-star, *tel.* (02974) 2010
Buena Vista, Pound St, 2-star, *tel.* (02974) 2494
Dorset, Silver St, 2-star, *tel.* (02974) 2482
St Michael's, Pound St, 2-star, *tel.* (02974) 2503
Restaurant: Drake's, 14-15 Monmouth Rd, 2-fork, *tel.* (02974) 2079
Guesthouses: Coverdale, Woodmead Rd, *tel.* (02974) 2882
Kersbrook Hotel & Restaurant, Pound Rd, *tel.* (02974) 2596
Rotherfield, View Rd, *tel.* (02974) 2811
White House, 47 Silver St, *tel.* (02974) 3420

Selection only: see page 4

Maiden Newton, Dorset

Map Ref: 91SY5997

A rural village set in the valley bottom of the River Frome. Flint and brick cottages line the main road, but unlike many of the small country towns in Dorset it is not a picturesque place. This was once a railway junction, where the Bridport line joined the main Dorchester to Yeovil route. The lines were opened in 1857 but this did not result in prosperity for Maiden Newton.

A single shaft of Ham stone stands in its socket to mark the site of the 15th-century market cross, said to have been one of the finest in the country; it was removed in 1780 to make way for the turnpike road improvements.

The church claims the oldest door in England, a Norman one, still on its hinges. The key stone of the arch inside is a fine piece of Norman carving, but the rest of the arch has been rebuilt. High up on the same wall, the carved stone corbels are fun: a man sounding a horn, a snarling dog, and a dog with a bone. It is a peaceful little medieval church, well worth seeing.

Above: a detail of the richly carved, roofed market cross, Malmesbury
Right: the south side of Malmesbury Abbey

Malmesbury, Wiltshire

Map Ref: 85ST9387

A picturesque town of mellow Cotswold stone, Malmesbury occupies a strategic position between two rivers which join to the south-east to become the Bristol Avon. The High Street of pretty cottages leads up from the River Avon to the richly carved 15th-century market cross described by Leland as 'a right faire costley peace of worke' for 'poor folkes to stande dry when rayne cummith'.

In about AD640 a Celtic monk, Mailduib, settled here and founded a school; a monastery developed and Aldhelm, nephew of King Ine, became the first Abbot. After his death in 709 he was canonised and buried in the Abbey Church, thereby attracting pilgrims to the Abbey and the town.

The historic Abbey crowns the hilltop; from the Market Cross a solid square gatehouse opens into the 'close' to reveal the remains of a magnificent 12th-century church; the southern porch is a blaze of fine Norman carving. Inside, the nave is truncated at the crossing, where in the 15th century a massive tower crashed down destroying much of the east end. Although a fragment of its former size, the building constitutes one of the most impressive remains of Norman architecture in England.

After the Dissolution the Abbey was bought by a wealthy local clothier, William Stampe, who presented the surviving nave to the townspeople for their parish church.

The isolated steeple in the Abbey churchyard is the remnant of the 13th-century St Paul's Church, the parish church until 1541. This now serves as the bell tower for the Abbey church.

The façades of numerous buildings in the town belie far earlier interiors: the central portion of the Bell Hotel, for instance, was originally built as the Abbey guesthouse, and the Abbey House has 13th-century monastic foundations, despite its Elizabethan exterior.

Down by St John's Bridge, where the river which once powered the great silk mill rushes by, are Almshouses dating from 1694. Incorporated in the gable wall is a Norman arch from the Hospital of St John; the adjoining historic Court House was used as a free school.

AA recommends:
Hotels: Old Bell, Abbey Row, 3-star, *tel.* (0666) 822344
Whatley Manor, Easton Grey, 3-star, country house, *tel.* (0666) 822888

Marlborough, Wiltshire

Map Ref: 89SU1869

The motto on the borough arms reads *Ubi nunc sapientis ossa Merlini* – 'Where now are the bones of wise Merlin?' A tradition persisted until the 14th century that Merlin was buried beneath the mound at the west end of the town, now in the grounds of Marlborough College. The pre-history of the mound remains a mystery, comparable with Silbury Hill, but from the 11th century it was the heart of a royal castle. William I established a mint here, and King John married Hadwisa of Gloucester in the Castle Chapel.

Meanwhile the town grew up around the Green, beyond the east end of the High Street and St Mary's Church; the cellars of some of the cottages here are of Saxon origin, and the church has a fine Norman-arched entrance at its western end.

A fire in 1653, described by Samuel Pepys as 'the most furious fire that ever mortal creature saw', destroyed most of the High Street, St Mary's Church and the Town Hall. Lesser fires in 1679 and 1690 led to an Act of Parliament forbidding for ever the use of thatched roofs in Marlborough. The Hermitage, in Hyde Lane, is one of the few houses that escaped the fires and is probably the oldest house, dating from about 1629.

The broad High Street, overlooked by the elaborate Town Hall with cupola, coat of arms, balconied window and pillared entrance, retains a weekly market.

The buildings on either side of the High Street are a happy mixture of styles and sizes, 17th-century timber-framing, 18th-century bow-windowed shop fronts, tile hanging and brick. The pavement on the north side is shaded by a colonnade; Pepys described this as 'penthouses supported with pillars which makes it a good walk', when he was staying at the 'White Harte', now the Conservative Club.

St Peter's Church at the west end is 'redundant', but has been given a new lease of life as a concert hall, craft market and Tourist Information Centre. Eglantyne Jebb (1876-1928), founder of the Save the Children Fund, taught at St Peter's school, now the library on the corner of Hyde Lane.

Much of the character of old Marlborough is captured in the alleys or yards off the High Street, narrow thoroughfares dating from the 16th century: Neates Yard with cobbler's shop and pretty brick cottages; Hughenden Yard with a farmhouse cheese shop and traditional cabinet makers; Chandlers' Yard, almost unchanged after 300 years; and, behind the Town Hall, Patten Alley, where it was the custom for women attending church to leave their pattens (over-shoes).

Marlborough College, at the west end of town, was founded in 1843 as a public school. The gracious building at the far end of the carefully tended lawns of the college court was the 18th-century home of the Seymours; it later became the Castle Inn, and is now a school house. Best value for a quick snack is the school's Tuck Shop, on the corner.

AA recommends:
Hotels: Castle & Ball, High St, 3-star, *tel.* (0672) 55201
Ivy House, High St, 3-star, *tel.* (0672) 53188
Merlin, 36-9 High St, 2-star, *tel.* (0672) 52151

Marlborough: St Mary's Church tower, above shops at the west end of the High Street

Marshfield, Avon

Map Ref: 88ST7773

Three huge stones mark the ancient meeting place of the counties of Gloucestershire, Wiltshire and Somerset at the mere or marsh which may have given the town its name. Marshfield marks the easterly point of the Cotswolds' southerly hill edge, the pinnacled tower of St Mary's making a distinguished landmark high above the Avon vale.

Marshfield became a borough, with a regular Tuesday market and two fairs a year, all for the benefit of its lords, the canons of Keynsham Abbey. Today it is very much a Cotswolds town of attractive stone-built and stone-roofed houses and cottages.

This is corn-growing country which in the 17th and 18th centuries produced malt for Bristol and Bath, leaving large malthouses as relics in the town, and an impressive array of Queen Anne-style houses, the homes of prosperous maltsters.

Marshfield's importance in the coaching era, as the first or last stop on the Bristol to London run, is reflected in a number of eminent 18th-century inns offering hospitality to travellers then and now.

Every Boxing Day the Marshfield Mummers appear in the High Street, dressed in costumes covered in strips of newspaper and coloured paper, to present their play, a traditional cycle of death and resurrection, led by the Town Crier and starring Father Christmas, Little Man John, King William, Saucy Jack and other unlikely characters. The play lapsed for a time around the turn of the century, but was revived in 1931 by the vicar, the Rev Alford, who heard his gardener reciting some of the lines.

Countrymen's Smocks

The shape of a smock is not unlike that of the Roman 'tunica' which was still worn in England in Saxon times. Illuminated manuscripts of the Middle Ages depict labourers working in loose-fitting garments reaching to their knees, very similar to the 18th- and 19th-century smocks that have survived.

From the 17th century, illustrations of smocks, as protective over-garments worn usually by men, become more common. A playing card of 1676 shows a wagoner whose smock is described as 'straight and rather full, worn to just below the knees; the opening (at the neck) reaches almost to the waist and there is a small turned down collar; there is no smocking or decoration'. Smocks were worn as overalls and were the usual outdoor clothing of rural workers, especially shepherds and wagoners, who, more than most, were exposed to the inclemency of the English climate. In Wessex they were made of bleached linen or coarser cotton twill, but in other parts of the country they were sometimes dyed, blue in the Midlands, olive green in East Anglia. Some smocks were oiled to make them almost waterproof, and most had several

A Somerset smock. The broad collar gave extra protection against the elements

layers of material over the shoulders and a wide thick collar like a cape for extra protection.

The delicately embroidered decorations on the front panels of country smocks were thought to distinguish the occupations of the wearers; shepherds' smocks for example were thought to bear emblems of crooks, sheep and hurdles, while carters' smocks had wheels, whips and reins. Recent studies of smocks surviving in museum collections have shown that there is very little evidence for this theory; the various patterns are simply the 'basic stuff of untutored art'.

Thomas Hardy in *Under the Greenwood Tree* describes the rural scene in which 'stalwart ruddy men and boys were dressed mainly in snow-white smock-frocks, embroidered upon the shoulders and breasts in ornamented forms of hearts, diamonds and zigzags'. Some of these garments were too fine for everyday wear and were saved for Sunday best. There is a Wessex tradition of a 'smock' wedding dress, worn by the daughter of a poor family to indicate that she had nothing else to contribute as a dowry.

In 1874 Hardy noticed that 'the long smocked frocks and the harvest home have . . . nearly disappeared'; on more remote farms smocks continued to be worn until the 1920s. Now they are to be found packed in tissue paper in museum storerooms or used as dressing-up props for a Christmas pantomime.

Milton Abbas: grass steps lead to St Catherine's Chapel. Above: the 'model village' had troubled beginnings

Midsomer Norton and Radstock, Avon

Map Ref: 87ST6654

Midsomer Norton and Radstock were joined, administratively speaking, in 1933 to form the urban district of Norton-Radstock; since then their suburbs and housing estates have all but joined geographically. But the origins of the towns are clearly distinct and each has retained its individual character.

Both towns are sited in the very beautiful valley of the River Somer; Midsomer Norton was an offshoot of Stratton-on-the-Fosse, the 'north tun'; 'Midsomer' is a reminder of the annual midsummer fair. During the 19th century the village grew into a small mining town, surrounded by collieries at Welton, Old Mills and later Norton Hill. Remains of the old village can be deciphered round the parish church, the little square called The Island, and along the High Street.

At Radstock coal mining began in 1763 and the town that developed became the capital of the Somerset coalfield, obliterating any traces of the earlier village. The last colliery only closed in 1973.

For enthusiasts of industrial archaeology Norton-Radstock and the surrounding area offer rich pickings, and for others, the countryside around these towns is as lovely as anywhere in the region. To the south on the A367 is Stratton-on-the-Fosse with Downside Abbey monastery and school. The Abbey Church can be visited.

Milton Abbas, Dorset

Map Ref: 92ST8001

A thriving village grew up beside an ancient monastery, founded by Athelstan, in AD933, on the site of the present landscaped lawns of Milton Abbey House.

Virtually all the monastic buildings were destroyed by a fire; a huge new church was begun, and it is the east end of this 14th- and 15th-century work that survives. Massive as the church is, 136ft long, the nave was never built, so the west door leads straight into the crossing. The adjoining mansion was designed by Sir William Chambers for Lord Milton and built in 1774; Milton could not bear the village on his doorstep, so had it removed and rebuilt in a valley. This is the identical thatched pretty village of cottages we see today. In the middle, the church was erected in 1786 using stone and timber from the Abbey's tithe barn; the Tregonwell Almshouses are a rebuilding of the 17th-century houses from the original village.

From the grounds of Milton Abbey House, now a public school, a grass staircase of 111 steps leads up between solid yew hedges to St Catherine's Chapel. On this ridge, it is said, Athelstan and his army camped on their way to meet the invading Danes.

AA recommends:
Hotel: Milton Manor, 2-star, country house, *tel.* (0258) 880254
Self Catering: Little Hewish Farm (cottages), *tel.* (0258) 880326

Muchelney, Somerset

Map Ref: 90ST4224

Muchelney means 'great island'; and that is what it was, encircled by marshes, in the often-flooded valley of the River Isle. It was a suitably remote spot for the foundation of a Benedictine Abbey in the 8th century. The Abbey eventually prospered but was always overshadowed by the fame of nearby Glastonbury.

The remains are much ruined. The southern range containing the abbot's lodging is the best preserved and is interesting; the ornately carved fireplace, with an overmantel of crouching lions, gives an idea of the quality of the buildings that have been lost. There are also some wall paintings, medieval floor tiles and a very fine barrel-roof.

Shoulder-to-shoulder with the ruined Abbey Church is the Parish Church of St Peter and St Paul; the brightly painted roof of the nave is a riot of cherubs and angels in the firmament of sun, stars and clouds.

Over the road from the churchyard, the Priest's House has survived intact; it dates from the early 14th century when it had a small open hall. Alterations were made in the 15th and 16th centuries, but it remains a rare example of domestic architecture from this time.

The village is dotted with other old houses, most in blue Lias stone under thatched roofs; in one, John Leach, grandson of Bernard, runs the Muchelney Pottery.

Nailsea, Avon

Map Ref: 86ST4770

Nailsea could almost be described as a 'new town'; in the last 20 years it has grown from a quiet country village to a busy commercial town with a population nearing 16,000.

But behind the wide, sweeping roads, mown verges and neat estates, the story of Nailsea stretches back to the Saxon period. This was 'Neil's' or 'Niall's' island, slightly higher than the surrounding marsh, with a thriving farming settlement.

From the 14th century, if not earlier, coal was mined at Nailsea; pits were sunk in the Kingshill area and miners from other coalfields moved in to start work. During the 18th century the pits were deepened and the mining area was extended to Backwell and Nailsea Heath. Cottages were built for the miners, and Thatcher's Brewery opened to cater for their needs.

But Nailsea is best known for the decorative glassware of that name: unlikely objects, like walking sticks and rolling pins, made out of fine glass freckled with colours. It all began with J R Lucas from Bristol who chose Nailsea because of the combination, in the locality, of good quality coal, sand and limestone – the raw ingredients of glass. Production began in 1788.

The peak of activity was reached by the mid-19th century, when a rolling mill churned out plate glass; bottles and ornamental items were also made. The decorative items now commonly described as 'Nailsea' were probably made by skilled men working in their spare time, but some of the work attributed to Nailsea may not have been produced here at all.

The glassworks closed down in 1873 and the last glass cone was demolished just after the turn of the century.

Fine collections of Nailsea glass can be seen at Clevedon Court (see p 41) and at the Somerset County Museum, Taunton.

Norton St Philip, Somerset

Map Ref: 88ST7755

Norton St Philip, uncomfortably perched on the side of a hill, was one of the most important possessions of the Charterhouse at Hinton. Throughout the Middle Ages it was a collecting point for Mendip wool and the George Inn was built partly as a store for wool awaiting either the two annual fairs or the arrival of merchants from far afield.

The oldest parts of the building date from the 14th century. It claims to be one of the oldest licensed premises in the country. The ground floor is built of local reddish-brown stone, with jettied timber-framed first and second floors and a stone slate roof.

The Duke of Monmouth, illegitimate son of Charles II, stayed here shortly before being defeated at the Battle of Sedgemoor during his attempt on the throne in 1685; it is said that he narrowly missed being shot during a skirmish as he stood at one of the windows. He had many supporters in the Mendips, as is recalled by this whistling tune from Norton:

The Duke of Monmouth is at Norton Town
All a-fighting for the Crown,
Ho, boys, ho!

Lower down the hill, opposite the parish church, the village school is a fine example of early 19th-century Gothic, with castellated walls and gables, and little pinnacles decorating the corners.

The tower of the church is an odd design, planned, it is said, by a rich citizen of Norton, Jeffrey Flower.

Three miles east along the A366 Farleigh Hungerford Castle, an impressive ruin, dates from the mid-14th century. It was built to guard the crossing point of the River Frome by Sir Thomas Hungerford. The Hungerfords were one of the richest families in England. They could ride from here to Salisbury on their own land.

Landscape Gardens

Middleton, as Milton Abbas was first known, originally grew up around the abbey which was founded here in AD933. At the Dissolution the buildings went into private ownership and when, in 1752, the abbey and its estates came into the possession of Joseph Damer (later Lord Milton and Earl of Dorchester) the history of the village was to take a dramatic turn.

With the exception of the great abbey hall which Joseph Damer incorporated into a new mansion, everything else was to be swept completely away. Capability Brown was engaged to landscape the park, the woodlands and an entire new village. The old village lay in the valley south of the abbey, consisting of over 100 houses set in a number of streets, but it was Lord Milton's intention to flood this valley to create a massive lake. The provision of a new village may seem philanthropic, but he has been described as 'rude, proud and domineering' in his determination to create a tranquil setting for his stately home. To enable him to do this he began to acquire and to demolish the old village and to re-house the villagers in the present street. This was stubbornly resisted by many, but Lord Milton persisted, even introducing Acts of Parliament to remove the local grammar school to Blandford. Although the village was demolished, it appears never to have been drowned as there was insufficient head of water to realise the scheme. Today's humps and bumps between the abbey and the lake mark the sites of the former houses.

Milton Abbas may be seen as a prime illustration of the astonishing 18th-century phenomenon of re-creating the English rural landscape. In Wessex as throughout the country, the wealthy owners of country estates such as Stourhead in Wiltshire and Kingston Lacy in Dorset were to spend vast sums of money on damming streams, creating lakes, moving hills, building temples and monuments, and planting trees by the thousand, in order to re-shape their parks and gardens. In some cases, the landowners were influenced by what they had seen on their travels abroad, as at Stourhead where Henry Hoare recreated classical landscape paintings seen on the Grand Tour. In all, changing tastes and fashions in literature, art and architecture were reflected in the landscape designs of such men as William Kent, Henry Hoare, Lancelot 'Capability' Brown and Humphry Repton.

Autumn colours at Stourhead, the quintessential landscape garden

Nunney, Somerset

Map Ref: 88ST7345

The village of Nunney grew alongside the brook which was responsible for the prosperity brought by the woollen and edge-tool industries.

It is an unlikely setting for a castle; but Sir John de la Mare was licensed to crenellate his manor house here in 1373 and he modelled the building, it is said, on the Bastille. It consists of four great drum towers at the corners of a rectangular block, four storeys high. It was ruined during the Civil War when a Parliamentary force, well equipped with artillery, bombarded it to surrender. It remains a picturesque ruin, surrounded by a moat fed from the stream.

Until the 18th century the village was an important cloth centre; the sloping cobbled bank of the Brook, where the medieval market cross now stands, was a 'pavement and place to wash wool'. Nunney later had a Fussells ironworks.

The pretty village streets are lined with 17th- and 18th-century grey stone cottages, leading to the focal point at the old market place.

Lanes go north to Mells, where 16th-century Thomas Horner acquired the manor by possibly dubious means – he is the 'Little Jack' of the nursery rhyme.

AA recommends:
Guesthouse: George, Church St (Inn), tel. (037384) 458

Pewsey, Wiltshire

Map Ref: 89SU1660

The Vale of Pewsey is about 12 miles long and no more than 5 miles across. Its southern border, a wall of chalk hills, is steep and impressive, but the range on the north side is even more so, a series of towering hills, Milk Hill and Tan Hill rising to over 900ft.

The slopes of the Downs have provided a huge canvas for carved hill figures. Nothing can be seen now of the first Pewsey White Horse, carved by Robert Pile in about 1785. The one that can be seen today was cut in 1937, by the local fire brigade, to commemorate the coronation of George VI.

Pewsey developed as the market town for the Vale, the commercial centre of some of the richest farming country in England. William Cobbett visited in 1826 and enthused: 'It would be impossible to find a more beautiful and pleasant country than this.'

Pewsey is charming, unspoilt and rural, with a pleasing mixture of Wiltshire thatched cottages and Georgian houses. At the crossroads the statue of King Alfred is a reminder that this was part of a Saxon royal estate. The Parish Church of St John the Baptist is said to have been built on foundations of sarsen stones laid in Saxon times, and is one of several fine churches in the vale.

About a mile out of town, at the French Horn Inn, Pewsey Wharf is an ideal starting point for exploring the Kennet and Avon Canal (see p. 31).

AA recommends:
Garages: Pewsey Motors, Market Pl, tel. (0672) 62371
Whatley & Co, Avonside Wks, tel. (0672) 62404

Piddletrenthide, Dorset

Map Ref: 91SY7099

The delightfully named River Piddle lends its name to a string of villages down its valley – Piddlehinton, Puddletown, Tolpuddle, Affpuddle, Bryants Puddle and Turners Puddle. Piddletrenthide has the distinction of being the first, near the head of the valley. The village is strung out, following the B3143 and the river, from the Parish Church of All Saints down to the Methodist Chapel and Sunday School.

The church claims the earliest use of Arabic numerals on any building in England, in the date, 1487, inscribed over the west door of the tower. The tower is one of the

The weathervane on the roof of the Poacher's Inn at Piddletrenthide. Inset: Nunney Castle's imposing towers have stood firm for 600 years in spite of damage done during the Civil War

finest in the county, with an amazing array of gargoyles.

In the middle of the village the pretty flint and brick school was provided by John Bridge, of the Manor House, in 1848; the iron gates came from a tomb in Westminster Abbey, either Mary Queen of Scots' or Lady Margaret Beaufort's, no one is quite sure. There are two pubs, both with attractive gardens by the river, the Poachers' Inn and the Piddle Inn.

AA recommends:
Hotel: Old Bakehouse, 2-star, *tel.* (03004) 305
Guesthouse: The Poachers (Inn), *tel.* (03004) 358

Pilton, Somerset

Map Ref: 87ST5840

A scattered village of grey stone cottages and farmhouses on either side of the Whitelake River.

The Church of St John is near the bottom of the valley, where, it is said, Joseph of Arimathea landed – the valley bottom is close to sea level and boats may have reached this far inland.

The Abbot of Glastonbury had one of his many residences at what is now the Manor House of Pilton Vineyard; the Abbot grew vines here too, in the 12th century. The present house is a mixture of styles, mainly Georgian with a castellated top; the vaulted cellar, dovecote, and remains of a possible cloister suggest its more ancient origin. The village's associations with Glastonbury are also demonstrated by the shell of the medieval barn, on the south side of the valley: its gables are decorated with symbols of the Evangelists, as at the Abbey Barn at Glastonbury.

AA recommends:
Guesthouse: Long House, *tel.* (074989) 701

Poole, Dorset

Map Ref: 93SZ0190

Canute chose Poole harbour as his first base, in AD1015, for ravaging far and wide in Wessex before he moved on to besiege London. It is easy to see why: the harbour is sheltered from the westerlies with a narrow mouth protected by the sweep of Studland Bay and Sandbanks. Poole had the advantage of a deep-water harbour, so, as other ports like Wareham silted up, Poole rose to prominence.

From the 16th century the fishing fleet based in Poole ventured further afield, particularly to Newfoundland for cod. A triangle of trade developed in which the ships took salt and provisions to Newfoundland, returned to the Mediterranean with salt fish, and then went back to Poole laden with wine, olive oil and dried fruit. The quay and harbour-side still bustle with boats, and the old warehouse, now the Maritime Museum, Customs House and Harbour Office are substantial memorials to that past activity.

In the old town, between the railway and the quay, the Guildhall houses a local history museum. Market Street and Church Street are closely packed with 18th-century town houses, some modern infill and some earlier building, notably the Almshouses. In the heart of the old town St James Church, glistening white Purbeck limestone, is a 19th-century replacement of a medieval building.

This must be one of the very few towns in Britain where a railway actually crosses the main shopping street, the High Street. There is a handy footbridge in cast iron by Ransomes and Rapier of London, 1872. The modern shopping precinct of Falklands Square is dedicated to all those who took part in the liberation of the islands in 1982.

Poole Park, to the east of the town, was opened in 1885 by the Prince of Wales; its formal gardens look out over the harbour and there is a good zoo of smaller animals.

In the middle of Poole Harbour, Brownsea Island is now owned by the National Trust and is accessible by ferry from Poole Quay and Sandbanks. Henry VIII built a blockhouse here to defend the

The Custom House, Poole, a reminder of the busy trading days of the past. Today Poole is famous for its pottery (left)

harbour; in the 18th century it was transformed into an imitation castle and at the same time Humphrey Sturt set about attempting to 'improve' the island. Now the heath and woodland have returned and it has glorious rhododendrons; 200 acres are given over to a nature reserve, a sanctuary for ducks, geese and waders. There is a flourishing heronry, a black-headed gullery and a colony of common tern. Baden Powell held a camp here in 1907 to see if his idea of 'Boy Scouts' was feasible, and scouts and guides are the only visitors allowed to stay on the island.

AA recommends:
Hotels: Harbour Heights, Haven Rd, 3-star, *tel.* (0202) 707272
The Mansion House, Thames St, 3-star, *tel.* (0202) 685666
Salterns Hotel, 38 Salterns Way, 3-star, *tel.* (0202) 707321
Fairlight, 1 Golf Links Rd, 1-star, *tel.* (0202) 694316
Restaurants: The Warehouse, The Quay, 2-forks, *tel.* (0202) 677238
Le Select, 129 Parkstone Rd, 1-fork, *tel.* (0202) 740223
The Rajpoot, High St, 1-fork, *tel.* (0202) 676330
Self Catering: 28 Banks Rd, *tel.* (0202) 708600
8 Brownsea Rd, *tel.* (0202) 708600
25/29 Longfleet Rd, *tel.* (01) 993 2095
31/33/35 Longfleet Rd, *tel.* (01) 993 2095
Guesthouses: Ebdon House Hotel, 21 St Clair Rd, *tel.* (0202) 707286
Grovefield Hotel, 18 South Pinewood, *tel.* (0202) 766798
Redcroft Private Hotel, 20 Pinewood Rd, *tel.* (0202) 763959
Westminster Cottage Hotel, 3 Westminster Rd East, *tel.* (0202) 765265
Garages: Grand Parade Mtrs, Poole Rd, Branksome, *tel.* (0202) 763361
Horizon Mtr Co, 397 Ringwood Rd, Parkstone, *tel.* (0202) 740270
Magna Mtr Co, 410-16 Poole Rd, Branksome, *tel.* (0202) 768383
Wadham Stringer, 573 Wallesdown Rd, *tel.* (0202) 519191

Selection only: page 4

Portishead, Avon

Map Ref: 86ST4676

On the east side of Portishead the reclaimed marshes lead towards the Royal Portbury Dock and the Severnside Industrial Area, but the original settlement and the church are on the other side of the town, with tree-lined lanes and a charming rural atmosphere. The church, which is mainly 15th-century, has a Norman font and is approached from the south through an avenue of pollarded willows. The 16th-century manor house beside the church path has a hexagonal tower, and the farm buildings include a two-storey barn with storage above the arched cattle stalls.

Over the hill the old cliff line was first developed with a stylish terrace of early 19th-century villas backing on to Battery Lane. The Battery, at Portishead Point, was defended in the 16th century against the possibility of Spanish invaders. It was then refortified when Napoleon threatened, but the fort was dismantled soon after the First World War. An open-air heated swimming pool has been built into the side of the headland, overlooking the esplanade, park and muddy beach.

The country village and select resort have almost been swamped by commercial development, particularly since the arrival of the railway in 1867, the creation of the dock in 1879, and more recently by dormitory housing estates. In the Severnside Industrial Area, one firm has the distinction of making most of Britain's horseshoes.

AA recommends:
Garage: Wheelers, 141 High St, *tel.* (0272) 842373

Portland, Dorset

Map Ref: 90SY6971

Although the Isle of Portland is not really an island, being connected to the mainland by Chesil Beach and since 1839 by a road, its character is so bleak and strange compared with the rest of Dorset that it might as well be an island. It is a windswept and almost treeless lump of limestone, tapering to Portland Bill at the southern tip, which is marked by two lighthouses, one in action, the other a bird observatory. The quarrymen's cottages and villages, Fortuneswell and Easton, are reminiscent of the industrial north-east of England.

On either side of the road to the Bill are common fields, the relics of medieval strip farming. Rare survivors, too, are the local breed of Portland sheep; small and hardy, they were once common but are now seldom seen outside rare breeds farms.

In the latter half of his reign, Henry VIII was nervous of the possibility of invasion by the joint forces of Roman Catholic Spain and France, and organised a programme of fortification right round the south coast. Portland Castle, now inside the modern Naval base, was part of this chain, and is particularly well preserved. Together with Sandsfoot Castle, on the mainland, it was designed to defend the harbour at Weymouth from attack by sea. It is an excellent example of military architecture of that period, now in the care of English Heritage.

Rusty chains, cranes and bollards and great angular blocks of white Portland stone, like giants' building blocks, mark the quarries. It was not until after the Great Fire of London that the stone was used in quantity. Sir Christopher Wren

The naval base at Portland, seen from the Verne. Inset: Portland stone, durable but easily carved

Monastery Barns

The great medieval landowners of Wessex, the monastic houses, left a precious legacy of awe-inspiring buildings. Many of these were destroyed at the time of the Reformation when rampant vandalism made quarries of the most magnificent churches and their cloisters, and of those buildings that have survived the centuries it is the humble but massive barns that demonstrate most clearly the extent and power of those monastic estates. The barns remain simply because they were essential to the purposes of farming. At Abbotsbury the 14th-century barn survives while there is scarcely more than a trace of the rest of the abbey.

All the barns follow the same basic pattern: a large unencumbered floor space under a high roof, with entrance doors and porches on opposite sides, wide and high enough to allow loaded wagons to be drawn inside, unloaded, and then, without turning, to emerge through the doors on the opposite side. The barns at Bradford-on-Avon and Doulting, near Shepton Mallet, which belonged to the nunnery at Shaftesbury and the abbey at Glastonbury respectively, each have four porches, to facilitate the separation of different crops within the one building, and to allow access – particularly important at Bradford-on-Avon where the barn is 168ft long, the second largest such barn in the country.

The great barn of the abbey at Abbotsbury, one of the largest in England

The structure of the barns' roof timbers is frequently of great interest to architectural historians, partly because it is usually exposed and therefore can be studied relatively easily, but also because these roofs represent examples of the medieval carpenters' craft in its simplest and purest form. The Abbey Barn at Glastonbury has a brilliantly designed two-tier cruck roof, the 'cruck' being the inverted V formed by two curved beams. Dating from the 1340s, it has lower cruck blades linked by a collar beam at high level, eliminating the need for a tie beam lower down; and smaller pairs of crucks stand on that collar beam to join at the apex.

The barns were built for the storage of the corn harvest and needed to be large enough to contain the whole crop at harvest time. During the winter the corn was threshed, and the draughty area between the great doors of the barns was traditionally used as the threshing floor, hence the word 'threshold'.

The medieval barns at Bradford-on-Avon and Glastonbury are open to the public. Others at Abbotsbury, Cerne Abbas, Doulting, Pilton, Stoke sub Hamdon, Wells and West Pennard can be seen from the roadside. Tisbury's barn has a magnificent thatched roof. The late 17th-century barn at Avebury is open to the public as a museum of Wiltshire folk life.

---

chose it for the new St Paul's and for many of the new City churches, and by the 19th century 25,000 tons were being exported annually. The use of the stone for carving, by such sculptors as Gaudier-Brzeska and Henry Moore, is commemorated annually by an open-air exhibition of modern sculpture in Tout Quarries.

Construction of the massive breakwater began in 1847 to create an anchorage sufficient for the largest ships in the Royal Navy. A prison was built on the island so that the convicts could provide labour. In 1872 the breakwater was officially opened by Albert Edward, Prince of Wales. The ceremonial stone is inscribed 'These are Imperial Works and Worthy of Kings'. In addition a great citadel was built on the Verne, the highest point of the island, to guard the harbour. Today the prison has become a Borstal institution while the Verne Citadel is used as a prison.

One cottage, at the southern end of Wakeham, is open to the public as the Portland Museum.

AA recommends:
Hotels: Portland Heights, Yeates Corner, 3-star, *tel.* (0305) 821361

Pennsylvania Castle, Pennsylvania Rd, 2-star, *tel.* (0305) 820561
Garages: Chesil Beach Motors, Easton Ln, *tel.* (0305) 820483
Easton Motor Services, 26-8 Easton Sq, *tel.* (0305) 820084

Priddy, Somerset

Map Ref: 87ST5251

High on the Mendip plateau, 800ft or so above sea level, Priddy is a windswept village of farms and low cottages sheltering behind rubble limestone walls. The large triangular green forms the centre, but the houses are not clustered around it; the focal point on the green is a stack of sheep hurdles, with a little thatched roof to protect them from the weather, like a lonely haystack. It is a permanent reminder of the annual invasion of sheep at the summer fair (about 21 August). The village, usually empty save for a few tired potholers, suddenly comes to life for one hectic day and is packed with farmers, travellers, animals and activity.

The fair was transferred to Priddy from Wells in 1348, possibly to avoid the excessive tolls charged by the city, or perhaps because of the plague, when the sheep farmers preferred to stay up on the hills of the Mendips rather than go down into the crowded town where their chances of picking up the disease would have been that much greater; and it has stayed ever since. There is a local proverb that 'the first rain after Priddy Fair is the first rain of winter', and another that the fair will only survive if the hurdles on the green are preserved.

On the skyline above Priddy, north-east of the village, the humps of the prehistoric Priddy Nine Barrows can be seen; and beyond them, less visible but impressive from aerial photographs or maps, lie the three Neolithic Priddy Circles, each about 200yds in diameter.

On the edge of the village Priddy Church, with its squat square tower, is set in a huge churchyard. Inside there is a large Norman font. The barrel roof rests on stone corbels carved as heads of kings and queens and women with wimples. The altar frontal in a glass case is 500 years old, beautifully embroidered in fine damask.

AA recommends:
Campsite: Mendip Heights Caravan & Camping Park, Townsend, 2-pennants, *tel.* (0749) 870241

Puddletown, Dorset

Map Ref: 92SY7594

The 'new' village and the rebuilding on the main roads were the result of work by an enthusiastic squire in the 1860s and 1870s. Some of the building is austere, but down by the Square and towards the church the old village has character and style. The village shop with a pillared first floor bay window faces the old market place. In the shelter of the canopy is an old shop sign 'Stephens & Co'.

Puddletown Church has some splendid tombs and one of the finest figures is that of Sir William Martyn of 1503

The church is a time-warp – a perfect 17th-century interior, complete with all its dark stained woodwork: box pews (with hat pegs), font cover, pulpit and especially the balcony, dated 1635 and scrawled with 17th- and 18th-century graffiti. Underneath the balcony hang four 19th-century heavy canvas fire buckets from an insurance company. The tombs and memorials in the southern aisle are exceptional, particularly the effigies of a 13th-century knight and his lady, carved in Ham stone; the knight is in full armour, and the lady in a veil and wimple.

Athelhampton House, just off the A35, is an architectural gem. Built on the legendary site of King Athelstan's palace, the buildings date from the 15th century. The baronial Great Hall, with tapestries, halberds and antlered skulls, has a spectacular timber roof structure. The house is surrounded by formal gardens.

AA recommends:
Garage: Olds, *tel.* (030584) 456

Salisbury, Wiltshire

Map Ref: 93SU1429

On top of a bleak hill two miles north of the present city of Salisbury are the massive ramparts and earthworks of the original settlement of Old Sarum. Once an Iron Age hillfort and later inhabited by Romans, Saxons, Danes and Normans, Old Sarum was the place where William the Conqueror inspected his victorious army in 1070. His nephew, Bishop

Salisbury Cathedral (above) – its clean lines, the simplicity of its plan and the uniformity of its design make it the perfect expression of the Early English style. Its most famous feature is the spire which, with a height of 404ft, is the tallest in England.
Overlooking part of the Cathedral Close is Mompesson House, a beautifully proportioned Queen Anne town house of 1701 noted for its elegant plasterwork ceilings (detail, right)

Osmund, later St Osmund, built a castle and a magnificent cathedral in 1078. Only five days after its consecration it was struck by lightning and largely destroyed; the nave alone survived to be incorporated into the cathedral of Bishop Roger's restoration.

Roger also built a new castle, which doubled as the Bishop's palace. After his death in 1139, King Stephen took over the castle and trouble brewed between the governors of the castle and the bishops. The problems are summed up in a papal bull:

Situated within a castle, the church is subject to such inconvenience that the clergy cannot stay there without danger to their persons. The church is exposed to such winds that those celebrating the divine offices can hardly hear each other speak. The fabric is so ruinous . . . Water is so scarce . . . and access to it is not to be had without the governor's permission . . . The whiteness of the chalk causes blindness.

All these moans did the trick, and in 1226 the bishop moved to a new site and a new town, New Sarum, the place we know as Salisbury.

Salisbury Cathedral is stunning; particularly so because it is built in a single style and therefore appears to be an exceptionally unified design.

In fact it was built in two phases, 1220-58 when most of the building including the nave was constructed; and 1334-80 when the tower was heightened and the spire put up.

The spire, a landmark for miles around, shoots up to a height of 404ft. Inside, at the crossing, the giant piers of clustered dark, Purbeck marble columns were intended to support the original low tower, but since the 14th century they have been required to bear the extra 6,500 tons of the heightened tower and spire.

Several tombs, including those of Bishops Roger and Joscelin, and the shrine of St Osmund were moved here from Old Sarum.

The Chapter House, a most beautiful octagonal room, has one central column supporting a delicately carved roof, and eight giant windows.

The Close is the largest in England and contains a rich variety of architectural styles, from the 13th century to the present day. Of particular interest, both for its architecture and contents, is the King's House, on the west side, which is now the home of the Salisbury and South Wiltshire Museum; apart from its archaeological treasures from Old Sarum and Stonehenge, there are the Salisbury Giant and Hob Nob, and a reconstructed, pre-NHS doctor's surgery.

On the north side of the Close, facing Choristers' Green, is Mompesson House (National Trust, open to the public). Built in 1701 by Charles Mompesson, it is well furnished and displays a rare collection of English drinking glasses.

General Pitt-Rivers

One of the greatest names in 19th-century Wessex was General Augustus Pitt-Rivers, the first Inspector of Ancient Monuments, the founder of scientific archaeology, and the owner, from 1880 to 1900, of the Cranborne Chase Estate in Dorset and Wiltshire.

Born Augustus Henry Lane Fox on 14 April 1827 in Yorkshire, he had to change his name to Pitt-Rivers when he inherited Cranborne Chase under the terms of the will of Lord Rivers.

As the youngest son of a youngest son, Augustus Fox's chances of inheriting anything were slight and, with no prospects in sight, he was sent off to join the Army. One of his tasks in the 1850s was to test rifles which were about to be introduced to replace muskets. It was characteristic of him that he not only produced a first-class manual, *Instruction of Musketry*, but also began a collection of weapons, to illustrate their development, which he arranged systematically and carefully catalogued.

After taking part in the battle of Alma in the Crimea, he returned to more mundane duties and was appointed Assistant Quartermaster General for the southern district of Ireland. Here he carried out his first archaeological field-work and continued to build up his collections, turning to ethnological artefacts to demonstrate his theories of cultural evolution.

Pitt-Rivers' achievement was to turn the excavation of ancient sites into a systematic study, rather than an idle pastime or looting exercise. His principal excavation in the 1870s was at Cissbury hillfort, near Worthing, where his interest in objects developed into a broader understanding of the societies he was investigating.

It was only through a series of family coincidences that Cranborne Chase and the new surname passed to Fox. The estate covered some 28,000 acres, and included Rushmore Lodge where the Pitt-Rivers lived. The wealth of archaeological sites on the estate occupied him for the rest of his life and filled four huge volumes with excavation reports and sketches.

Having given most of his collections to Oxford University, he built a private museum in the grounds for his models of the archaeological sites, and for local collections of rural life.

Pitt-Rivers died at Rushmore in 1900 and was cremated at Woking. He is commemorated by a carved urn at the west end of Tollard Royal church, where his wife and children are buried. His real memorials are his collections, in the Pitt-Rivers Museum in Oxford and in the Salisbury and South Wiltshire Museum, Salisbury.

Between these two, the Wardrobe was built as the Bishop's storehouse in 1254; altered and extended it now houses the museum of the Duke of Edinburgh's Royal Regiment.

Away from the environs of the Cathedral, Salisbury is still a delight. Between the Close and the Market Square to the north there remains an intriguing network of medieval streets and alleys, lined with half-timbered, jettied houses and enjoying names like Fish Row, Butcher Row, Silver Street, Blue Boar Row, Ox Row and Oatmeal Row. At the centre of it all is a small square with the 15th-century Poultry Cross, the last of four market crosses in the City.

As a cultural centre, Salisbury has yet more to offer with an annual Festival and permanent facilities at the Playhouse Theatre and the Arts Centre. The Cathedral is also a perfect setting for concerts.

AA recommends:

Hotels: Red Lion, Milford St, 3-star, *tel.* (0722) 23334

Rose & Crown, Harnham Rd, Harnham, 3-star, *tel.* (0722) 27908

White Hart, St John Street, 3-star, *tel.* (0722) 27476

Cathedral, Milford St. 2-star, *tel.* (0722) 20144

Guesthouses: Byways House, 31 Fowlers Rd, *tel.* (0722) 28364

Glen Lyn, 6 Ballamy Ln, Milford Hill, *tel.* (0722) 27880

Hayburn Wyke, 72 Castle Rd, *tel.* (0722) 24141

Old Bell, 2 St Ann Street (Inn), *tel.* (0722) 27958

Campsite: Coombe Nurseries Touring Park, Race Plain, Netherhampton, 3-pennants, *tel.* (0722) 28451, (2m SW off A3094)

Garages: Anna Valley Motors (Campbell Symonds) Ltd, Brunel Rd, *tel.* (0722) 23522

W Goddard & Co, 41-5 Winchester St, *tel.* (0722) 336681

Henlys, Southampton Rd, *tel.* (0722) 335251

Wood Motors, Middleton Rd, *tel.* (0722) 24343

Selection only: see page 4

Shaftesbury, Dorset

Map Ref: 92ST8622

A hilltop town, 700ft above sea level, commanding the Blackmoor Vale. By the time King Alfred founded a nunnery here in AD888, there was already a Saxon settlement on this naturally strategic site. Alfred appointed his daughter, Ethelgiva, as the first abbess. In AD 978 the remains of Edward the Martyr were brought from Wareham to the Abbey church for reburial, ensuring the popularity of the place for pilgrims and therefore consequent prosperity. In fact Shaftesbury became the wealthiest nunnery in the country, as evidenced by the huge tithe barn at Bradford-on-Avon, the centre of just one of its estates. At the Dissolution the Abbey buildings were demolished and provided a quarry for building stone; the remaining ruins are little more than a pile of rubble.

Elsewhere the town repays exploration on foot; there are superb views especially from Castle Hill, as far as Glastonbury Tor, and from the gardens of Park Walk. Steeply cobbled Gold Hill will be familiar to many as the location of the Hovis advertisement on television; on one side it is lined by 18th-century cottages, on the other by a heavily buttressed retaining wall, possibly the medieval wall of the Abbey precinct. At the top of the Town Hall, the southern end of the market place, was originally open on the ground floor to provide shelter for traders' stalls. The museum, by St Peter's Church, must be visited if only to see the unique 'Bysant', a strange relic of an annual ceremony to confirm the town's right to have water from Enmore, at the foot of the hill.

Modern Shaftesbury is a busy market town; its position on the A30 has brought light industry and distribution services for a wide area. Amenities include a swimming pool, an arts centre and even an airstrip, albeit grass, at nearby Compton Abbas.

AA recommends:
Hotels: Grosvenor, The Commons, 3-star, *tel.* (0747) 2282
Royal Chase, Royal Chase Roundabout, 3-star, *tel.* (0747) 3355
Garages: Causeway, Sherborne Causeway (A30), *tel.* (0747) 2479
Five Square Motors, Salisbury Rd, *tel.* (0747) 2295

Gold Hill, Shaftesbury, one of the few cobbled streets left in southern England

Shepton Mallet, Somerset

Map Ref: 87ST6143

The town is graced by some of the finest wool merchants' and clothiers' houses in the region, their stables and service buildings now converted to desirable residences.

In the heart of the town is the Square, with the Market Cross, which was rebuilt in 1841, and next to it an original 15th-century roofed market stall, a 'scamel' or 'shambles'. Between the Square and the church, lying over to the east, its tower dominating the town, the stylish Shepton Mallet Centre offers facilities for banquets, exhibitions, cinema and theatre; it was financed by Showerings, the firm that created Babycham, which has its headquarters in the town. The drink industry is not new to Shepton – the magnificent shell of the Anglo-Bavarian Brewery building, seen from Commercial Road, dates from about 1890.

The prosperity of the woollen industry, before its decline in the 19th century, is reflected in many of the town houses; the 17th-century terrace in Great Ostry is particularly noteworthy.

The blind towering walls of Shepton prison were imaginatively transformed into those of a German castle for the filming of *The Dirty Dozen*. Coincidentally, the prison played its own valuable part in the war effort as the temporary safe storage depot for treasures from the Public Record Office, including Domesday Book.

Two miles south of the town, between the A37 and A371, is the showground of the annual Royal Bath and West Show.

AA recommends:
Hotel: Shrubbery, Commercial Rd, 2-star, *tel.* (0749) 2555
Restaurants: Bowlish House, Coombe Ln, Bowlish, 2-fork, *tel.* (0749) 2022 (on the Wells Rd, A371)
Thatched Cottage, Frome Rd, 2-fork, *tel.* (0749) 2058
Blostin's, 29 Waterloo Rd, 1-fork, *tel.* (0749) 3648
Guesthouse: King's Arms, Leg Sq (Inn), *tel.* (0749) 3781
Garages: Arthur's Bridge, Arthur's Bridge, Ditcheat, *tel.* (074986) 297
Charlton, (G A William & Son), *tel.* (0749) 2517

Sherborne, Dorset

Map Ref: 91ST6316

A gorgeous and prosperous town of rich yellow stone buildings, enhanced by the wonderful Abbey.

The church or minster here became a cathedral in about AD 705, with St Aldhelm as the first bishop, and remained the seat of a bishop until 1075. A Benedictine monastery was established in 998. The Abbey church includes Saxon, Norman and Early English work, but it is predominantly of the 15th century. The fan vaulting of the nave and choir is breathtaking.

The monastic buildings on the north side of the Abbey have been converted into the chapel and other buildings of Sherborne School.

Cheap Street is the main shopping street, stretching from the

The most famous prehistoric monument in Britain, Stonehenge

Green down to the Conduit. This was originally built as a *lavatorium* or washing place in the Abbey's cloisters. After the Dissolution it was moved to this site to act as a market house, although over the years it has had many uses. Down the footpath behind the Conduit is Sherborne Museum, with good local exhibits including a section on the 18th-century silk industry here.

To the east of the town, Sherborne's castles are worth visiting; the old one dates from the early 12th century. In 1592 it passed to Sir Walter Raleigh. He attempted to convert it into a house but gave up and built Sherborne Lodge, or the 'new' castle, instead, in the grounds.

AA recommends:
Hotels: Post House, Horsecastles Ln, 3-star, *tel.* (0935) 813191
Half Moon, Half Moon St, 2-star, *tel.* (0935) 812017
Restaurant: Grange Hotel, Oborne, 2-fork, *tel.* (0935) 813463 (1½m NE off A30)
Garage: Westbury, Westbury, *tel.* (0935) 814781

Somerton, Somerset

Map Ref: 90ST4828

A quiet unspoilt town on a ridge overlooking Sedgemoor, its claim to be the 'ancient capital of Wessex' is more folklore than fact, although the ridge was part of the estates of the Saxon and medieval royal house.

The 17th-century former town hall and castellated market cross are surrounded by elegant town houses and old inns, all built in the local blue Lias stone.

Off the beaten track and surrounded by a working farm, Lytes Cary, two miles south of the town, is one of the National Trust's most homely manor houses. This was the home of the Lyte family for five hundred years; Henry Lyte published his *Niewe Herball*, based on the garden here, in 1578.

AA recommends:
Hotel: Lynch Country House, Behind Berry, 3-star, *tel.* (0458) 72316
Guesthouse: Church Farm, School Ln, Compton Dundon, *tel.* (0458) 72927
Garage: Somerton Service Centre, West St, *tel.* (0458) 72439

The New Castle, Sherborne, where Sir Walter Raleigh lived before his execution

Steep Holm, Avon

Map Ref: 90ST2260

Flat Holm, Steep Holm and Brent Knoll were created, so the saying goes, by the Devil. In order to spoil the Mendip ridge he began by digging out Cheddar Gorge; he flung his first spadeful into the Bristol Channel, forming Steep Holm and Flat Holm, but his second did not reach the coast, hence the Knoll.

The islands are lonely outcrops of limestone, lying six miles or so out, west of Brean Down, swept by fierce currents and tides. The isolation of these islands has meant that relics have survived far longer than on the mainland. Such isolated rocks appealed to the ascetic; in the 6th century St Gildas lived on Flat Holm and visited a community on Steep Holm; by the 13th century, if not earlier, there was an Augustinian priory on Steep Holm.

From the 14th century until about 1750 the island seems to have been left uninhabited; then a couple of limekilns were built, and by about 1800 there was an inn, a farmhouse and Cliff Cottage.

In the 1860s Steep Holm was fortified as one of a chain of forts across the Bristol Channel, but at the end of the century the island was again vacated. During World War II, after Dunkirk, a decision was taken to refortify Steep Holm.

Steep Holm is owned by the Kenneth Allsop Memorial Trust and protected as a nature reserve; consequently it has become a haven for birds. One hundred and twenty-eight species have been spotted. The flora includes a rare Mediterranean peony, *Paeonia mascula*, difficult to find.

Boats run out to the island from Weston-super-Mare on Saturdays and Bank Holidays throughout the summer, weather and tides permitting.

Stonehenge, Wiltshire

Map Ref: 89SU1242

This mystical and awe-inspiring stone circle, set in the middle of Salisbury Plain, is one of the most famous prehistoric monuments in Europe and one that has created endless speculation for archaeologists concerned with its interpretation.

The first preconception to be shattered is that Stonehenge had any connection with the Druids; they had nothing to do with this or any other monument of the Bronze Age or indeed of any earlier period in the British Isles.

In the five parishes surrounding Stonehenge there are well over three hundred barrows or burial mounds. There can be little doubt that Stonehenge was the centre of some sort of religious ceremony but precisely what is not known.

The main axis of the stones is aligned with the sun on Midsummer's Day, and it is thought that through various combinations of alignments a calendar of annual festivals was devised.

Stonehenge was started about 5,000 years ago, but it was altered and remodelled several times in the following 1,500 years. The encircling ditch and bank belong to about 2,800BC. In about 2,100BC the great Blue Stones (over 80 of them weighing more than 2 tons each) were brought from the Preseli Hills in south-west Wales and erected in the middle with sarsens around the edge of the bank.

They were dismantled while incomplete and great sarsen stones, sandstone blocks weighing over 50 tons each, were dragged from the Marlborough Downs, 20 miles north; they were erected, as seen today, in an outer ring with lintels, and an inner horseshoe of five pairs of uprights with lintels. The uprights and lintels were carefully matched and joined by mortises and tenons cut in the stones. Some time later the Blue Stones were re-erected and the avenue was lengthened.

Numerous theories have been put forward, but we will probably never understand the complexity and organisation of the society that devised the monument and arranged the labour necessary for both transport and construction.

Stourhead, Wiltshire

Map Ref: 88ST7733

Glorious gardens are the prime feature of the National Trust headquarters for the Wessex region.

In 1741 Henry Hoare II returned from his Grand Tour, influenced by the gardens and landscapes he had seen in Italy, and, more particularly, by the Classical landscapes of the artists Claude Lorraine (1600-82) and Nicholas Poussin (1594-1665).

He determined to subdue his patch of Wiltshire and to create a replica of such a landscape round his house. First he dammed the River Stour, then diverted the medieval fishponds to make a large triangular lake; then he began his plantings of deciduous trees and conifers, 'ranged in large masses as the shades in a painting'. Brilliant colour was provided by daffodils, bluebells, rhododendrons and azaleas. The next step was to build focal points, in Classical style, which could be viewed and admired from specific vantage places – the Temple of Flora and the Grotto; also the Gothic Cottage, the Pantheon, the Temple of Apollo and the Iron Bridge.

The house was the product of Henry Hoare I, the banker son of a Lord Mayor of London; it was built in the 1720s but many of its contents were sold in 1883, and it suffered a fire in 1902. The

Stourhead: ornamental temples and trees reflected in the water of the lake

furniture by Thomas Chippendale, especially the library table, is very fine, and there are a number of paintings, some collected by Henry Hoare II in Italy and clearly an inspiration for the gardens.

Street, Somerset

Map Ref: 86ST4836

The expansion of Street in the 19th century from a little village to an industrial town was thanks to the Clark brothers, Cyrus and James, who established a sheepskin business here in the 1820s; they made sheepskin slippers, 'Brown Peters', from skins too small for rugs, and within twenty years slippers and shoes had overtaken the rug side of the business. As a Quaker family, the Clarks influenced the development of the town in a paternalistic and sober way: the Friends' Meeting House (1850) stands close to the factory gates; a workers' club and library were started up; and a temperance hotel, the Bear Inn, opened in 1894. Originally, manufacturing was largely on an outwork basis, but as demand increased, machinery requiring a regular labour force was centralised in the factory.

The success story has continued to the present day. Clarks, still a private company, has shoe factories throughout the world. A shoe museum, illustrating both the history of the firm and the development of the shoe from Roman times, has been opened in the factory; the entrance is beneath the clock-tower.

In the High Street bargain shoe shops offering factory seconds attract coach tours from far and wide to the area which has been dubbed 'Shoeshire'.

AA recommends:
Hotels: Bear, 53 High St, 3-star, *tel.* (0458) 42021
Wessex, High St, 3-star, *tel.* (0458) 43383
Garages: Abbey, 189 High St, *tel.* (0458) 47147
Foundry, Leigh Rd, *tel.* (0458) 42013
Leigh Road (Arnie Levic), *tel.* (0458) 42707
North Park, High St, *tel.* (0458) 45332

Sturminster Newton, Dorset

Map Ref: 92ST7814

An important market town on the River Stour, serving Blackmoor Vale, Sturminster Newton has the largest calf market in England. Market Day is Monday.

In the 18th century the cloth industry flourished here particularly with the making of a coarse white woollen cloth called 'swanskin'. It was used for military uniforms and by Dorset fishermen, being especially warm and wind-proof.

William Barnes, the popular Dorset poet, was born at Bagber, a mile or so west, in 1801; he attended school in Sturminster until he was 13, then worked as a solicitor's clerk, before moving to Dorchester. He is particularly remembered for his dialect poems, such as *Linden Lea*:

Ithin the woodlands, flow'ry-gleaded,
By the woak tree's mossy moot,
The sheenen grass-bleades, timber-sheaded,
Now do quiver under voot;
An' birds do whissle over head,
An' water's bubblen in its bed,
An' there vor me the apple tree
Do lean down low in Linden Lea.

The town is attractive, with a mixture of building materials. The Swan Inn has especially elaborate 18th-century brickwork. A 16th-century stone bridge leads across the river to Newton. Beside the weir is the mill, open to the public, who may watch the complete milling process.

AA recommends:
Restaurant: Plumber Manor, 2-fork, 1-rosette, *tel.* (0258) 72507, (2m SW on Hazelbury Bryan Rd)
Self Catering: The Cottage, *tel.* (02586) 348
Guesthouse: Holbrook, Lydlinch (farmhouse), *tel.* (02586) 348
Garage: Sturminster Motor Co, Station Rd, *tel.* (0258) 72155

Swanage, Dorset

Map Ref: 93SZ0378

A classic, 19th-century seaside resort, Swanage developed later than the other popular holiday towns on the Dorset coast largely because the railway did not reach here till 1885.

Before tourism took off, the port was busy with the export of Purbeck stone and marble. John Mowlem (1788-1868), a local man who worked as a stone contractor in London, and his nephew, George Burt, arranged an unusual trade back to their home town: any unwanted architectural bits and pieces from London were transported back here as ballast in their sailing ships. So Swanage acquired a Town Hall façade from Mercers' Hall, Cheapside, re-erected here in 1883, a clock(less) tower from London Bridge, put up near the lifeboat station in 1868, and several inscribed posts and bollards from various parts of London.

Behind the Town Hall is a tiny lock-up, built in 1803. Shore Road is backed by municipal gardens, complete with bandstand and ornamental flower beds; there are seaside cafés and rock shops along the front and an easy-going bucket-and-spade friendliness everywhere. The pier, built in 1896, is now the boarding point for various local ferry services.

Swanage Station was fortunately saved from destruction when the branch line from Wareham closed in 1972: enthusiasts started working on the restoration of the track in order to run steam trains from the station again.

To the west is pretty, stone-built Worth Matravers, with access to the sea at Winspit and fine, high walks along the Dorset Coast Path.

AA recommends:
Hotels: Grand, Burlington Rd, 3-star, *tel.* (0929) 423353
Pines, Burlington Rd, 3-star, *tel.* (0929) 425211
Suncliffe, Burlington Rd, 1-star, *tel.* (0929) 423299
Self Catering: Alexander Court, Grosvenor Rd, *tel.* (0929) 424606
Carlton Lodge, 22 Ulwell Rd, *tel.* (0929) 423295
Gulls Way Flat 4, Osborne House, Seymer Rd, *tel.* (0929) 426360
Marston Flats, 16 Burlington Rd, *tel.* (0929) 422221
Guesthouses: Eversden Private Hotel, Victoria Rd, *tel.* (0929) 423276
Havenhurst Hotel, 3 Cranbourne Rd, *tel.* (0929) 424224
St Michael Hotel, 31 Kings Rd, *tel.* (0929) 422064
Seychelles Private Hotel, 7 Burlington Rd, *tel.* (0929) 422794
Campsite: Ulwell Cottage Caravan Park, Ulwell Cottage, Ulwell, 3-pennants, *tel.* (0929) 422823, (1½m N on Studland Rd)
Garage: St Michaels, Valley Rd, *tel.* (0929) 480221

Selection only: see page 4

Several historic locomotives are on view in the GWR Museum in Swindon

Swindon, Wiltshire

Map Ref: 89SU1584

As an industrial and engineering city Swindon frequently gets a bad press, but increasingly as our industrial heritage becomes appreciated Swindon's story will be revealed and enjoyed.

In the early 19th century the population of Swindon was about a thousand. In *Beauties of Wilts* Britton described it thus:

The pleasantness of its situation, combined with other circumstances, have induced many persons of independent fortune to fix their residence at Swindon

That was the 'Old Town', still a

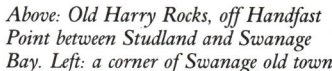

Above: Old Harry Rocks, off Handfast Point between Studland and Swanage Bay. Left: a corner of Swanage old town

pleasant enough spot, with the Bell Hotel, the old market, and parkland of gravel walks and mature trees.

Then in 1839, the Marquess of Ailesbury refused to allow the Great Western Railway to cross his estate, Savernake, on the direct route from London to Bristol and Swindon was chosen for a junction on the alternative route. New Swindon was created down in the valley.

By 1900 the population of New Swindon had mushroomed to 40,000; 4,000 were employed directly by GWR in the locomotive and carriage workshops and a railway village was built to house the workers and their families. Now the village is a Conservation Area and the best part of the town.

The 'model lodging house', at the corner of Faringdon Road, for workers who arrived daily from all over the country, has become the Great Western Railway Museum.

Although the railway workshops have now gone, the town remains well connected by road and rail routes and has attracted a host of light industries.

AA recommends:
Hotels: Blunsdon House, Blunsdon, 4-star, *tel.* (0793) 721701, (3m N off A419)
Crest, Oxford Rd, Stratton St Margaret, 3-star, *tel.* (0793) 822921, (3m NE A420)
Post House, Marlborough Rd, 3-star, *tel.* (0793) 24601
South Marston Hotel & Country Club, South Marston, 3-star, *tel.* (0793) 827777
Garages: Bath Road, 40 Bath Rd, *tel.* (0793) 24217
Gorse Hill Motors, Chapel St, *tel.* (0793) 612600
Greens, Marlborough Rd, Old Town, *tel.* (0793) 27251
Swindon Automobiles, Dorcan Way, *tel.* (0793) 612091

Selection only: see page 4

St Mary's Church, Tarrant Rushton, has 3 delightful decorated squints, each filled with stone tracery

The Tarrants, Dorset

Map Ref: 92ST9204

The Tarrants are small, pretty villages on the River Tarrant, a tributary of the Stour. Following the valley from north to south they are Tarrant Gunville, Tarrant Hinton, Tarrant Launceston, Tarrant Monkton, Tarrant Rawston, Tarrant Rushton, Tarrant Keynston and Tarrant Crawford.

Tarrant Gunville once had a huge mansion, Eastbury Park, designed by Vanbrugh and finished in 1738. The cost of upkeep, however, soon proved too great and most of it was demolished. All that remains is part of the stable block and some gateways.

Tarrant Rushton is a delightfully quiet village of cob and brick cottages. In the church there are three fine leper squints; the carved lintel over the south door dates from the 12th century; and also of interest are the earthenware jars, set on their sides in the east face of the chancel arch. They were installed, it is thought, in the 15th century to amplify the voice of the priest.

The little church at Tarrant Crawford is decorated with a series of 14th-century wall paintings. One describes the life of St Margaret of Antioch. Just behind the church, the old barn is all that remains of the great Cistercian nunnery of Tarrant Kaines. The barn, whose walls have probably survived since the Abbey's foundation in about 1200, has a magnificent hammer beam roof.

AA recommends:
Garage: Ashley Wood Service Station, Tarrant Keynston, *tel.* (0258) 52595

Taunton, Somerset

Map Ref: 90ST2224

Somerset's county town lies in the fertile vale of Taunton Deane, a rich bowl bounded on the north by the Quantock Hills and on the south by the Blackdown Hills.

The historic centre of the town, Taunton Castle, is hidden from view and can easily be missed. King Ine's fortress, destroyed in AD722, was on this site. The remains of the huge square keep of the later Norman castle can be seen in the gardens of the Castle Hotel. The castle buildings that now house the Somerset County Museum date from the 13th century. The Great Hall, inside the Castle, was the scene of part of Judge Jeffreys' 'Bloody Assize' after the Monmouth Rebellion of 1685 and the rout of the Battle of Sedgemoor, the last battle to be fought on English soil.

Under protection of the castle, a thriving market town grew up with a mint, a priory and a cloth industry whose prosperity is reflected in the soaring tower of St Mary's Church. Hammett Street was opened in 1788 to show this magnificent tower off to full advantage.

Taunton has been developed as an administrative and commercial centre, and for shops it is unrivalled in the region: modern shopping precincts include the Old Market Centre, off the High Street, and County Walk, East Street. More characterful shops can be found in Bath Place, through an entrance off the High Street, where once an open drain ran with 'all the abominations from courts in the High Street and the Crescent houses'. Now there is a pleasant passageway of boutiques, cafés, the Quaker Meeting House, and, at the far end, the Dragon Bookshop.

West of the bridge over the Tone, riverside walks lead quickly out past Goodland Gardens to French Weir Park and the meadows beyond; to the east the Brewhouse Theatre offers both good entertainment and first class food.

Taunton's associations with cider are longstanding – cider has been made in the county for at least 700 years. In 1911 a master cidermaker, Arthur Moore, started the Taunton Cider Company at Norton Fitzwarren. Sheppy's, on the A38 west of Taunton, won gold medals for cider at the Paris exhibition in 1892; the farm is open to visitors and includes a rural museum.

Three miles north east of Taunton, off the A361, is Hestercombe House with its

Top right: a Roman mosaic, one of several exhibits of local archaeology in Somerset County Museum in Taunton Castle. Somerset and the cider making business: oak vats (above) for the Taunton Cider Company and (right) a press at Sheppy's traditional farm cider making museum

delightful formal gardens; the lawns and terraces were laid out between 1904 and 1909 by Gertrude Jekyll and Sir Edwin Lutyens. The design is reminiscent of Elizabethan gardens, with raised walkways, sunken lawns and water gardens.

AA recommends:
Hotels: Castle, Castle Gn, 4-star, red-star, 1-rosette, *tel.* (0823) 72671
County, East St, 3-star, *tel.* (0823) 87651
Falcon, Henlade, 2-star *tel.* (0823) 442502, (3m E A358)
St Quintin, Bridgwater Rd, Bathpool, 2-star, *tel.* (0823) 59171
Restaurant: Rajpoot Tandoori, Corporation St, 2-fork, *tel.* (0823) 79300
Guesthouses: Meryan House Hotel, Bishop's Hull Rd, *tel.* (0823) 87445
Ruishton Lodge, Ruishton, *tel.* (0823) 442293
Rumwell Hall, Rumwell, *tel.* (0823) 75268
White Lodge Hotel, 81 Bridgwater Rd, *tel.* (0823) 73287
Campsite: St Quinton Hotel Caravan & Camping Park, Bridgwater Rd, Bathpool, 3-pennants, *tel.* (0823) 59171
Garages: Auto Safety Centre, Castle St, *tel.* (0823) 85691
Co-operative Retail Service, Magdalene St, *tel.* (0823) 75321
South West Motors, Cornishway North, *tel.* (0823) 77805
Taunton Auto-Elec & Diesel Co, Priorswood Rd, *tel.* (0823) 89111

Selection only: see page 4

Thornbury, Avon
Map Ref: 84ST6490

The 'thorny burh', the original settlement, was probably on the low ground beside the church, where there was a market recorded in Domesday Book. In the mid-13th century Richard de Clare, Earl of Gloucester, whose family had the castle, developed a new town up the hill to the south. He advertised it by promising that any who took up houses would have the same liberties and free customs as he had already granted to Tewkesbury.

The grand castle, now a restaurant, can be glimpsed through the north wall of the churchyard; the building dates from the early 16th century and was the work of Edward Stafford, Duke of Buckingham. Unfortunately he was executed in 1521 before he could finish it. When Henry VIII and Anne Boleyn visited in 1535, Bristol sent them 10 fat oxen, 40 sheep and a gilt cup. In 1720, it was partly restored, and in 1854 it was completed by Anthony Salvin.

In the Middle Ages there was a flourishing cloth industry; but by the 16th century this had died out and Leland reported that:

there hathe bene good clothing in Thornebyrry, but now Idelnes much reynithe there.

The town survived as a market centre; three streets converge on the large market place, the area bounded by High Street, Silver Street and St Mary Street. There are many good Georgian and earlier houses, and a variety of Victorian revival styles.

AA recommends:
Hotel: Thornbury Castle, 3-star, country house, 1-red-star, 1-rosette, *tel.* (0454) 418511

The Tolpuddle Martyrs

Late in 1833 the men of Tolpuddle established a Friendly Society of Agricultural Labourers, 'to preserve ourselves, our wives, and our children from utter degradation and starvation'. Inspired by George Loveless, a farm labourer and local Methodist preacher, the society planned to force farmers, by withholding labour, to increase wages from seven or eight shillings a week to ten shillings.

The authorities, fearful of a repetition of the wave of rural unrest and riots that had swept across southern England in 1830, quickly ordered the arrest of the six ringleaders, James Brine, James Hammett, who was mistaken for his brother John, George Loveless and his brother James, George's brother-in-law Thomas Stanfield and his son John. The Union in itself was not illegal, so the men were charged with administering secret oaths – which were. They were brought to trial in Dorchester on 17 March 1834, and were sentenced to seven years' transportation in Australia. As he left the court, George Loveless tossed a paper to the crowd on which he had written:
God is our guide! No swords we draw.
We kindle not war's battle fires:
By reason, union, justice, law,
We claim the birthright of our sires:
We raise the watchword Liberty:
We will, we will, we will be free!
Protests and petitions began to bombard Parliament and there was a massive trades union rally in London. The London Dorchester Committee was set up to help the families of the six, who had been refused parish relief by the magistrates and evicted from their cottages.

Two years after the trial, with continued efforts by the protestors, pressure to indict the king's brother for administering secret oaths as Grand Master of the Orange Order forced the king to grant a free pardon to the Tolpuddle men. It took a further two years for the news of their freedom to reach them, and George Loveless first read of his in an old newspaper given to him by his old master.

On their return, great celebrations were held in London, and money was raised to lease two farms for them in Essex. After six years' farming, five of them decided to go to Canada with their families to make a fresh start; James Hammett returned to Tolpuddle and was to die in Dorchester Workhouse.

On the green in the village of Tolpuddle, there is an old sycamore tree under which the Martyrs used to meet. There is a thatched shelter, erected by Sir Ernest Debenham as part of the centenary celebrations in 1934. On the west side of the village are the TUC Memorial cottages, built in 1934, with a small museum devoted to the Martyrs and trades unions.

Four of the Tolpuddle Martyrs, portrayed in Cleave's Penny Gazette *in 1838, the year they returned home from Australia*

Trowbridge, Wiltshire

Map Ref: 88ST8557

Trowbridge is neatly sited between the escarpment of the downlands of Salisbury Plain to the south, and the limestone landscape stretching to the north from Bradford-on-Avon. The town is surrounded by rich pastureland, although it lies largely on a narrow stony ridge of 'cornbrash' running east–west.

The name Trowbridge, the first syllable rhyming with 'throw', not 'cow', is derived from the Anglo-Saxon words for 'tree' and 'bridge'.

By the 12th century, there was a castle here of some importance, held by supporters of Queen Matilda. There are no standing remains of this castle, but the curving line of Fore Street from the Town Hall to the Town Bridge evidently follows the line of the castle's outer defences. The name Wicker Hill for the lowest part of Fore Street came from a reinforcement of the sides of the moat or ditch by wickerwork or hurdles.

By the time Leland looked at the town on his travels in 1540, the castle was 'clene down', and the place was 'flourishing by drapery'. Trowbridge's woollen cloth earned a high reputation for its quality and its design.

Five mills continued to operate until the 1950s, when only one remained in operation. That finally closed in 1982. The industry has bequeathed a legacy of historic buildings of great interest: several imposing clothiers' houses of the 17th and 18th centuries survive, as do some of the mills dating from the early 19th century.

Another building associated with the industry worth finding is the 'Handle House', which straddles the river and has walls of open brickwork to allow free circulation of air inside. It was intended for the storage of teazles, which were used for raising the nap of woollen cloth.

The old Parish Church of St James is a monument to that earlier prosperity; the slender, well-proportioned tower, 150ft high, is the tallest in Wiltshire after Salisbury Cathedral, on which it must have been modelled. The church dates from the 14th and 15th centuries, but was drastically restored in the 1840s. The tower has a peal of 12 bells. The tuneful chimes played on them at the hours and quarters were specially composed by the late Sir Walter Alcock, organist of Salisbury Cathedral, for a new clock given by the late Thomas Charles Usher, of the local brewery.

Beside the Town Bridge, the Blind House or lock-up, with two cells, was built in 1757; from the knob at the apex of its roof comes the traditional town nickname 'Trowbridge Knobs'.

Trowbridge is the administrative seat for both West Wiltshire District Council and Wiltshire County Council, but it is not the historic 'county town'. That honour belongs to Salisbury. Trowbridge was chosen as the county's headquarters because in the days of universal rail travel it was within easy reach of both Swindon and Salisbury and more or less equidistant between the two. The 'new' County Hall, opened in 1939, was designed by Philip Hepworth, brother of the sculptress, Barbara.

Trowbridge: the Handle House which straddles the river is of red brick with ventilation gaps for drying teazles

AA recommends:
Hotel: Hilbury Court, Hilperton Rd, 1-star, *tel.* (02214) 2949
Garages: Lesters, Duke St, *tel.* (02214) 2077
Marks (Riverway MOT Centre), Riverway, *tel.* (02214) 68445

Wareham, Dorset

Map Ref: 92SY9287

This charming town remains confined within the earth embankments of the 10th-century 'town walls', as if on a platform above the flood plains of the rivers Piddle and Frome which form its north and south boundaries. At the main crossing point of the Frome, where until the 14th century a sizeable seaport developed, the town was of great strategic importance and the scene of frequent skirmishes between the Anglo-Saxons and the Danes.

The Saxon nave of the Church of Lady St Mary was demolished in 1841; some stone fragments in the north-east corner of the plain Victorian building that replaced it included a Purbeck marble coffin thought to have been used for the burial of the murdered King Edward in AD987. The Edward Chapel is a strange place to find a Russian icon; apparently it was saved by a Wareham man from a church in Moscow which had been set on fire by the Bolsheviks in 1917.

At the north end of the town, St Martin's Church is a far more rewarding experience; it is the only Saxon church in Dorset in anything like its original state. The full size effigy of T E Lawrence, 'Lawrence of Arabia', in Arab dress is here.

Wareham's side streets are lined with 18th- and 19th-century cottages, mainly in brick, many having been rebuilt after a disastrous fire in 1762, the date on the United Reformed Church in Church Street. The old quay beside the Frome is a pleasant haven of warehouses and pubs, and somewhere to sit outside in the summer and watch the river, busy with pleasure boats.

The plain brick house on the corner of North Street and Cow Lane was where Mrs Dinah Maria Craik wrote *John Halifax Gentleman* in 1857. Notice the sign in Cow Lane: *Traction Engines and Heavy Motors prohibited*.

The Church of Lady St Mary, Wareham, and close by it the River Frome

AA recommends:
Hotels: Priory Church Gn, 3-star, *tel.* (09295) 2772
Springfield Country, Grange Rd, Stoborough, 3-star, *tel.* (09295) 2177, (1½m S off A351)
Kemps Country House, East Stoke, 2-star, *tel.* (0929) 462563
Worgret Manor, 2-star, *tel.* (09295) 2957
Restaurant: Kemps Country House, see Hotels, above
Priory, see Hotels, above
Guesthouses: Luckford Wood, East Stoke (farmhouse), *tel.* (0929) 463098
Redcliffe (farmhouse), *tel.* (09295) 2225
Campsites: Hunter's Moon Caravan & Camping Site, Cold Harbour, 3-pennants, *tel.* (09295) 6605
Lookout Park, Corfe Rd, Stoborough, 3-pennants, *tel.* (09295) 2546
Manor Farm Caravan Park, Manor Farm Cottage, East Stoke, 3-pennants, *tel.* (0929) 462870
Garages: Purbeck Motor Co, Corfe Rd, Stoborough, *tel.* (09295) 2151

Selection only: see page 4

Lawrence of Arabia

T E Lawrence, 'Lawrence of Arabia', spent the last 12 years of his enigmatic life based in Dorset.

Thomas Edward was born in a boarding house at Tremadoc, North Wales, on 16 August 1888, the illegitimate son of Thomas Robert Tighe Chapman and the Chapman family nursemaid, Sarah Maden, or Junner. In order to mask their unmarried status, his parents changed their names to 'Lawrence', as Mrs Chapman steadfastly refused to divorce her husband.

The family (Sarah produced five boys) settled in Oxford from 1896, and the boys attended Oxford High School. In 1907 T E Lawrence was awarded an exhibition to read history at Jesus College; he became fascinated by medieval architecture and spent his vacations on bicycle tours visiting sites throughout England and France. In the summer of 1909, encouraged by friends at the Ashmolean Museum, he set off on a hazardous study tour of castles in Syria. He was excused his late return to college after a dramatic saga of adventures, and his thesis on 'Crusading Castles of Syria' won him a first-class degree. From 1910 to 1914 he worked as an assistant archaeologist on excavations of the ancient city of Carchemish in Syria.

Lawrence's experience of the Middle East and his affection for the Arabs fitted him perfectly for his role, soon after the outbreak of war, as Intelligence Officer based in Cairo.

His later exploits, fighting with the Arabs and disguised as one of them in white robes, have been dramatically described in book and film. Lawrence's own book, *Seven Pillars of Wisdom*, recounts his Arabian extravaganza with a mixture of fact, legend and imagination.

In 1922 Lawrence joined the RAF as J H Ross and later when he entered the Royal Tank Corps he changed his name to Shaw, attempting on each occasion to escape his fame. The remote house he eventually bought in Dorset, Clouds Hill, a mile north of Bovington Camp, was to provide him with the privacy he sought.

The house was surrounded by rhododendrons and trees making an almost impenetrable screen; inside Lawrence slept downstairs, on a leather daybed, where two sleeping bags were kept marked 'Meum' and 'Tuum' for himself and the friend of the night. Upstairs he kept a horn gramophone and his record collection. There were no cooking facilities and no refrigerator.

Lawrence died in 1935 following a motorbike accident on the road between Bovington Camp and Clouds Hill. Mystery still shrouds the details of the crash and at the time all news about it was handled by the War Office. His funeral at Moreton Church was attended by more than one hundred mourners, including Winston Churchill, Lady Astor, Mrs Hardy and Siegfried Sassoon. The inscription on his tombstone says simply 'Fellow of All Souls Oxford'.

In the tiny Saxon Church of St Martin at Wareham there is a large reclining effigy of Lawrence dressed in his Arab robes. It was designed to be placed in Salisbury Cathedral, but the Dean refused to accept it: Lawrence was not forgiven the murkier side of his life.

T E Lawrence as he is familiar to all, in Arab robes. Below: his effigy

Warminster, Wiltshire

Map Ref: 88ST8744

In the 1820s, William Cobbett was impressed by the town when he rode in:

A very nice town: everything belonging to it is solid and good. There are no villainous gingerbread houses running up, and no nasty, shabby-genteel people; no women trapsing about with showy gowns and dirty necks.

Warminster lies to the south-west of Salisbury Plain, amid chalk downlands rich in prehistoric barrows and earthworks. Battlesbury Camp, 1½ miles from the town, is one of the more impressive Iron Age forts in Britain.

The town is of Saxon origin; it developed as an important market centre for corn, and later, in the Middle Ages, for wool and cloth. At a major road junction, it also became a regular stopping place for coaches as the Anchor, Bath Arms and Old Bell inns recall.

In the High Street the little Chapel of St Lawrence was founded by the Maudit family, Lords of the Manor of Warminster, in the early 13th century as a chapel of ease. It is unusual in being under the control of 'Twelve, Ten or Eight of the principal honest and discreet men of the Parish of Warminster' known as the feoffees. The Minster Church of St Denys has traces of Norman work, but is mainly 14th-century, with a 15th-century tower; its organ was originally built for Salisbury Cathedral.

Warminster is the modern headquarters of various military activities; the workshops of the Royal Electrical and Mechanical Engineers are here, the School of Infantry, and Battlebury Barracks; and there is a comprehensive museum of weapons.

AA recommends:
Hotels: Bishopstrow House, Boreham Rd, 4-star, country house, 4-red-star, *tel.* (0985) 212312
Old Bell, Market Pl, 2-star, *tel.* (0985) 216611

Wedmore, Somerset

Map Ref: 86ST4347

Wedmore lies on the sheltered side of a natural ridge that divides the Levels west of Cheddar, eventually petering out at Mark; on either side stretch the moors, rich verdant pasture fringed by pollarded willows and rhynes.

It was here that the 'Peace of Wedmore' was agreed, in AD878, between King Alfred and the newly baptised Danish leader, Guthrum; Wedmore was a royal estate near the minster at Cheddar and itself perhaps also the site for a palace and a minster.

Much of the fabric of the parish church dates from the 12th century. The most magnificent feature is the south doorway, very likely designed and carved by masons from Wells Cathedral. There are two murals of St Christopher, one painted over the other, and beautifully sculpted oak bench ends. Some of these are modern but equally fine, and interesting in that they depict symbolically the rural crafts and industries associated with the area: peat, willows, strawberries, apples and cheese.

The small town, or large village, is spacious and elegant with a number of double-fronted Georgian and Victorian houses enclosing a square of gardens and orchards.

Local farmhouse Cheddar and Caerphilly cheeses, and Somerset 'scrumpy' cider are advertised at the roadside.

AA recommends:
Self Catering: The Ciderbarn (cottage), *tel.* (0934) 712007

Wells Cathedral, within and without. The majestic west front (right) is unique and has hundreds of medieval statues

Wells, Somerset

Map Ref: 87ST5445

England's smallest city gained its name from the fresh springs of water that bubble up in the bottom of a pool in the bishop's garden.

The west front of the Cathedral has been described as the finest sculpture gallery in Europe. There are 356 statues set in ornate niches, dating from the early 13th century. Inside the Cathedral, the main feature of the nave is the astonishing inverted arch inserted about 1350 beneath the central tower to prevent it from collapsing.

The tops of many of the piers or pillars are decorated with carvings of foliage and scenes from life in the 13th century, such as a man with tooth-ache, or another trying to dig a thorn out of his foot. The medieval clock is in the north transept: it performs every quarter of an hour, with jousting knights on horseback, and a little seated figure known as Jack Blandiver. From the north transept a flight of stone steps leads to the octagonal Chapter House with its fine, stone, fan-like vaulted roof. From here, a bridge across the road links the Cathedral to the Vicars' Hall.

From the Cathedral Green, Penniless Porch, where beggars hoped for good pickings from the churchgoers, opens into the bustling everyday life of the Market Place. It is dominated on the north side by a row of bay-fronted stone buildings built by Bishop Beckington in the 15th century. Opposite, the timber-framed coaching inn, the Crown, has a plaque to commemorate a speech made by the Quaker William Penn in 1695. The Town Hall was built in 1779 with an open ground floor for a covered market and now houses the Tourist Information Office and city archives. An arched gateway, known as 'the Bishop's Eye', on the east side of the Market Place, gives access to the moated Bishop's Palace and gardens.

A feature of the narrow High Street is the water, fed from the springs, flowing through the gutters beside the pavements, and directed through the streets to promote cleanliness. St Cuthbert's Church, at the west end of the High Street, sometimes mistaken for the cathedral, is the largest parish church in Somerset with a magnificent tower, 122ft high. The 15th-century timber roof of the nave has been brightly restored to its original colours, with bosses of angels and mythical beasts.

Vicars' Close, Wells, a little medieval street where the terraced houses on each side, all with tall chimneys, were originally identical in plan

AA recommends:
Hotels: Swan, Sadler St, 3-star, *tel.* (0749) 78877
Crown, Market Pl, 2-star, *tel.* (0749) 73457
Ancient Gate House, Sadler St, 1-star, *tel.* (0749) 72029
Guesthouses: Bekynton House, 7 St Thomas St, *tel.* (0749) 72222
Coach House, Stobery Pk, *tel.* (0749) 76535
Home, Stoppers Ln, Upper Coxley (farmhouse), *tel.* (0749) 72434, (2m SW off A39)
Southway Farm, Polsham, *tel.* (0749) 73396
Campsite: Homestead Caravan & Camping Park, Wookey Hole, 3-pennants, *tel.* (0749) 73022
Garages: Easton Service Station, Easton, *tel.* (0749) 870053
Gunnings, Priory Rd, *tel.* (0749) 73089
Harris Motors, Glastonbury Rd, *tel.* (0749) 72626
Provincial, New St, *tel.* (0749) 72099

Selection only: see page 4

Westbury, Wiltshire

Map Ref: 88ST8751

Hill figures cut into the chalk escarpments are an idiosyncratic feature of this region, and the Westbury White Horse, on Bratton Down, is the oldest of the white horses in Wiltshire. It is best seen from the B3098 about 1½ miles from Westbury. It was cut in 1778 by a connoisseur of horseflesh who had been irritated for many years by an earlier figure on the same site. The earlier horse was smaller, a long narrow creature with short legs, more like a dachshund. It could possibly have been Saxon, but was more probably 17th- or 18th-century.

When William Cobbett explored the little town in the 1820s he was not impressed: 'A nasty odious rotten-borough, a really rotten place.' He did notice, however, that it was 'a place of great ancient grandeur'.

Away from the traffic of the main roads the Market Square has elegance and style. The Town Hall, on Tuscan pillars, was built by Sir Massey Lopes, Baronet, Recorder of the Borough, in 1815 and is the finest in the county. Also in the Square is the Lopes Arms which claims a history of more than 600 years as an inn. It was originally called the St George and Dragon.

The Parish Church of All Saints is surrounded by a peaceful close of Georgian houses, and Maristow Street has a number of very attractive 19th-century shop fronts.

At the bottom of Newtown Hill, the Victorian school is being used as a pottery, specialising in big practical pots, all thrown by hand – chimney pots, huge jardinières, large flower pots and bread crocks.

The Westbury White Horse, one of several in Wiltshire, cut out of the turf on the chalk downs and visible for miles

Weston-super-Mare, Avon

Map Ref: 86ST3161

Weston is in a splendid bay created by Worlebury Hill to the north and the Mendip promontory of Brean Down to the south. Views extend to the Quantock Hills and to the coast of Wales 12 miles across the Bristol Channel.

Until the 19th century the village of Weston consisted of no more than a handful of houses, the homes of fishermen and smugglers, and the population was only 163 in 1811. A hundred years later it had rocketed to over 20,000, the result of growing enthusiasm for ozone and bracing seaside walks. Weston was promoted by the British Quaker physician, Dr Edward Long Fox, and his son Francis, who developed the first baths and swimming pool at Knightstone Island.

The coming of the railway in 1841 was the real turning point in Weston's history as the seaside became available to everyone (the scene of a family arriving at the station for their summer holiday appropriately makes the introduction to the Woodspring Museum, in Burlington Street). The terraces and crescents of Italianate and Tudor-style villas spread as prosperity and popularity followed.

The Old Pier, linking Birnbeck Island with the mainland at the northern end of the resort, was officially opened in 1867. Before that, in about 1845, Fred Martell considered the island was a:

charming little oasis in the midst of the brown waters . . . It had only a rough little hut in the centre, where the gull yeller used to stay in the fishing season, to shout the gulls away from the nets

Birnbeck served as the landing stage for the thousands of visitors who arrived by pleasure steamer from Bristol and South Wales. The Grand Pier opened in 1904; its theatre was destroyed by fire in 1930 and was replaced by a large indoor amusement area which remains to the present day.

The summer season now is hectic: the Esplanade and Grand Pier are thronged with visitors and amenities are constantly changing and improving. A recent one is 'Tropicana Pleasure Beach', with a fun pool, wave machine and extraordinary giant tropical 'fruits', ensuring that even when it is raining visitors can enjoy (simulated) surf.

Woodspring, the District of which Weston is the administrative capital, gets its name from the Priory, more correctly Worspring, 4 miles north beyond Kewstoke. It was founded in 1230 by the grandson of one of the murderers of Thomas Becket. The church and the remains of the infirmary and gatehouse survive. The monastic barn is in use and not open to the public.

AA recommends:
Hotels: Grand Atlantic, Beach Rd, 3-star, *tel.* (0934) 26543
Royal Pier, Birnbeck Rd, 3-star, *tel.* (0934) 26644
Rozel, Madeira Cove, 2-star, *tel.* (0934) 415268
Beachlands, 17 Uphill Rd North, 1-star, *tel.* (0934) 21401
Self Catering: Moorfield Holiday Flats, 150 Milton Rd, *tel.* (0934) 23687
Guesthouse: Baymead Hotel, Longton Grove Rd, *tel.* (0934) 22951
Milton Lodge, 15 Milton Rd, *tel.* (0934) 23161
Newtown House, 79 Locking Rd, *tel.* (0934) 29331
Shire Elms, 71 Locking Rd, *tel.* (0934) 28605
Campsites: Country View Caravan Park, Sand Rd, Sand Bay, 3-pennants, *tel.* (0934) 27595
West End Farm Caravan & Camping Park, Locking, 3-pennants, *tel.* (0934) 822529, (3m E off A371)
Weston Gateway Caravan Site, West Wick, 3-pennants, *tel.* (0934) 510344
Ardnave Caravan Park, Crooks Ln, Kewstoke, 1-pennant, *tel.* (0934) 22319
Garages: Passey & Porter, Locking Rd, *tel.* (0934) 28291
Reakes, 6-8 Baker St, *tel.* (0934) 23995
Uphill Motor Co, Winterstoke Rd, *tel.* (0934) 417886

Selection only: see page 4

Westonzoyland, Somerset

Map Ref: 91ST3534

In 1685, at nearby Sedgemoor, was fought the last great battle on English soil, when Monmouth and his rebels were ruthlessly routed by James II. Five hundred of Monmouth's men spent a horrific night locked up in Westonzoyland Church, wounded and awaiting their ghastly fate in the morning.

A register in the church has an entry describing the battle. Another tells how frankincense was bought to purify the church after the prisoners had gone.

The magnificent 15th-century tower is a landmark for miles around. Inside the church is a beautiful 15th-century nave roof, richly carved with figures of angels.

Weymouth, Dorset

Map Ref: 91SY6779

At the mouth of the River Wey two settlements originally developed. Melcombe Regis on the north side and Weymouth on the south. After years of competition they were united in 1571 and Weymouth came to be the

Fishing boats, ferries and yachts at anchor in the old harbour, Weymouth

dominant name, although Melcombe Regis was larger and has since been the area of growth.

Weymouth was one of the first towns on the Dorset coast to attract visitors for sea bathing. As early as 1748 wooden bathing houses were being erected. The Duke of Gloucester spent the winter of 1780 in the town, and soon after had a great house built on the front, now the Gloucester Hotel. He persuaded his brother, George III, to come and from 1789 to 1805 the king and his retinue arrived almost every summer, bringing great publicity and prosperity. George's bathing machine, an octagonal box mounted on four great cart-wheels, is preserved in the Weymouth Museum.

The great feature of the town was and is the Bay. The gently sloping sandy beach is perfect for young children. The Esplanade is backed by Georgian-fronted hotels and houses; many have been converted to provide every sort of seaside facility.

An extraordinary sight in Weymouth is trains actually running in the road. From the Railway Station at the bottom of King Street, those trains that connect with the cross-Channel or Channel Island ferry services from the port continue down Commercial Road to the quayside.

Over the bridge, Trinity Road and Hope Square have retained the flavour of 'old' Weymouth. There are pleasing back streets of terraced cottages and the Devenish Brewery. On the headland the landscaped gardens lead to Nothe Fort, an impressive stronghold built to defend the harbour in the 1860s and well worth a visit.

At Lodmoor, on the A353 just east of town, a country park has been developed. Among the varied attractions two are particularly good for a rainy day – the Sea Life Centre and a Butterfly Farm.

AA recommends:
Hotels: Glenburn, Preston Rd, 2-star, *tel.* (0305) 832353
Prince Regent, The Esplanade, 2-star, *tel.* (0305) 771313
Rembrandt, Dorchester, 2-star, *tel.* (0305) 780384
Rex, The Esplanade, 2-star, *tel.* (0305) 773485
Restaurant: Sea Cow Bistro, Custom House Quay, *tel.* (0305) 783524
Self Catering: Hursey Farm Cottages, Broadwindsor, *tel.* (0308) 68323
The Lilacs, The Street, Charmouth, *tel.* (0297) 60747
Guesthouses: Millmead Country GH, Portesham, *tel.* (Abbotsbury) 432
Sou'west Lodge, Rodwell Rd, *tel.* (0305) 783749
Turks Head Inn, Chickerell, *tel.* (0305) 783093
Westwey House, 62 Abbotsbury Rd, *tel.* (0305) 784564
Garages: C M Elliot, 174 Dorchester Rd, *tel.* (0305) 785042
Hewitt, Dorchester Rd, *tel.* (0305) 782222
Marsh Road, Marsh Rd, *tel.* (0305) 776116
Olds, 172 Dorchester Rd, *tel.* (0305) 786311

Selection only: See page 4

Fred Darrington puts the finishing touches to a sand carving in Weymouth

The Duke of Monmouth and the Prince of Orange

In 1685 and 1688 the West of England caught the attention of the nation. In June 1685 a handsome, dashing and popular prince arrived with some 80 men at Lyme Regis and received a hero's welcome. In November 1688 a much less handsome prince landed at Brixham. Both came from Holland, the first in a campaign which ended in disaster and death, the second on an enterprise which gave him the English throne.

James, Duke of Monmouth, illegitimate son of Charles II, came to the west as the champion of Protestants who feared the rule of the Catholic James II. The Protestant political leaders, the Whigs, however, stayed at home when the small farmers and craftsmen of east Devon, west Dorset and Somerset flocked to his banner, and at Taunton hailed him king.

The rebel army, perhaps 7,000 strong at the most, won at Norton St Philip but was cut to pieces on Sedgemoor, near Westonzoyland. Monmouth was executed at the Tower, and many of his followers were sentenced by Judge Jeffreys either to hanging and quartering or to transportation to the West Indies. Those who survived lay low.

But Monmouth was finally justified. James II added cruelty to his reputation for bigotry, and the freedom which many had fought for in the Civil War seemed lost. The Whig politicians plotted again and invited William, Prince of Orange, Monmouth's one-time friend and protector, to come over and take control.

William landed at Brixham on 5 November 1688 with 15,000 men, but the people of Wessex did not rise in his support – their enthusiasm had been quenched by the hangings.

What stood between William and London was James II and his great army. That began to melt away as those who had fought against Monmouth joined the prince in the same cause as he advanced from Exeter through Axminster, Chard and Wincanton towards Salisbury. And at Salisbury, where the king decided on retreat, even John Churchill, later Duke of Marlborough, architect of the king's success against Monmouth, threw in his lot with the invader. James II was forced to leave his kingdom; Wessex, and soon the whole country, declared for William of Orange.

The landing of William, Prince of Orange, in 1688

The Palladian Bridge in the grounds of Wilton House. Right: woollen warps at the Royal Wilton Carpet factory

Wilton, Wiltshire

Map Ref: 89SU0931

The town on the River Wylye – the river and the town gave their names to the county of Wiltshire. Wilton can justify its claim to be an ancient capital of Wessex. It could even be said to have been the first capital of all England, for here in AD838 King Egbert was formally acknowledged as overlord of all the English kingdoms. Egbert founded a Benedictine convent in the town which brought great prosperity; in its heyday Wilton is said to have had a dozen churches.

Unfortunately the Abbess of Wilton was not predisposed to help the Bishop of Salisbury when he asked her to provide land for his new cathedral; so New Sarum was created, far too close for comfort, and certainly too close for both towns to prosper.

At the Dissolution Henry VIII presented the abbey buildings to Sir William Herbert, 1st Earl of Pembroke, who demolished most of the abbey and used the stones to build Wilton House. After a fire in 1647 the house was rebuilt to designs by Inigo Jones and John Webb. The Palladian Bridge in the gardens was built in 1737.

Meanwhile the little town began to recover. Carpet weaving was revived by the 8th Earl of Pembroke who smuggled over two skilled French Huguenot weavers to set up a carpet factory. This was such a success that in 1699 it was granted 'royal' status by William III. The Royal Wilton Carpet Factory in King Street is open to visitors.

At the centre of the town the Market Square has an 18th-century Town Hall and a Saxon church. There are pretty streets of 17th- and 18th-century cottages.

AA recommends:
Garage: F W Marks & Sons, 19-23 Shaftesbury Rd, *tel.* (0722) 743237

Wimborne Minster, Dorset

Map Ref: 93SU0100

The two squat square towers of the Minster identify the town from every direction. Despite considerable new building in recent years Wimborne retains its historic charm and is a delightful place.

The Minster church is very special and quite breathtaking. Much Norman masonry survives, particularly the central tower and the toothed arches of the nave. Much of the rest of the church is Early English or Decorated. The astronomical clock in the west tower was made about 1320. Up on the tower outside, the Quarter Jack strikes two bells every quarter, and on a freestanding stone pillar, dated 1676, is a sundial. In the south vestry, the Chained Library, founded in 1686, was the first free library in the country. Although the chains were made in Wimborne they are an exact copy of those designed by Michelangelo for the Lorentian Library in Florence.

Opposite the Minster is the Priest's House Museum of local history.

AA recommends:
Hotel: King's Head, The Square, 3-star, *tel.* (0202) 880101
Guesthouses: Riversdale, 33 Poole Rd, *tel.* (0202) 884528
Stour Lodge, 21 Julian's Rd, *tel.* (0202) 888003
Campsites: Merley Court Touring Park, Merley, 4-pennants, *tel.* (0202) 881488, (1m S A349)
Wilksworth Farm Caravan Park, Cranborne Rd, 3-pennants, *tel.* (0202) 883769
Charris Caravan Park, Candy's Ln, Corfe Mullen, 2-pennants, *tel.* (0202) 885970, (2m W off A31)
Garages: Auto Service, 41 Leigh Rd, *tel.* (0202) 887163
Wimborne Ford, (C J Manns), Poole Rd, *tel.* (0202) 886211

Wincanton, Somerset

Map Ref: 91ST7128

Wincanton is a charming unpretentious country town of steep streets and back alleys with views over the Blackmoor Vale.

Interest is focused on the town for the National Hunt race-meetings. Horses played a part in the earlier history of Wincanton when the town became an important resting place and change-over point for the horses that hauled the Royal Mail and travellers' coaches to and from London and the West Country. Evidence of the hospitality then offered to passengers can still be seen in the elegant coaching inns on either side of the High Street.

In 1688 William of Orange stopped in Wincanton on his way from Torbay to London. First blood in the Revolution was shed here when his troops were attacked by a party of James II's dragoons.

In the 18th century there were more than 80 weaving looms working in the town making the material used for mattress ticking. The elongated windows of the weavers' workshops can be seen at first or second floor level in some of the older cottages. The industry collapsed in the 19th century, faced with competition from the North of England and abroad.

AA recommends:
Hotels: Dolphin, High St, 2-star, *tel.* (0963) 32215
Holbrook House, Castle Cary Rd, Holbrook, 2-star, country-house, *tel.* (0963) 32377

Restaurant: Paupers Bistro, 6 South St, 1-fork, tel. (0963) 32752
Guesthouse: Hatherleigh, (farmhouse), tel. (0963) 32142
Campsite: Wincanton Racecourse (TRAX) Caravan Club Site, 2-pennants
Garages: Cuss Car Care, Bennetts Field Trad Est, tel. (0963) 32800
Southgate, Southgate, tel. (0963) 33950

Winchester, Hampshire

Map Ref: 85SU4829

The ancient 'capital' of Wessex and of England, Winchester lies steeped in history in the heart of the Hampshire countryside.

The present day High Street follows almost exactly the line of the main street of the important Roman town of *Venta Belgarum*. Overlooked at one end by St Giles Hill, the site of a medieval fair, and at the other by the Westgate, a fortified medieval gateway into the City, the historic High Street is lined with interesting buildings.

In Saxon times Wessex was the predominant kingdom in England and Winchester the national 'capital'. King Cenwealh built the first Saxon cathedral in 648.

Wessex was constantly attacked by hordes of pagan Vikings during the 9th century. Tradition has it that St Swithun, Bishop of Winchester from 852 to 862, built the great wall around the city that saved the inhabitants from the Danes. Later, King Alfred, who may have been a pupil of St Swithun and who certainly was both married and crowned in Winchester Cathedral, successfully fought off the Danes and established a network of fortified towns, or burhs, throughout Wessex. The monumental statue of Alfred in the Broadway was erected in 1901.

In 1079 the Old Minster was demolished to make way for the new Norman cathedral, begun by Walkelyn, the first Norman bishop. The substantial remains of the Norman work are now largely overlaid by successive rebuildings and alterations. The nave was remodelled during the 14th century, to make this the longest cathedral in Europe.

Unwisely the Cathedral had been built on a marsh and over the centuries the foundations began to rot, causing grave concern about the future stability of the building. So for a period of seven years, between 1906 and 1912, a local diver, William Walter, 'Diver Bill', worked 6 hours a day in the murky marsh water replacing the sodden peat with bags of concrete.

The tombs of St Swithun, William of Wykeham, Jane Austen, Izaak Walton and Diver Bill are among those of interest in the Cathedral. The library, dating from 1150, is one of the oldest in the country. Among innumerable treasures is the 12th-century Winchester Bible. The Cathedral has a remarkable collection of Norman and medieval sculpture.

Winchester Castle, begun in the 11th century, largely rebuilt by Henry III (1216-72), was besieged, then captured by Cromwell who eventually ordered it to be demolished in 1651. The magnificent Great Hall is all that remains. It houses the Round Table, supposed to be that used by King Arthur and his knights.

The city continued to thrive in medieval times, and the power and wealth of the bishops of Winchester increased. Bishop Henry of Blois rebuilt Wolvesey Castle and in 1136 established the Hospital of St Cross, the oldest charitable institution in the country where the Wayfarer's Dole of bread and ale may still be claimed from the Porter's Lodge. In 1382 Bishop William of Wykeham founded Winchester College.

Winchester is a busy modern city but there are peaceful parks and quiet corners where the hurly-burly of the traffic can be forgotten, and the rich pageant of its history can come alive in the imagination.

Winchester: the Cathedral and Deanery. Left: the Wayfarer's Dole of bread and ale can still be claimed at the Hospital of St Cross, founded in 1136

AA recommends:
Hotels: Wessex, Paternoster Row, 4-star, tel. (0962) 61611
Lainston House, Sparsholt, 3-star, country-house, tel. (0962) 63588 (3m NW off A272)
Royal, St Peter St, 3-star, tel. (0962) 53468
Restaurants: Cellar Peking, 32/33 Jewry St, 2-fork, tel. (0962) 64178
Old Chesil Rectory, 1 Chesil St, 2-fork, tel. (0962) 53177
Guesthouse: Harestock Lodge Hotel, Harestock Rd, tel. (0962) 881870
Campsites: Mornhill Caravan Club Site, Morn Hill, 2-pennants, tel. (0962) 69877
Winchester Recreation Centre, Gordon Rd, 2-pennants, tel. (0962) 69525
Garages: Easton, (Mould & Thompson), Easton, tel. (096278) 319
Gordon Holland, 12/14 City Road, tel. (0962) 62244

Wookey Hole, Somerset

Map Ref: 87ST5347

The village of Wookey Hole straddles the River Axe as it emerges from its rocky lair beneath the Mendip Hills. The main street scarcely copes with the daily influx of visitors to the attractions in the caves, which have drawn tourists since the 15th century. In 1709 a party of six people paid 2s 6d for an unguided visit. They were, however, given candles and beer.

In 1973 Madame Tussaud's purchased the caves and since then an unusual tourist complex has been created, with caves, a papermaking mill and a fairground collection.

Visitors purchase a comprehensive ticket which allows access to all the attractions. A guide leads parties through the caves, a startling wonderland of underground caverns and lakes, now paved and dramatically lit. Archaeologists have found evidence of the human occupation of the caves from 250BC to AD400: pottery, weaving equipment, grain stores and possibly the remains of a human sacrifice (which perhaps helps to explain the origin of the Witch of Wookey legend).

Paper is once again made by hand in the 19th-century mill buildings where visitors can see cotton rags swilling about in great troughs and the paper-maker filling a meshed tray. At one time bank-note paper was made here, with exquisite watermarks; it remains one of the few places where high quality hand-made paper can be purchased.

Lady Bangor's fabulous collection of fairground art includes a garish menagerie of richly carved and painted beasts from roundabouts, a steam-powered Marenghi organ, gilded merry-go-rounds, moonrockets and painted cars from mechanical rides.

The final bizarre attraction is the Madame Tussaud's 'Cabinet of Curiosities': for 30 years, before she opened her waxwork displays permanently in Baker Street, London, Marie Tussaud toured Britain, and this exhibition recreates an imaginary show about to open in a Georgian town.

Wool, Dorset

Map Ref: 92SY8486

Modern housing estates straggle along the A352, but off the main road and towards the church the old village is discreetly caring for its various charms. Behind the bakery, Spring Street is bordered by a stream with little bridges across to each pretty thatched cottage; behind, watermeadows and rolling green fields mingle with woodland.

There are some exceptionally good examples of modern conversions of older buildings, like

A colourful medley of fairground beasts has found a home at Wookey Hole

the old coach house and the Poorhouse barn. The Roman Catholic Church of St Joseph, back on the main road, designed by Anthony Jaggard and built in 1972, is a striking modern building in its own right.

Over the railway crossing the 16th-century bridge on the River Frome has a cast-iron notice threatening to transport anyone defacing it. Woolbridge Manor, close by, is an odd conglomeration of cottages, manor, barns, gatehouse and cowsheds dating from the 16th century. It was in the Manor that Tess and Angel Clare spent their tragic honeymoon in Hardy's *Tess of the d'Urbervilles.*

Bovington Tank Museum, about 2 miles north, claims to have the largest collection of armoured fighting vehicles in the world. That plus a cut-in-half Centurion tank and the opportunity to clamber inside some of the exhibits make it a place worth visiting.

AA recommends:
Self-catering: Braeside, Lulworth Rd, *tel.* (0929) 462057
Whitemead Lodge, *tel.* (0929) 462241
Campsite: Whitemead Caravan Park, East Burton Rd, 3-pennants, *tel.* (0929) 462241
Garage: Wool & Bovington Motors, Dorchester Rd, *tel.* (0929) 462248

Yeovil, Somerset

Map Ref: 91ST5515

A prosperous and expanding town in the south of Somerset, on the banks of the River Yeo; a commercial centre with a wide range of manufacturing industries. Thomas Gerard described the market in 1633 as 'one of the greatest I have seen' – it was famous for its cheeses, hemp and linen thread.

The 14th-century Church of St John has survived. Known as 'the Lantern of the West', for the number and size of its windows, it is a masterpiece of design by the master-mason of Wells Cathedral, William Wynford. The tower, decorated with grotesque gargoyles, is a dominant landmark.

Glovemaking was a major cottage industry, using skins from the sheep of the Mendip Hills and Dorset Downs. There is still a Glovers' Walk in town, and some specialist glove manufacturers, but it was the arrival of the railway that really boosted economic activity in the 19th century, together with the success of the Petter engineering company. More recently the Westland Aircraft Company and its various subsidiaries became the largest employer. The firm started during World War I.

Yeovil Museum, housed in the old coach house of Hendford Manor, has firearms, costume, glassware and Yeovil memorabilia.

Two of the most beautiful historic houses in the region are close by. Montacute House is a large Elizabethan mansion of Ham stone, warm and delicate, set in formal gardens and surrounded by lush countryside. The long gallery, reputed to be the longest in England, houses an exhibition of 16th- and 17th-century portraits from the National Portrait Gallery.

Brympton d'Evercy is smaller in scale, presenting a picture of rural seclusion and perfection. As well as the principal rooms of the house, the church, priest's house, stables and a rural museum can be visited. The latest venture is a vineyard on the south facing slopes of the valley.

AA recommends:
Hotels: Four Acres, West Coker, 3-star, *tel.* (093586) 2555, (3m W A30)
Manor Crest, Hendford, 3-star, *tel.* (0935) 23116
Preston, 64 Preston Rd, 1-star, *tel.* (0935) 74400
Restaurant: Little Barwick House, 2-fork, *tel.* (0935) 23902, (2m S off A37)
Guesthouse: Carents, Yeovil Marsh, (farmhouse), *tel.* (0935) 76622
Campsite: Partway Lane Caravan Park, Hartington Mandeville, 2-pennants, *tel.* (093586) 2863, (4m SW off A30 beyond W. Coker)
Garages: A M Motors, Unit 7, Enterprise Mews, Lynx Trad Est, *tel.* (0935) 73574
Abbey Hill Motor Sales, Boundary Rd, Lufton Trad Est, *tel.* (0935) 29111
Vincents, Market St, *tel.* (0935) 75242
Wincanton, Addlewell Ln, *tel.* (0935) 74842

Selection only: see page 4

Directory

Spools of yarn at Wilton carpet factory

ANGLING

Two of England's best coarse fisheries are Wiltshire's River Avon and the Stour in Dorset, which are renowned for specimen barbel, pike, chub and roach. The Brue, Parrett, Tone and Axe also offer good coarse fishing. On all rivers and stillwaters in Wessex the coarse season is from 16 June until 14 March inclusive. High quality stillwater fly fishing for rainbow and brown trout can be found in Blagdon, Chew Valley, Durleigh, Hawkridge, Otterhead and Sutton Bingham reservoirs.

There is chalk stream fishing for trout, which is first class but mostly preserved and permits are difficult to obtain. You can find very good sea fishing for bass and other species on some south coast beaches and there is boat fishing for a wide range of species.

Platforms for disabled anglers have been constructed at some fisheries and for full details of these, and other fishing information, write to the Chief Fisheries and Recreation Officer, Wessex Water Authority, Wessex House, Passage Street, Bristol BS2 0JQ. *Fishing in England's West Country* is also available free from West Country Tourist Board, Trinity Court, Southernhay East, Exeter EX1 1QS.

CRAFTS

Two Craft Guilds are useful sources of information about traditional and contemporary crafts in Wessex: Alan Dean, Dorset Craft Guild, Walford Mill Craft Centre, Knobb Crook, Stone Lane, Wimborne Minster BN21 1NL and Rev R Wild, Somerset Guild of Craftsmen, Yard End, Carters Lane, Crowcombe, Taunton TA4 4AA. Oustanding in the area are:

Wilton
At the *Royal Carpet Factory* a working exhibition of traditional weaving crafts can be seen alongside the full woven carpet manufacturing process. Tours open: all year, Mon to Fri. *Tel.* Salisbury (0722) 742441

Beaminster
Parnham House is a Tudor manor house and now the home of John Makepeace's famous *furniture-making workshops*. Open: Apr to Oct, Wed, Sun and Bank Holidays. *Tel:* Beaminster (0308) 862204

Stoke St Gregory
In the Somerset Levels willows are grown, processed and made into *baskets*. All aspects of the industry can be seen at the Willows and Wetlands Visitor Centre, Meare Green Court.
Open: all year, Mon to Sat.
Tel. North Curry (0823) 490249

CYCLING

The Wiltshire Cycleway is a 160-mile circular route along mainly quiet lanes, passing many of the county's most attractive places to visit. A free leaflet is available from Wiltshire County Council, County Hall, Trowbridge BA14 8JN.

There are shorter cycleways in the Bath/Bristol area and parts of the Ridge Way Path can be used.

West Dorset District Council publishes the *West Dorset Cycleway* leaflet, giving detailed information about a 110-mile route. Available from the council's offices, High West Street, Dorchester DT1 1UZ.

GOLF

In 1888 Wessex was the setting for one of the game's very first professional matches, played over 18 holes at the still-flourishing Royal Winchester Club, and 18 holes at Burnham, a testing championship links course. Visiting golfers now have a choice of other courses by the sea and many inland courses which enjoy spectacular views. The Vale of Taunton Deane lies beneath Pickeridge in the Blagdon Hills, and from the plateau of Came Down there are glorious views over Portland. In the Bath and Bristol area there are courses to test players of all handicaps.

The AA *Guide to Golf in Great Britain* is an annual publication which gives descriptions, telephone numbers and local arrangements for courses in the region.

INFORMATION CENTRES

National Trust
The National Trust runs houses, gardens, prehistoric sites, areas of coast and countryside, and other places of interest in Wessex. Full details are given in the annual National Trust Handbook; write to the National Trust, Queen Anne's Gate, London SW1H 9AS, *Tel.* 01-222 9251.

English Heritage
English Heritage runs houses, gardens, prehistoric sites and other places of interest in Wessex. For a complete guide to sites, write to English Heritage, PO Box 43, Ruislip, Middlesex HA4 0XW (for latest price information, *Tel.* 01-734 6010).

TOURIST INFORMATION CENTRES

There are more than 50 Tourist Information Centres in Wessex and all can provide more information about local accommodation, opening times and admission charges, and ideas for places to visit.

Addresses are given for Tourist Information Centres in cities and larger towns. For a list of other Tourist Information Centres in the region write to West Country Tourist Board, Trinity Court, Southernhay East, Exeter EX1 1QS.

Bath, Avon
Abbey Churchyard
Tel. (0225) 62831

Bournemouth, Dorset
Westover Road
Tel. (0202) 291715

Bristol, Avon
Colston House, Colston Street
Tel. (0272) 293891/20767

Salisbury, Wiltshire
Fish Row *Tel.* (0722) 334956

Swindon, Wiltshire
32 Arcade, Brunel Centre
Tel. (0793) 30328/26161 ext 3056

Taunton, Somerset
Library, Corporation St
Tel. (0823) 74785/70479

Wells, Somerset
Town Hall, Market Place
Tel. (0749) 72552

Winchester, Hampshire
The Guildhall, Broadway
Tel. (0962) 65406

PLACES TO VISIT

Wessex is exceptionally rich in beautiful houses, gardens, prehistoric sites and other places to visit. Brief details are given below. This is *a selection only*, and sources of further information are given on page 75.

Details may change: it is wise to check with a Tourist Information Centre before visiting. National Trust and English Heritage properties are marked (NT) and (EH) respectively.

CASTLES

Corfe, Dorset
Corfe Castle (NT) stands dramatically over the picturesque village in the heart of the Isle of Purbeck.
Open Mar to Oct, daily;
Nov to Feb, Sat and Sun.

Farleigh Hungerford, Somerset
Farleigh Castle (EH) 14th-century with moats and towers.
Open Apr to Sep, daily;
Oct to Mar five days a week.

Nunney, Somerset
Small but impressive *Nunney Castle* (EH). Built in the late 14th century it has towers at the angles and stands in a moat.
Open all year, daily.

Portland, Dorset
Portland Castle (EH) Erected by Henry VIII and added to in the 17th century, to defend the southernmost coast of Wessex.
Open Apr to Sept, daily.

Sherborne, Dorset
The 12th-century *Sherborne Old Castle* (EH) was once occupied by Sir Walter Raleigh. Open all year, daily. In 1594 he built the new *Sherborne Castle* on the site of a nearby Tudor hunting lodge.
Open Easter to Sept, Thu, Sat, Sun and Bank Holidays.

Tisbury, Wiltshire
Ruins of *Old Wardour Castle*. (EH)
Open daily Mar to Oct; otherwise weekends.

CAVES

Cheddar, Somerset
Cheddar Caves are the show caves at the foot of scenic Cheddar Gorge, and feature a museum, fantasy grotto and caving trips. Open: Gough's Cave, all year, daily; other attractions: Easter to Sep, daily.

Wookey Hole, Somerset
The spectacular caves and tunnels are the most impressive features of Wookey Hole Caves, which also boasts a working Victorian papermill. Open all year, daily.

'Witch of Wookey' by J Hassell (inset) and Cheddar Gorge

FOOD AND DRINK

Chewton Mendip, Somerset
Chewton Cheese Dairy Working dairy where you can see Cheddar cheese being made by hand.
Open all year, daily.

Dowlish Wake, Ilminster, Somerset
Perry's Cider Rural life display and cidermaking. Open daily.

Moorlynch, Somerset
Spring Farm Vineyard, where vineyard and winemaking can be seen. Open May to Sep.

Sturminster Newton, Dorset
Sturminster Newton Mill
Commercial, working watermill producing animal feeds and wholemeal flour.
Open May to Sep, Tue, Thu, Sat, Sun and Bank Holidays.

Taunton, Somerset
Sheppy's Farmhouse Cider Orchards, the press room and a delightful farm and cider museum. Traditional farmhouse cider for sale.
Open Apr to Dec, daily.

GARDENS

Abbotsbury, Dorset
The 20 acres of *Abbotsbury Sub-Tropical Gardens,* woodland and formal gardens are famed for their tender outdoor plants and their peacocks. Open all year, daily.

Castle Cary, Somerset
Hadspen House Gardens include rare plants in 8 acres. Open Apr to Oct Tue to Sun and Bank Holidays. Nov to Mar (except Jan) Tue to Sat.

Cerne Abbas, Dorset
Lovers of rhododendrons visit *Minterne Gardens,* landscaped in the 18th century with lakes, cascades and streams. Open Apr to Oct, daily.

Cheddon Fitzpaine, Somerset
Hestercombe House has gardens by Gertrude Jekyll.
Open all year Tue to Sat.

Crewkerne, Somerset
Clapton Court Gardens have 10 acres of both formal and woodland settings and a 'garden for all seasons'. Open all year, Sun to Fri; also Easter Sat and Sats in May.

Devizes, Wiltshire
Broadleas Medium-sized garden of rare and unusual plants. April and May are outstanding for magnolias, azaleas and rhododendrons. Open Apr to Oct, Wed, Thu and Sun.

Ilminster, Somerset
see HISTORIC HOUSES, below.

Stourhead, Wiltshire (NT)
The temples and grottoes around the lake at the Stourhead garden are as famous throughout the world as the trees and shrubs of this idyllic landscape. Open all year, daily.

HISTORIC HOUSES

Athelhampton, Dorset
Athelhampton, a family home for 500 years, is a fine example of 15th-century architecture, and its attractive gardens include fountains and waterfalls. Open Easter to Oct, Wed, Thu, Sun and Bank Holidays; also Mon and Tue in Aug.

Beaminster, Dorset
Parnham Tudor manor house, embellished by John Nash in 1810, and with 14 acres of gardens. Now John Makepeace's workshops. Open Apr to Oct, Wed, Sun and Bank Holidays.

Bradford-on-Avon, Wiltshire
Westwood Manor (NT) 15th-century stone manor house. Open Apr to Sep, Sun, Mon and first Wed in month.

Calne, Wiltshire
Robert Adam's 18th-century *Bowood House* features some interesting collections, a landscaped park and its own interpretation centre. Open Easter to Sep, daily.

Chippenham, Wiltshire
Ancient manor house, *Sheldon Manor*. Fine 13th-century porch and early English oak furniture. Ancient yew trees and rare and interesting shrubs. Open Easter to Oct, Thu, Sun and Bank Holidays.

Clevedon, Avon
Clevedon Court (NT) is a 14th-century manor house set in a terraced garden. Thackeray stayed here while writing *Vanity Fair*. Nailsea glass and Eltonware. Open Apr to end Nov, Wed, Thu, Sun and Bank Holiday Mons.

Chipping Sodbury, Avon
Horton Court (NT) Cotswold manor house with 12th-century Norman Hall and early Renaissance features. Detached from the house is an ambulatory. Open Apr to end Oct, Wed and Sat.

The upper marble staircase at Kingston Lacy, recently restored

Dyrham, Avon
Built at the end of the 17th century, *Dyrham Park* (NT) is an imposing mansion house whose rooms have been little changed. A herd of deer roam the surrounding parkland. Open Apr, May and Oct, Sat to Wed; Jun to Sep, Sat to Thu.

Higher Bockhampton, Dorset
Hardy's Cottage (NT) Garden open daily, Apr to Oct. Interior by appointment with tenant.

Ilminster, Somerset
Barrington Court (NT) is a 16th-century Ham stone house with gardens by Gertrude Jekyll. Open Easter to Sep, Sun to Wed.

Kingston Lacy, Dorset (NT)
Recently restored by the National Trust, splendid Kingston Lacy (near Wimborne Minster) has a collection of paintings, a park and garden. Open Apr to Oct, Sat to Wed.

Lacock, Wiltshire
Lacock Abbey (NT) has been the home of the Talbots since the Dissolution. Open Apr to Oct; Wed to Mon (house); gardens daily.

Littlecote House, Wiltshire
Seven miles east of Marlborough this early 16th-century house has a unique collection of Cromwellian armour, a rare breed farm, riverside railway and a period village reconstruction.
Open Apr to Oct, daily.

Longleat, Wiltshire
On the county border with Somerset, Longleat is a grand Elizabethan house and family home with outstanding collections of books and pictures.
Open all year, daily.

Lytes Cary Manor, Somerset (NT)
Manor house near Somerton with 14th-century chapel.
Open Apr to Oct, Wed and Sat.

Poundisford Park, Somerset
Tudor house near Taunton. Open May-Sep, Wed, Thu and Bank Holidays; and Fri, Jul to Aug.

Purse Caundle, Dorset
Purse Caundle Manor has a Great Hall and minstrel's gallery.
Open Easter to Sep, Thu, Sun and Bank Holidays.

Salisbury, Wiltshire
Mompesson House (NT), a graceful 18th-century house with walled garden. Open Apr to Oct, Sat to Wed.

Tisbury, Wiltshire
Pyt House, Palladian mansion. Open May-Sep, Wed and Thu.
Wardour Castle, Palladian mansion. Open school summer holidays, Mon, Wed, Fri, Sat.

Westbury, Wiltshire
Chalcot House. Mansion with paintings and Boer War collection. Open Jul, Aug, daily.

Wilton, Wiltshire
Wilton House's magnificent state rooms, including the Double Cube room by Inigo Jones, and its fine art collection are the highlights of this lovely 17th-century house.
Open Easter to Oct, Tue to Sun and Bank Holidays.

Winchester, Hampshire
Pilgrims' Hall, with its outstanding 13th-century hammer-beam roof, is in Cathedral Close, one of the most attractive and interesting parts of the city. Open all year, daily.

Yeovil, Somerset
Brympton d'Evercy Priest house museum, extensive gardens and a vineyard. Open May to Sep, Sat to Wed.
Montacute House (NT) Built of golden Ham stone in the late 16th century. Collection of Tudor and Jacobean art. Open Apr to Oct, Wed to Mon.

MUSEUMS

Avebury, Wiltshire
Great Barn Museum of Wiltshire Folk Life. Open daily Easter to Oct; weekends Nov to Easter.
Alexander Keiller Museum (EH) Local prehistoric finds. Open daily Apr to Sep; weekends Oct to Mar.

Bath, Avon
In the *Assembly Rooms* is the city's *Museum of Costume.* Open all year, daily.
The *Holburne of Menstrie Museum.* Silver, porcelain, Old Master paintings, furniture and 20th-century crafts. Open Apr to Nov, daily; Feb and Mar, Tue to Sun.
Pump Room, Georgian social centre of the city, where spa water can be drunk. Open daily.
Roman Baths Museum Extensive remains of Roman baths, and hot spring. Open daily. Also *toy, bookbinding, postal, geology, costume, photography* and other museums, and *Botanic Gardens.*

Bovington Camp, Dorset
Seven miles west of Wareham is the *Tank Museum*, a collection of more than 150 armoured vehicles. Open all year, daily.

Bournemouth, Dorset
Big Four Railways Museum. Open weekdays all year, closed Bank Holidays.
Russell Cotes Art Gallery and Museums. Ship models, shells, orientalia. Open all year except Sun.

Bristol, Avon
City Docks, including *Industrial Museum*, *National Lifeboat Museum* and SS *Great Britain*. Maritime, wine, ephemera, and other museums. The *Arnolfini Gallery* has contemporary visual art and performances of contemporary theatre, music, dance and film. Open all year, Tue to Sun.

Claverton, Avon
American Museum in Britain Rooms in period style, folk art, galleries of silver, pewter and glass, patchwork quilt collection, and an arboretum. Open Easter to Oct, Tues to Sun and Bank Holidays.

Devizes, Wiltshire
Devizes Museum Best collection of prehistoric Wessex material. Open Tue to Sat.

Dorchester, Dorset
The *Dorset County Museum* Archaeology, natural history and material relating to Thomas Hardy. Open all year, Mon to Sat.
Dinosaur Museum. Open daily.

Glastonbury, Somerset
The *Somerset Rural Life Museum.* Open all year, daily.

Lacock, Wiltshire
Fox Talbot Museum (NT), with Fox Talbot photographs. Open daily, Mar to Oct, except Good Friday.

Salisbury, Wiltshire
The Pitt-Rivers Wessex collections form part of the displays of local history in the *Salisbury and South Wiltshire Museum*. Open all year, Mon to Sat also Jul and Aug, Sun.
Duke of Edinburgh's Royal Regiment Museum. Open Apr to Oct, Sun to

Part of a board of Bronze Age artefacts now in Somerset County Museum, Taunton which is housed in the town's medieval castle

One of many exhibits from the days of steam at Swindon's Railway Museum

Thurs; to Sat in Jul and Aug; Nov to Mar, Mon to Fri.

Sparkford, Somerset
Sparkford Motor Museum Classic, veteran and vintage motor cars and motor cycles. Open all year, daily.

Street, Somerset
Shoe Museum Shoes from Romans to modern day.
Open Easter to Oct, Mon to Sat.

Swindon, Wiltshire
In the *Great Western Railway Museum* and *Railway Village Museum* there are historic locomotives, posters, tickets and a foreman's house furnished to recreate a Victorian home. Open all year, daily. Also *Richard Jefferies* and *Coate Agricultural Museum.*

Taunton, Somerset
Taunton Castle, dating from the 13th century and associated with Judge Jeffreys' 'Bloody Assize' of 1685, houses the *Somerset County Museum.* Open all year Mon to Fri; also Sat in summer.
Closed Bank Hols.

Winchester, Hampshire
Great Hall of Winchester Castle Only part left of castle, with 'Round Table of King Arthur'. Open daily.
Westgate Museum, Medieval city gate, with armour display.
Open daily (except Mon, Oct to Mar). *Winchester City Museum*, Prehistory and history of city and area, well displayed. *Winchester Gallery* Modern art and crafts in monthly-changing exhibitions.
Open all year, Mon to Fri.

Yeovilton, Somerset
Fleet Air Arm Museum. Over 50 historic aircraft, including the Concorde 002 prototype, a Kamikaze Exhibition and a Falklands Campaign Exhibition. Open all year, daily.

PREHISTORIC SITES

These sites are open all year.

Abbotsbury, Dorset
Kingston Russell Stone Circle

Avebury, Wiltshire
Avebury Ring (EH) Stone circle and embankment around the village. *Avenue* Double row of sarsen stones. *Silbury Hill* (EH) Huge, baffling artificial mound. *West Kennett Long Barrow* (EH) Chambered tomb. *Windmill Hill* (EH) Neolithic causewayed camp.

Badbury Rings, Dorset (NT)
Hillfort near Wimborne, Dorset

Barbury Castle
Prehistoric camp near Marlborough

Cerne Abbas, Dorset
Cerne Giant (NT) Figure cut in chalk.

Dolebury Warren, Avon (NT)
Exceptionally fine hillfort with drystone walling near Churchill.

Dorchester, Dorset
Maiden Castle Huge hillfort.
Maumbury Rings Neolithic site used as Roman amphitheatre.

Ham Hill Camp, Somerset
Iron Age hillfort with inn, near Montacute.

Ridge Way
Long distance footpath based on prehistoric route. See *WALKING*.

Salisbury, Wiltshire
Old Sarum. (EH) Site of old city with earthworks, originally Iron Age.

South Cadbury, Somerset
South Cadbury Castle (NT) Iron Age hillfort used in the Dark Ages, perhaps King Arthur's Camelot.

Stonehenge, Wiltshire (EH)
World-celebrated stone circles near Amesbury.

Westbury, Wiltshire
Bratton Camp (EH) Prehistoric camp with white horse cut in chalk.

Woodhenge, Wiltshire (EH)
Site of rings of wooden posts, near Amesbury.

Weston-Super-Mare, Avon
British Encampment 10¼-acre encampment.

WILDLIFE

Abbotsbury, Dorset
Abbotsbury Swannery Unique colony of mute swans, managed here since the 14th century.
Open May to Sep, daily.

Bristol, Avon
Bristol Zoo Includes gorillas, white tigers and a reptile house.
Open all year, daily.

Skeletons found at Maiden Castle and now in the County Museum, Dorchester

Cricket St Thomas, Somerset
Four miles east of Chard this wildlife park and countryside museum was the location for BBC TV's *To The Manor Born.*
Open all year, daily.

Longleat, Wiltshire
The *Lions of Longleat Safari Park* lets you drive amidst lions, cheetahs, giraffes and monkeys, and offers a wide range of other attractions for the family.
Open Mar to Oct, daily.

Rode, Somerset
Tropical Bird Gardens Hundreds of brilliant, exotic birds in beautiful surroundings, including flower gardens and ornamental lakes.
Open all year, daily.

Weymouth, Dorset
The largest display of marine life in Britain, the *Sea Life Centre* features baby leopard sharks, huge rays, octopus and conger eels.
Open Mar to Nov, daily.

WALKING

The South West Peninsula Coast Path
This footpath, the longest of all long distance paths in England, begins at Poole Harbour in Dorset and goes right round the peninsula. A favourite route is eastwards from Lyme Regis with the prevailing winds behind for 72 miles, along a coastline designated an Area of Oustanding Natural Beauty and famous for its fossils. A descriptive leaflet is available from the Countryside Commission, John Dower House, Crescent Place, Cheltenham GL50 3RA.

Ridge Way Path
Following the ancient Wessex Ridge Way and Icknield Way the path passes through an area of considerable archaeological interest. A descriptive leaflet is available from the Countryside Commission.

The Avon Walkway and Kennet and Avon Canal
The Walkway and the towpath of the canal provide a continuous walk across Avon and Wiltshire, including Bristol and Bath.

The West Mendip Way
This linked series of footpaths runs from near Weston-super-Mare over the Mendip Hills and into the cathedral city of Wells.

Country Parks
There are six country parks recognised by the Countryside Commission in Wessex. As well as their attraction to walkers they offer a variety of opportunities for family recreation.
Barbury Castle, near Swindon
Barton Farm, near Bradford-on-Avon
Cotswold Water Park, near Swindon
Durleston, near Swanage
Ham Hill, near Yeovil
Upton Park, near Poole

NATURE TRAILS

Details are given in *Walking in England's West Country* (below).

WOODLAND

For information about woodland walking write to The Forestry Commission, 231 Corstorphine Road, Edinburgh EH12 7AT.

Walking in England's West Country is available free from West Country Tourist Board, Trinity Court, Southernhay East, Exeter EX1 1QS

WATERSPORTS

The large natural harbour at Poole, with its many marinas and yacht charter bases, is just one of the Dorset coastline's sites for watersports enthusiasts. There are other marinas at Christchurch, Wareham and Weymouth – and Lyme Regis and West Bay have their harbours. To the north, on the Bristol Channel, there are marinas at Bridgwater, Bristol and Weston-super-Mare.

Waterskiing and windsurfing can be practised at all the main resorts and tuition is often available. There are many opportunities for sub-aqua divers, for example the Purbeck Marine Wildlife Reserve.

Inland there are reservoirs and lakes which also offer facilities for the whole range of watersports. Further information on these is available from Wessex Water, Wessex House, Passage Street, Bristol BS2 0JQ.

DIRECTORY

CALENDAR OF EVENTS

Many of the remarkable Wessex carnivals are staged in October and November. Highlights of the carnival season come in Bridgwater and Taunton, and there are traditional carnival processions in Bristol, Burnham-on-Sea, Glastonbury, North Petherton, Shepton Mallet, Wells and Weston-super-Mare, to name only a few.
Check with tourist information centres for details of events.

March
Bath Spring Antiques Fair

April
Badminton Horse Trials
Complete Home and Garden Exhibition, Bristol
'Aerojumble', Yeovilton
Bristol Eisteddfod

May
West of England Antiques, Bath
Chippenham Folk Festival
Great Wishford Oak Apple Day
Bath International Festival
Weymouth Harbour Trawler Race
Royal Bath and West Show, Shepton Mallet
Bristol Proms
Beer Festival, Winchester
May Fair, Wells
North Somerset Show

June
American Indian Weekend, Claverton
Bristol Tennis Trophy
Bristol Power Grand Prix
Wessex Game and Country Fair, Cricket St Thomas

July
Hat Fair, Winchester
World Wine Fair, Bristol
Portland Navy Days and Air Display
Glastonbury Children's Festival
Tolpuddle Martyrs' Rally
Badminton Air Day
Chard Show
Royal Bath and West Summer Show, Shepton Mallet
RNLI Lifeboat Week, Lyme Regis
Great Weston Air Days, Weston-super-Mare

August
Bournemouth Carnival Week
Woman's World Exhibition, Bristol
Dorset County Arts and Crafts Association Exhibition, Puddletown
Priddy Sheep Fair, near Wells
Weymouth Carnival
Bristol International Balloon Fiesta
British Fuchsia Society South Western Show, Chippenham
Poole Yachting Week
Bristol Harbour Regatta
Taunton Flower Show

August/September
Bristol Flower Show

September
Great Dorset Steam Fair, Blandford
Salisbury Festival
West of England Open Amateur Golf Championship, Burnham-on-Sea
Pewsey Carnival
Frome Cheese Show

October
Carnivals – see note above
Pack Monday Fair, Sherborne
South Western Dairy Show, Shepton Mallet
Marlborough Mop Fair
Weston-super-Mare Enduro Motor Cycle Beach Races
Bath Autumn Antiques Fair

November
Carnivals – see note above
Avon Poetry Festival
Great Western Beer Festival, Bristol
Antique and Collectors' Fair, Shepton Mallet

Balloons at Bristol, August

WESSEX
Atlas

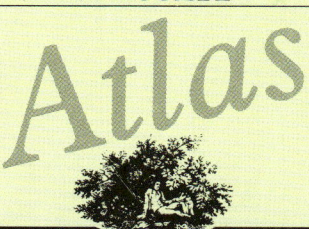

The following pages contain a legend, key map and atlas of Wessex, four motor tours and sixteen Wessex coast and countryside walks.

Above: Thatchers at work near Bridport

82 AA/OS WESSEX GUIDE

Wessex Legend

TOURIST INFORMATION

- Camp Site
- Caravan Site
- Information Centre
- Parking Facilities
- Viewpoint
- Picnic site
- Golf course or links
- Castle
- Cave
- Country park
- Garden
- Historic house
- Nature reserve
- Other tourist feature
- Preserved railway
- Racecourse
- Wildlife park
- Museum
- Nature or forest trail
- Ancient monument
- Telephones : public or motoring organisations
- PC Public Convenience
- Youth Hostel

ORIENTATION

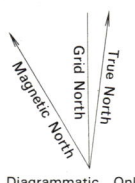

True North
At the centre of the area is 20'E of Grid North

Magnetic North
At the centre of the area is about 5½°W of Grid North in 1987 decreasing by about ½° in three years

Diagrammatic Only

GRID REFERENCE SYSTEM

The map references used in this book are based on the Ordnance Survey National Grid, correct to within 1000 Metres They comprise two letters and four figures, and are preceded by the atlas page number.

Thus the reference for Salisbury appears 93 SU 1429

93 is the atlas page number

SU identifies the major (100km) grid square concerned (see diag)

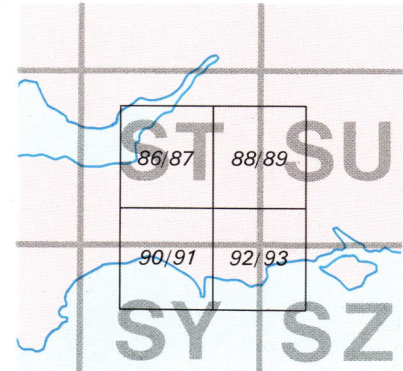

1429 locates the lower left-hand corner of the kilometre grid square in which Salisbury appears

Take the first figure of the reference 1, this refers to the numbered grid running along the bottom of the page. Having found this line, the second figure 4, tells you the distance to move in tenths to the right of this line. A vertical line through this point is the first half of the reference.

The third figure 2, refers to the numbered grid lines on the right hand side of the page, finally the fourth figure 9, indicates the distance to move in tenths above this line. A horizontal line drawn through this point to intersect with the first line gives the precise location of the places in question.

KEY-MAP 1:625,000 or 10 MILES to 1"

ROAD INFORMATION

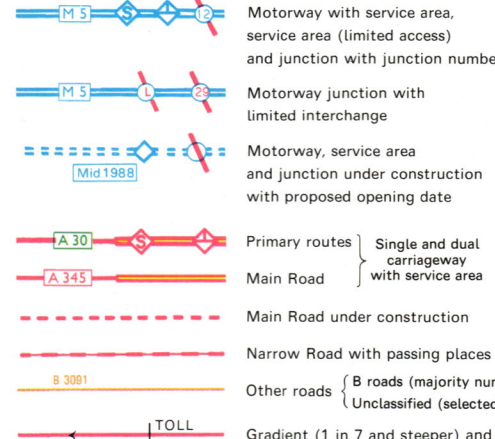

Motorway with service area, service area (limited access) and junction with junction number

Motorway junction with limited interchange

Motorway, service area and junction under construction with proposed opening date

Primary routes } Single and dual carriageway
Main Road } with service area

Main Road under construction

Narrow Road with passing places

Other roads { B roads (majority numbered)
{ Unclassified (selected)

Gradient (1 in 7 and steeper) and toll

Primary routes and main roads

Motorways

Primary Routes   These form a national network of recommended through routes which complement the motorway system. Selected places of major traffic importance are known as Primary Route Destinations and are shown on these maps thus YEOVIL. This relates to the directions on road signs which on Primary Routes have a green background. To travel on a Primary Route, follow the direction to the next Primary Destination shown on the green backed road signs. On these maps Primary Route road numbers and mileages are shown in green.

Motorways   A similar situation occurs with motorway routes where numbers and mileages, shown in blue on these maps correspond to the blue background of motorway road signs.

Mileages are shown on the map between large markers and between small markers in large and small type

1 mile = 1·61 kilometres

GENERAL FEATURES

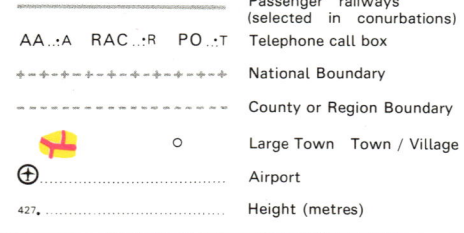

Passenger railways (selected in conurbations)

Telephone call box

National Boundary

County or Region Boundary

Large Town   Town / Village

Airport

Height (metres)

WATER FEATURES

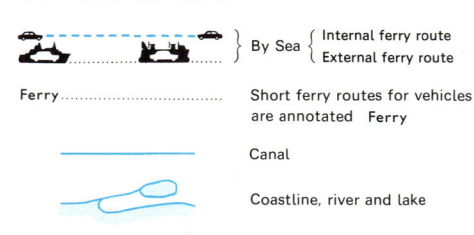

By Sea { Internal ferry route
{ External ferry route

Ferry .... Short ferry routes for vehicles are annotated Ferry

Canal

Coastline, river and lake

AA/OS WESSEX GUIDE 83

ATLAS 1:200,000 or 3 MILES to 1"
TOURS 1:250,000 or 4 MILES to 1"

ROADS Not necessarily rights of way

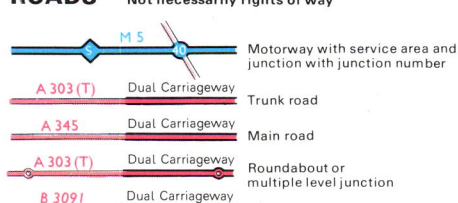

RAILWAYS

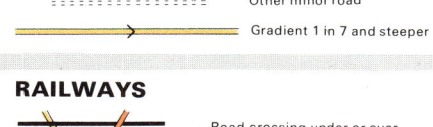

WATER FEATURES

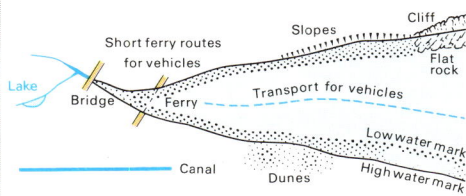

ANTIQUITIES

                  Native fortress

---------- Roman road (course of)

Castle • Other antiquities

CANOVIVM • Roman antiquity

GENERAL FEATURES

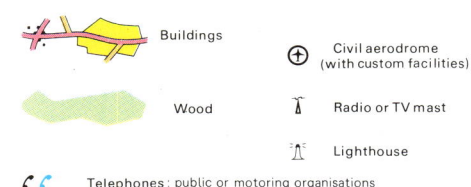

Telephones: public or motoring organisations

RELIEF

Feet	Metres	
		.274 Heights in feet above mean sea level
3000	914	
2000	610	
1400	427	
1000	305	Contours at 200 ft intervals
600	183	
200	61	
0	0	To convert feet to metres multiply by 0.3048

WALKS 1:25,000 or 2½" to 1 MILE

ROADS AND PATHS Not necessarily rights of way

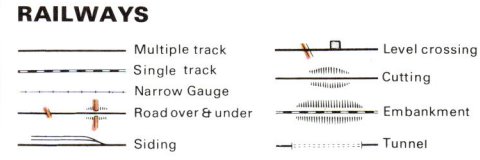

RAILWAYS

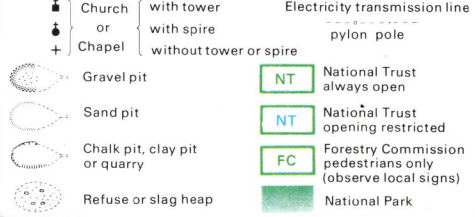

GENERAL FEATURES

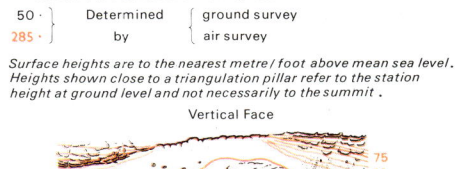

HEIGHTS AND ROCK FEATURES

Contours are at various metres / feet vertical intervals

Surface heights are to the nearest metre / foot above mean sea level. Heights shown close to a triangulation pillar refer to the station height at ground level and not necessarily to the summit.

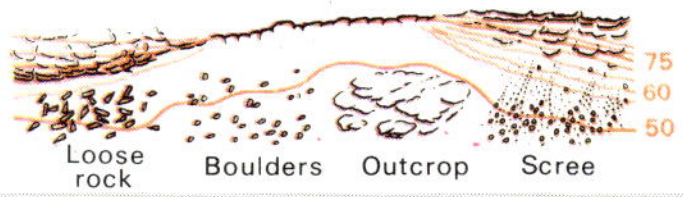

PUBLIC RIGHTS OF WAY

Public rights of way shown in this guide may not be evident on the ground

- - - - -   Public Paths { Footpath / Bridleway

+ + + + +   By-way open to all traffic

+ + + + +   Road used as a public path

Public rights of way indicated by these symbols have been derived from Definitive Maps as amended by later enactments or instruments held by Ordnance Survey between 1st Nov 1968 and 1st Nov 1984 and are shown subject to the limitations imposed by the scale of mapping

Later information may be obtained from the appropriate County Council.

The representation on this map of any other road, track or path is no evidence of the existence of a right of way.

WALKS AND TOURS (All Scales)

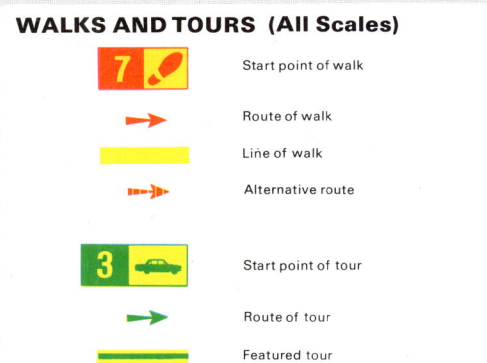

TOUR 1 63 MILES

Cheddar Gorge, Wells and Bath

This is a tour that is both rich in history and of great geological beauty and interest. It takes you over the Mendip Hills and through the rugged grandeur of Cheddar Gorge. You can see the stalagmites and stalactites of the Cheddar Caves and Wookey Hole Caves, occupied by Stone Age and Iron Age man. You can stop off in the medieval cathedral city of Wells, and in Bath with its rich Roman and Georgian inheritance.

The drive starts from Bristol (see page 36), a place with a rich heritage, both maritime and industrial, and now a blend of ancient and modern.

From the city centre follow signs Taunton, The South West, A38. As you skirt the northern side of the Floating Harbour along Hotwell Road there are brief views of *SS Great Britain* to the left. *After 1¼ miles follow signs The South West to cross the impressive Cumberland Basin Swing Bridge then continue with Taunton signs. In 1 mile turn left (one-way) then right and right again, then turn left to the A38. After ¼ mile, at the Cross Hands Public House, branch left signed Bishopsworth on to an unclassified road.*

Proceed through suburbs and after 1 mile keep forward at a mini-roundabout then shortly branch left. Proceed through Withywood and shortly begin the winding ascent (10 per cent gradient) of Dundry Hill. The drive reaches a height of 669ft but the actual summit of 764ft lies away to the right. There are views ahead to the Chew Valley Lake from the start of the descent. *In 1½ miles cross a main road, signed Chew Stoke and ¾ mile further on turn right on to the B3114, signed West Harptree, and go through Chew Stoke.*

One mile beyond the village the drive passes at several points the attractive Chew Valley Lake, a reservoir opened in 1956. *Beyond the Blue Bowl Inn (edge of West Harptree) keep forward on to an unclassified road signposted Cheddar. In ½ mile cross the main road and ascend on to the main Mendip ridge. At the crossroads immediately beyond the Wells Way Inn, turn right and in ¼ mile at the next crossroads turn left signed Cheddar to cross high open agricultural land. In 1¼ miles at a crossroads go forward on to the B3371. Continue through open scenery for some distance before descending into a shallow valley and turning right at a T-road on to the B3135.*

From here the drive starts the long, winding and at first thickly wooded descent of Cheddar Gorge. This is a huge natural chasm nearly 500ft in depth at its greatest point. At the mouth of the gorge the drive passes the entrance to the Cheddar Caves with their magnificent stalagmite and stalactite formations (see page 39).

In Cheddar village (see page 39) continue with the Wells road and in ¼ mile at the market cross turn left on to the A371. The drive then proceeds along the foot of the escarpment, with the broad flat Axe Valley to the right. *After about 5 miles at Easton, on the nearside of the Church, turn left (no sign) on to a narrow unclassified road. Climbing over a low hill the drive reaches the car park and entrance to the spectacular Wookey Hole Caves and Paper Mill* (see page 74). There are weird formations within this complex of prehistoric caves, now run by Madame Tussaud's.

Continue on the Wells road passing the Wookey Hole Inn and in 1½ miles turn left on to the A371 for the centre of Wells, a charming cathedral city that has retained its medieval atmosphere (see page 68).

Leave the city following signs for Bath A39 and begin a long gradual climb to an 850ft summit on the Mendip scarp. Prominent to the left is the television transmitter on the summit of Pen Hill (1,002ft).

Continue across undulating country and pass through Chewton Mendip. The church has a 15th-century tower, 126ft high, one of the highest parish church towers in the county. *Continue north with the A37 and ¾ mile beyond Farrington Gurney village turn right to rejoin the A39, signposted Bath. Proceed through Hallatrow then High Littleton and then 1 mile further turn right on to the B3114, signposted Timsbury. Continue through agricultural countryside to pass through the villages of Timsbury and Tunley. 1¾ miles beyond Tunley turn left on to the A367 and after a further 1½ miles at a roundabout keep forward signposted City Centre to enter the city of Bath by the Wells Road. At the next roundabout (1¾ miles) take the 2nd exit under a railway bridge and cross the River Avon before turning left to enter the city centre.* See page 30 for details of Bath and its associations with Roman and Georgian high society.

Leave Bath following signs Bristol A4 along either the Lower or Upper Bristol roads. In 4¾ miles the drive passes through Saltford. After a further 1¼ miles at a roundabout take the 2nd exit. In 2 miles at the next roundabout take the 2nd exit again to pass through the suburbs of Bristol, returning to the city centre along the Bath Road.

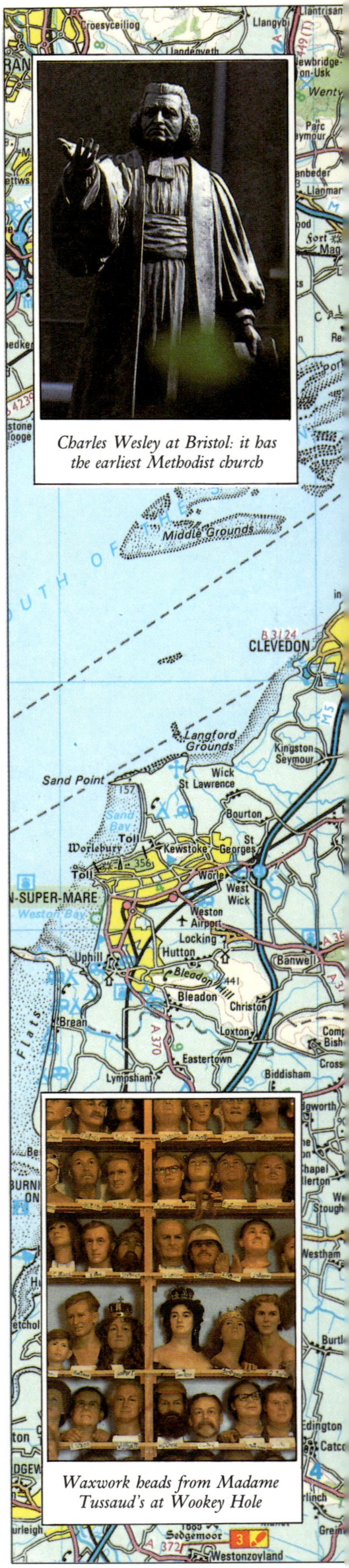

Charles Wesley at Bristol: it has the earliest Methodist church

Waxwork heads from Madame Tussaud's at Wookey Hole

TOUR 1

63 MILES

The Royal Crescent in Bath was designed by John Wood the Younger and inspired by Classical architecture. Behind the uniform façades, houses were tailored to individual owners' wishes

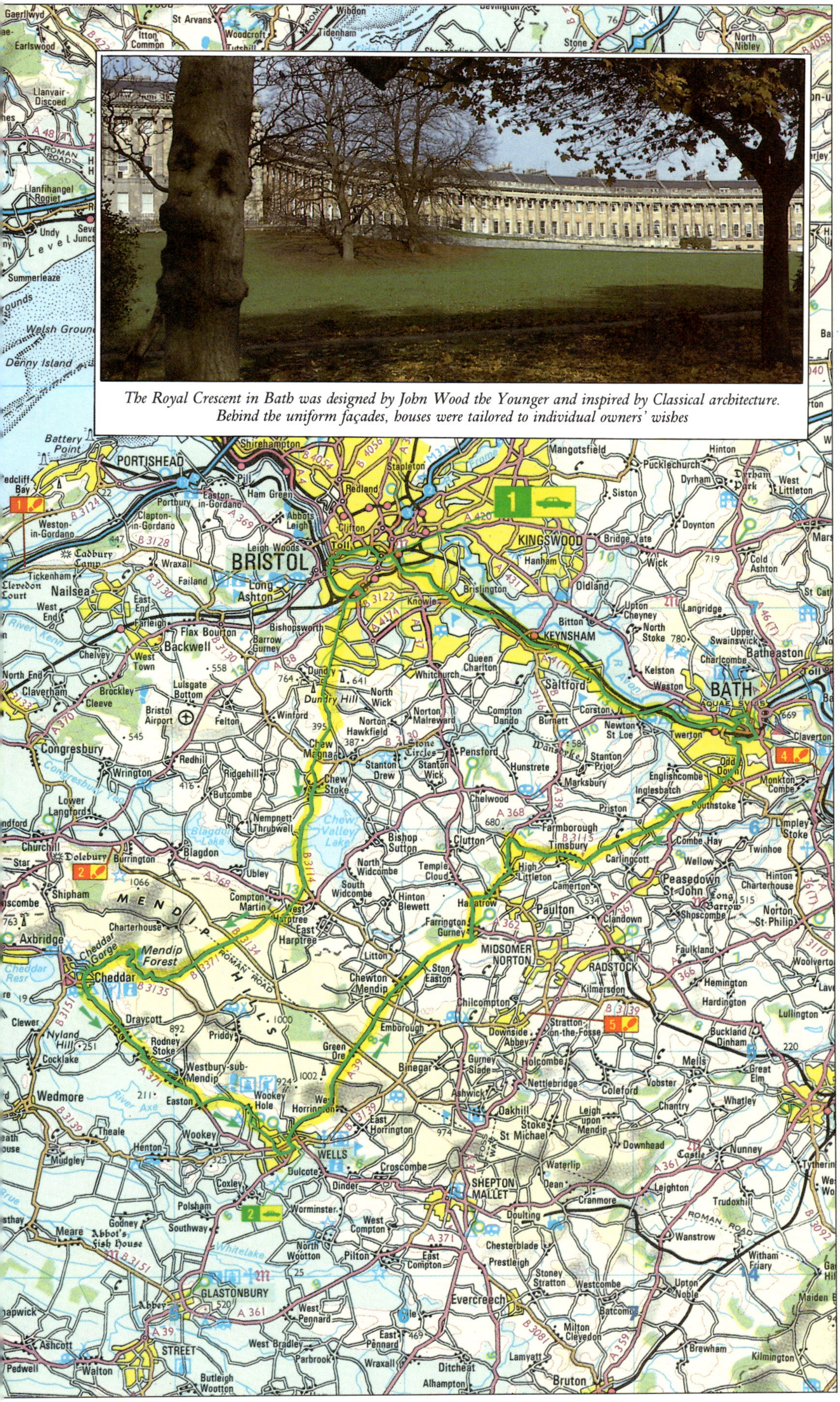

SCALE 1:25 000

TOUR 2
Somerset Levels

71 MILES

A drive through a varying landscape that offers something of interest for all, from Arthurian legend to the Fleet Air Arm Museum.

The drive starts from **Wells** (see page 68).

Follow signs Glastonbury A39 and after 2 miles pass through the village of Coxley. You will soon be crossing part of Queen's Sedge Moor and the dyked Whitelake River. Visible ahead is Glastonbury Tor (521ft).

Continue to the historic town of Glastonbury, linked in legend with King Arthur and with Joseph of Arimathea (see page 45). Turn right, signed Bridgwater, to enter the town centre and in ¼ mile at the market cross turn right again (no sign) to leave by the Meare road B3151. Proceed through low-lying country to Meare. Interesting features here include the 14th- and 15th-century church, and the 14th-century Abbot's Fish House (NT).

Continue on the B3151 and in 1¼ miles at the edge of Westhay turn left, unclassified, signed Shapwick, then shortly, at a T-junction, turn left again. After 3 miles, at Shapwick, keep forward signed High Ham, Langport. In ¾ mile at a T-junction, turn left on to the A39, then shortly, at the Albion Inn, turn right, unclassified, signed Redwell, High Ham, Langport. Descend Pedwell Hill and at the bottom turn right, A361 signed Taunton. After 1 mile pass through Greinton and cross King's Sedge Moor to reach Othery. In 1¾ miles the road goes round Burrow Mump (NT) (see page 29), topped by an unfinished church.

At Burrow Bridge cross the River Parrett then turn left, unclassified (no sign). In just under ¼ mile keep forward signed Stathe, Langport. At Stathe follow Curry Rivel signs. In ¾ mile turn right to cross a railway bridge. The all-round views take in West Sedge Moor to the right.

In 1 mile the drive makes the sharp ascent of Red Hill (NT) with excellent views once again. *At the top turn right and in ¾ mile turn left, A378, to enter Curry Rivel. A quarter of a mile from the centre turn on to an unclassified road signed Drayton, Muchelney.* (see page 52).

Bear left at the Abbey with the Langport road and in 1 mile at a T-junction turn right. You will pass Huish Episcopi Church, noted for its magnificent 15th-century tower. *Turn right again, A372, signed Wincanton, Yeovil. Half a mile after the village of Long Sutton turn left, B3165, signed Somerton and in 2¼ miles turn right, signed Ilchester to enter Somerton.* Here there is an old market cross (AM) and a 12th- to 15th-century church.

Beyond the main square turn right into New Street, unclassified, signed Ilchester and ¼ mile further turn right again on to the B3151. After 2¾ miles turn right then left to cross the A372.

The main drive continues along the B3151 and in 1½ miles reaches a mini-roundabout at the edge of Ilchester. Here take the 1st exit, signed Yeovilton. Half a mile beyond the entrance to the Royal Naval Air Station is the Fleet Air Arm Museum. *A quarter of a mile beyond the museum turn right on to an unclassified road signed Queen Camel. At Queen Camel keep left to join the A359 before turning right shortly on to an unclassified road signed Sutton Montis. At the end of Sutton Montis village turn right, signed South Cadbury.* The road then rounds Cadbury Castle, believed by some to be Camelot.

Continue through South Cadbury and ½ mile beyond the village cross over the main road, signed North Cadbury, Castle Cary. After ¾ mile pass through the Ham stone village of North Cadbury.

Continue with the Castle Cary road and after ¾ mile turn right, A359. A quarter of a mile beyond Galhampton branch left, B3152, signed Castle Cary. In 1¼ miles enter Castle Cary. This pleasant town has the foundations of a Norman castle and a lock-up built in 1779. *Turn left with the one-way system, then left again signed Bath, Bristol (A371). In ¾ mile turn left, A371, signed Shepton Mallet, then shortly bear right across the railway bridge. In ½ mile, at the Brook House Inn, turn left, unclassified, signed Alhampton. Three quarters of a mile further enter Alhampton and turn right, signed Ditcheat. In 1 mile, on entering Ditcheat, turn left (no sign) at the T-junction, then at the Manor House Inn turn right signed Glastonbury.* The church has an angel roof.

Shortly keep left, signed East Pennard, Glastonbury. At Wraxall turn right, A37, signed Shepton Mallet. At the top of Wraxall Hill (1 in 7) turn left, unclassified, signed East Pennard. After ½ mile turn right, signed Pilton, and in 2½ miles enter Pilton and turn left. The church has a fine screen.

Beyond the church turn left, signed Shepton Mallet, and at a T-junction, turn right, A361, also signed Shepton Mallet. In 1 mile turn left, B3136, to reach Shepton Mallet (see page 60).

Leave the town following signs Wells A371 and continue to Croscombe. As the drive re-enters Wells, there are views of Pen Hill and of the Cathedral.

Wells Cathedral is remarkable for its sculpture

71 MILES TOUR 2

Swordfish bi-plane at the Fleet Air Arm Museum at Yeovilton, one of over 50 historic aircraft shown with models and other records of the Royal Naval Air Service and Fleet Air Arm

TOUR 3
Dorset Coast and Country

67 MILES

This tour takes you over chalk downs to Lulworth Cove and along the Purbeck Hills to Corfe Castle, through some attractive Dorset villages and on to Dorchester. A diversion may be made to the Swannery and Sub-Tropical Gardens at Abbotsbury.

The drive starts at Weymouth, a pleasant seaside town (see page 70).

Follow the Wareham signs to leave by the A353. After skirting the bay the route turns inland through Overcombe and Preston before ascending on to downland. To the left is White Horse Hill (519ft). The mounted figure cut into the chalk commemorates George III.

Shortly, pass the attractive village of Osmington and after 2¾ miles, at the roundabout, take the 3rd exit on to the A352. In another 3¾ miles, at the Red Lion Hotel, turn right, unclassified, signed Lulworth Cove. In Winfrith Newburgh, at the church, turn left and continue through chalk downland.

If you wish, after 2½ miles you can take the toll road on the right to a car park and the footpath to the arch in the rocks known as Durdle Door.

A descent is made into West Lulworth. Turn right, B3070, to visit Lulworth Cove. This round cove is almost land-locked. *Return along the B3070 through West Lulworth. Follow signs Wool, and ascend towards Lulworth Camp.*

From this point a scenic drive is made across the Purbeck Hills to Corfe Castle. This road may be closed by the army if they are using the nearby tank ranges. A large notice board indicates the situation. Alternative routes are available via the B3070 or B3071, thence A352 and Wareham.

Assuming the road is open, turn right with the B3070, signed Wareham, and in 1½ miles at the edge of East Lulworth turn right (unclassified) signed Whiteway Hill. In ¼ mile branch right (no sign), pass through an army barrier, then climb Whiteway Hill. At the summit (625ft) there is a magnificently situated car park with a picnic area and viewpoint.

Almost a mile further turn right on to the Church Knowle/Corfe Castle road. In ¾ mile pass the hamlet of Steeple and then the turning (on the right) to Kimmeridge. Near to this village, which overlooks Kimmeridge Bay, is the Jacobean and later building of Smedmore House. *Continue to Church Knowle, then in 1½ miles turn right on to the A351 and enter the attractive village of Corfe Castle* (see page 41).

Return along the A351 signed Wareham. In 2¾ miles at the roundabout take the third exit, unclassified, for Wareham. Wareham is a town of character with a history stretching back over 2,000 years (see page 66).

Follow signs Dorchester to leave by the A352. In 5 miles turn right, unclassified, signed Bovington Camp. After ½ mile turn left and enter Bovington Camp, home of the Royal Armoured Corps.

After 1¾ miles pass the entrance to Clouds Hill (NT). This cottage was the home of 'Lawrence of Arabia' immediately before his premature death.

At the next T-junction turn left, signed Dorchester, then in ¼ mile turn right, signed Bere Regis. Continue through dense woodland and after ½ mile turn left on to the Briantspuddle road. Pass through Briantspuddle, following the Bere Regis signs. Cross the River Piddle or Trent and in a mile turn left on to the A35, signed Dorchester, to enter Tolpuddle (see page 65). Another 1¼ miles along the A35 is Athelhampton House (see page 77).

Continue through Puddletown. This is the *Wetherby* of Thomas Hardy's novel *Far from the Madding Crowd*. Later descend Yellowham Hill, passing (on the left) the turning to Higher Bockhampton. Here you may see the cottage where Hardy was born. *Continue on the A35 to Dorchester* (see page 43). Dorchester is the county town of Dorset and Hardy's *Casterbridge*.

Follow the Bridport signs out of Dorchester, A35, and in 1 mile turn left, unclassified, signed Martinstown. In another 1½ miles turn right, B3159. Beyond the village of Martinstown turn left, unclassified, signed Portesham, and climb up on to downland. There are good views from the monument to Admiral Hardy, Nelson's flag-captain of 'Kiss me, Hardy' fame.

In ¾ mile, at the crossroads, turn left, then descend and later bear left to enter Portesham. From here a short detour can be made westwards along the B3157 to the beautiful stone-built village of Abbotsbury (see page 28). The two major attractions here are the Sub-Tropical Gardens and the Swannery.

At Portesham the main tour turns left onto the B3157, signed Weymouth. After Chickerell follow Town Centre signs to return to Weymouth.

Abbotsbury Swannery was started by monks in the 14th century

Weymouth: the Jubilee Clock celebrates Queen Victoria's reign

67 MILES # TOUR 3

*Folly on the Dorset Coast Path at Kimmeridge Bay, south of Steeple.
The shale rocks here have been pumped for oil for many years*

*Durdle Door: the sea has eaten away the surrounding rock, but left this fragment of limestone behind.
Man o' War Rocks and the Cow and Calf are similar formations on this coast*

TOUR 4
76 MILES

Cranborne Chase and Salisbury Plain

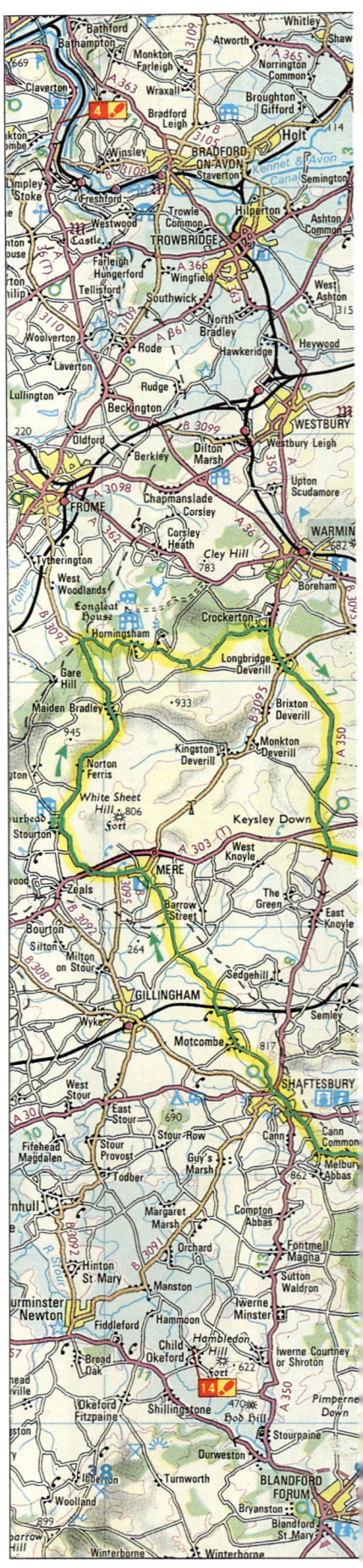

This is a tour which offers plenty of variety and several places to visit. It starts by going through the Ebble Valley villages and across Cranborne Chase to Shaftesbury, and continues via Mere to Stourhead and Longleat. It then crosses part of Salisbury Plain to the thatched villages of the Teffonts before returning via Wilton.

The tour starts from Salisbury (see page 58), one of England's most attractive cathedral cities.

Leave on the A354 following signs to Blandford. After 4 miles turn right in Coombe Bissett on to an unclassified road alongside the River Ebble, signed Bishopstone. Then keep left, signed Broad Chalke, to go through Bishopstone and into Broad Chalke. Broad Chalke is an attractive village with thatched cottages, barns and walls and a big 13th-century church.

At the Queen's Head Inn turn left, signed Bowerchalke, then in nearly ¼ mile, at the church, turn right and follow the road for 2 miles to Bowerchalke. Then follow signs to Sixpenny Handley and at the cross-roads turn right on to the B3081 signed Shaftesbury. Ahead of you is Cranborne Chase, an area of great beauty and rich in flora and fauna.

After 4 miles reach Tollard Royal, lying in a hollow on Cranborne Chase. General Pitt-Rivers, the archaeologist (see page 59) lived near here.

Follow the B3081 across Cranborne Chase and after 4 miles descend the aptly named Zig Zag Hill. After 1 mile, at a T-junction, turn right and in another mile turn left on to the A30, then at the roundabout take the 2nd exit, B3081 signed Town Centre, into Shaftesbury. Shaftesbury (see page 60) is a hilltop town of Saxon origins. Many royal names are linked with its Abbey, including that of King Canute.

From the centre follow signs All Through Traffic and then Gillingham. Shortly, at the T-junction, go left under a road bridge, then right (unclassified), signed Motcombe. In the village bear right, signposted Mere, and then at a T-junction, turn left. After ¾ mile turn left again at crossroads. After 5 miles enter Mere. Mere is a charming small town with some interesting inns and shops.

In Mere turn left on to the B3095 (no sign) and then straight ahead on the B3092, signed Frome. After 2½ miles turn left to Stourton. Here you may visit Stourhead House and its magnificent gardens (NT) (see page 62).

The tour continues on the B3092 to Maiden Bradley. After 2 miles turn right (unclassified), signed Horningsham, Longleat. At Horningsham a detour may be made to Longleat House and Safari Park (see page 48), famous for its lions.

One mile after Horningsham follow sign to Shear Water/Longbridge Deverill and after another 1 mile, at T-junction, turn left, and then take next left again. The road passes close to Shear Water before you reach Crockerton.

At the T-junction turn right, signed Blandford, and at the next T-junction right again, A350. After 1 mile enter Longbridge Deverill. This attractive village has some almshouses and a church with a Norman interior.

Five and a half miles after Longbridge Deverill turn left on to the B3089 signed Salisbury. After another 1½ miles reach Hindon. Follow the B3089 to Fonthill Bishop. Near to this village is the great arched entrance to Fonthill Park, erected in the 17th century. *Continue for 2¼ miles to Chilmark.* This is the home of Chilmark stone, used through the ages in many buildings, notably Salisbury Cathedral.

Follow the B3089 for another 1½ miles to Teffont Magna. Teffont Magna is a peaceful village with thatched cottages and little bridges over the stream. *At the Black Horse Inn, turn right on to an unclassified road, signed Tisbury, and enter Teffont Evias.* Teffont Evias is an equally pretty village, also by a stream, with an impressive church.

Shortly after the church, turn left and left again, signposted Salisbury. After ½ mile, at a T-junction, turn right and rejoin the B3089. After ¾ mile, at a crossroads turn right (unclassified), signed Fovant. On the downs above the village of Fovant are the regimental badges cut into the chalk hillside by World War I soldiers.

In Fovant turn left on to the A30, signed Salisbury and reach Wilton. Once the county town, Wilton is famous for the beautiful stately home, Wilton House, and for the Carpet Factory (see page 72).

At the roundabout at the end of Wilton, take the 3rd exit, A36, to return to Salisbury.

76 MILES **TOUR 4**

Stourbead was inspired by the imaginary landscapes of artists like Claude Lorraine and Nicholas Poussin. Henry Hoare II dammed the Stour, planted trees and built focal points to improve on nature

Salisbury Cathedral spire rises to a height of 404ft

WALK 1
Off The M5

Allow 3 hours

An energetic field and wildflower-wood ramble, over and under the M5, to Cadbury Camp. Parts may be very muddy.

To park, turn up Hill Lane off the B3130 about 3 miles east of Clevedon. At the top turn right. The rough track opens into a car park (ST437722). Start the walk by crossing the footbridge over the motorway. To the right the split-level elevated section begins.

At the end of the bridge turn right down the steep rocky track, which curves left. Continue downhill as a track joins from the left. Turn right on to the road at Norton's Wood and then almost immediately left, down Walton Drove. You are walking across drained peat.

On reaching Walton in Gordano, turn right on to the B3124. After 20 yards turn left on to the signposted public footpath. Go diagonally across the field, over three stiles and right, up through the wood. Snowdrops, violets, bluebells, aconites, anemones and other flowers may be seen here in season.

Eventually steps lead almost to the top of the wood. Keep going straight on up until you come through a clearing. At the cross-roads of paths turn right, continuing up to the top of Hack's Wood. Here the well-trodden path passes through ancient enclosures, burial mounds and hut circles.

Where the clearly-defined path forks, go left and re-enter the wood. Pass the sign 'All dogs must be on leads'. Eventually, at a T-junction of tracks, with several yellow arrows on a post, turn right. Go straight down through the wood, over the stile and left across the field. To the right is the dramatic elevated section of the M5, to the left the wood.

At the hedge, climb over the stile up near the wood to cross the field, keeping the wood to your left. Turn right at the next fence, go down and over a stile. Turn left on to the B3124 and walk with care to Weston in Gordano. The charming church has a rare stone pulpit, rood screen and rough misericords.

Continue east along the B3124 past the White Hart. Turn right down Cadbury Lane leading to Weston Drove and follow it straight to a wooden gate at a bridge at the end. Go over the gate and immediately right alongside the ditch. Go over the next wooden gate, left across the field, and over the stile by the metal gate. Go straight up towards the motorway, through the next gate and on up to the lane almost under the M5. Go left on to the road and then right at Wynhol Farm Kennels. Follow the bridle-path under the M5. Turn right just beyond the tall new house on the right. Follow the path up through the wood and turn right at the T-junction of tracks, on to Cadbury Camp Lane West. A detour can be taken around Cadbury Camp (NT), a 6½-acre hillfort.

The walk continues along Cadbury Camp Lane West for about a mile. Down on the left are the Somerset Levels, now drained, once sea and marsh. *The track goes through woods and finally descends to the car park.*

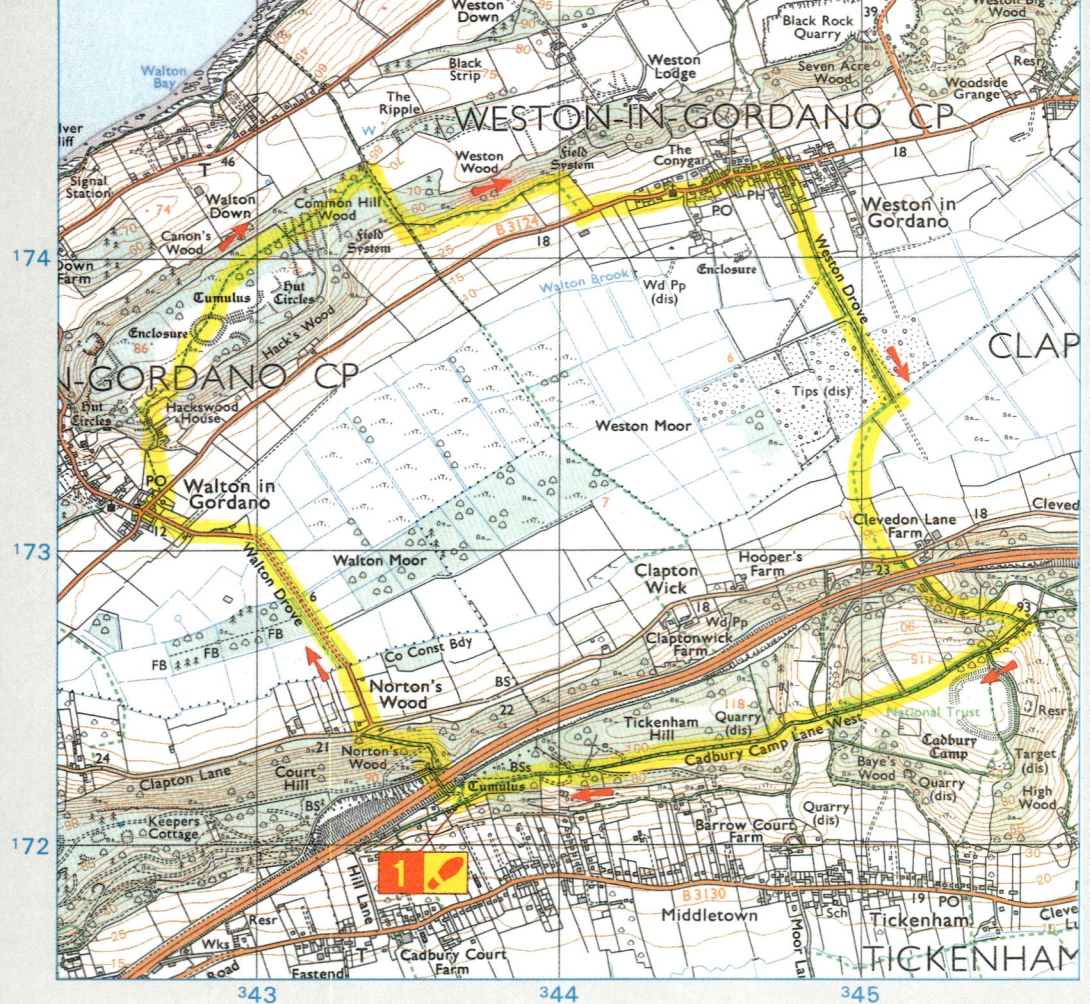

WALK 2

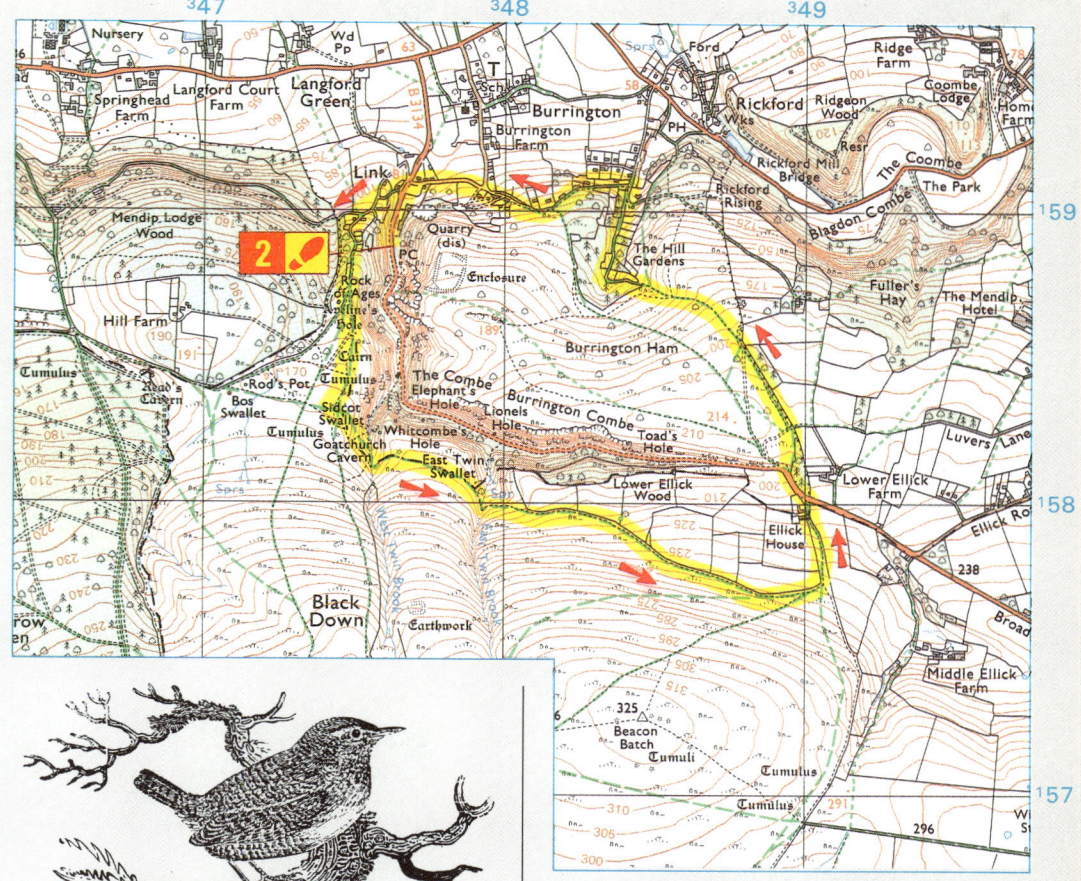

The wren's loud song may be heard in the woods

Mendip Ramble

Allow 2½ hours

An exhilarating, up-and-down ramble on the Mendip Hills, including streams and waterfalls. Care must be taken to follow the directions, as the heathland paths can be confusing. This walk must be tackled only in fine weather. Wear strong walking shoes or boots.

Park off the B3134 in the car park near the public conveniences just south of the Burrington pub (ST477588). Turn right on to the B3134, go past the Burrington pub and the garden centre, then cross with care and turn left up the lane by the postbox. The lane becomes a track. Keep going up, past a house on the right, until you reach a fire risk notice. Turn left on to the track in front of the notice and follow the broad track you see stretching across heathland.

After 200 yards on the bridle-path you come to a cross-roads of tracks. Turn left. Follow this well-trodden path ignoring a right turn after 20 yards and a wider fork to the left. At the next fork, go straight on where one branch of the path swings right uphill and a small path goes left. Follow the well-trodden path, used by horses, down to West Twin Brook. Cross the brook just below a small waterfall, and take the well-trodden path to the left. This takes you up and away from the brook. As you emerge from the valley, you should be able to see the rock face of the cliff above Burrington Combe, running parallel on your left. Artefacts of Early Stone Age people have been found in the cave called Aveline's Hole in the Combe.

The well-trodden path levels out and then goes down the steep-sided valley to East Twin Brook. The course of the stream goes underground at this point, but if you scramble to the right along the streambed, you can catch a glimpse of a waterfall.

Cross the streambed and take the well-trodden path, sharp left, out of the valley. Continue with fields to your left and heathland to your right for about ¾ mile. Eventually your path bends left as other tracks join from the right, and goes down between fields. Pass Ellick House on your left and reach the B3134. Turn left and walk down the B3134. After 40 yards, cross with care to the car park on the right. Take the rightmost broad track up and away from the road.

Go straight on through a gap in trees and on to a track used by cattle. The track veers left in front of a metal gate. Walk along the track with the hedge and then the wood on your right. At the junction of tracks keep going straight, heading downhill and ignoring two right turns. When you come to a distinct fork where both paths wind downhill and into trees, take the right fork and enter a wood.

Follow this track, which eventually bends sharp right round fir trees. Go down past Orchard Cottage on the right, then turn sharp left on the rough-surfaced road by the telegraph pole, with Hill Cottage and other houses on your right, and Burrington Common on the left. The rough road becomes a metal lane. Go straight on when it forks, keeping Burrington church on your right. The lane meets the B3134. Turn left and walk up past the garden centre and pub to your car.

SCALE 1:25 000

WALK 3

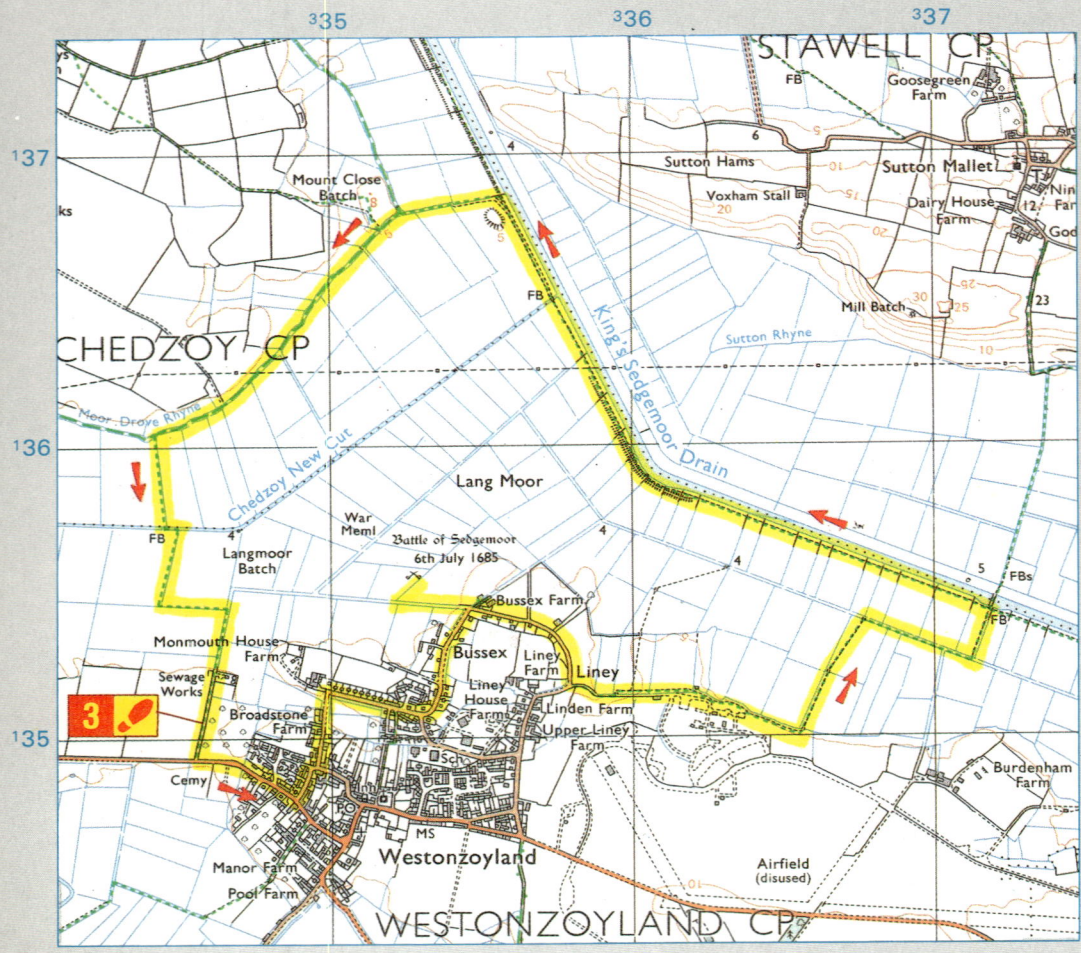

On Sedgemoor

Allow 2½ hours

This is a flat walk over the Somerset Levels, an extraordinary landscape rich in wildlife. The walk includes Sedgemoor Battlefield.

Park 50yds up the track ST346351 leading north from the A372 just west of Westonzoyland. Walk back to the road, turn left and go into Westonzoyland. Westonzoyland has a fine example of a tall, graceful, Somerset church tower.

Turn left down Standards Road and left again into Broadstone. Turn right into Monmouth Road and follow to Bussex Farm. Follow signs to the battlefield. Here hundreds of Monmouth's followers were killed in the rebellion of 1685.

Go back to the road and cross, to go down Liney Road. At a T-junction turn left down the private road (a right of way for pedestrians). Shortly go left across the ditch, through a metal gate, immediately right and walk parallel with the road, through a wooden gate and on beside the ditch. Go right at the next metal gate and back out on to the road. You are now walking through a disused air field.

At a small brick shelter where the road bends right, turn left down the track, keeping the drainage ditch on your left. Wooden tracks preserved in the peat show that people lived successfully in the swampland in prehistoric times. But a widespread drainage system was first dug only in the 13th century. Farmers still work together to adjust the water level so that rivers feed the land with rich silt.

Go through the removable barbed wire fence. Almost immediately go left across the ditch and continue alongside it. At the next hedge go through a metal gate, then left beside a row of trees and another ditch. Go through a metal gate and on until you meet another ditch. Go through a metal gate and right on to a well-used track with a largish drainage channel on your left. Go left over the fourth bridge and continue to King's Sedgemore Drain. In late spring and summer, spectacular dragonflies may be seen around the ditches, as well as butterflies and aquatic plants.

Just before the footbridge turn left and walk with King's Sedgemore Drain on your right, for about 1½ miles. Birdlife is rich: in spring and summer, look for lapwings, redshanks, kestrels and skylarks, with sedge warblers and whinchats in the reeds. There are freshwater mussels, and wildflowers flourish. In winter, green sandpipers may be seen. Wild Bewick's swans come here as do numerous waders, and you may be lucky enough to see short-eared owls or hen harriers.

After about 1¼ miles you go over Chedzoy New Cut. Note the sluice built into the bridge to contain the flow of water.

After the footbridge your track eventually veers left. It soon branches to the right but you continue straight on alongside Moor Drove Rhyne. Pass underneath the power cables, then count the drainage ditches coming in on your left. After the fifth drain go left through a metal gate; shortly there will be a hedge on your right. Cross the footbridge, go left and right along the hedge. At the next fence, turn left through a metal gate. At the main track, go right and back to your car.

WALK 4

Woods and Water

Allow 2 hours

Wandering by the River Avon and climbing steeply to delightful woods, this walk is close to the American Museum at Claverton, near Bath.

Park in the long layby a mile south of Claverton on the A36 (ST783625). At the lower end of the layby turn left. Walk down the track to the wharf by the canal.

Continue past the wharf to go up and across the higher bridge, then double back on the other side to cross the splendid Bath stone Dundas Aqueduct. This is where the Somerset Coal Canal meets the Kennet and Avon.

Turn left down some earth steps into the field just before the canal sweeps around to the right. Walk along the line of the trees and then down to the river.

Carry on walking across the fields. Ahead, up on the right, is Sheephouse Farm. Continue by the river until you meet the broad track leading to the farm. Follow the track. At the fork near the farmhouse bear left towards a step stile. Go into the farmyard and left out on to the road. Go left at the road and walk down. On your left you can see and hear the weir down at the river, and there is a lovely view across the valley to the handsome American Museum, above Claverton.

At a house called Hanover Square, follow the public footpath to the right, going steeply up over a field to Warleigh Wood. Cross the stile by a telegraph pole and continue the hard climb up through the wood. Wildflowers here include wood garlic, primroses, bluebells, aconites and wild strawberries.

Cross a stile and turn right down a well-marked footpath. In 10yds go left and up between two trees on another footpath. Climb for 20yds. The path goes right above the top of the wood, then levels out and follows the contour round the side of the hill. For a while you will walk parallel with a stone wall to your left. This is the Wiltshire/Avon boundary.

When the track forks, go right, down and into the wood on the well-defined path. Eventually you come to the edge of the woods, over a step stile and on to the road. Go left along the road and up through the wood until you come to a T-junction. Turn right, following the sign to Conkwell.

On reaching Conkwell go right, down the very steep hill. Where the road divides go left by Cromwell's Rest Cottage. The path enters a wood of bluebells (in season) and mossy boulders, past a little public footpath notice. When it joins another path at a right angle, you will see a fence directly in front of you. Turn right, and walk downhill keeping the wire fence on your left. Go over a step stile at the bottom of the wood and out into a field. The metal fence is still on your left. Eventually you pass through some beech trees and then over a step stile to get back to the Dundas Aqueduct. Cross the aqueduct and the bridge over the canal to re-trace your steps to the car.

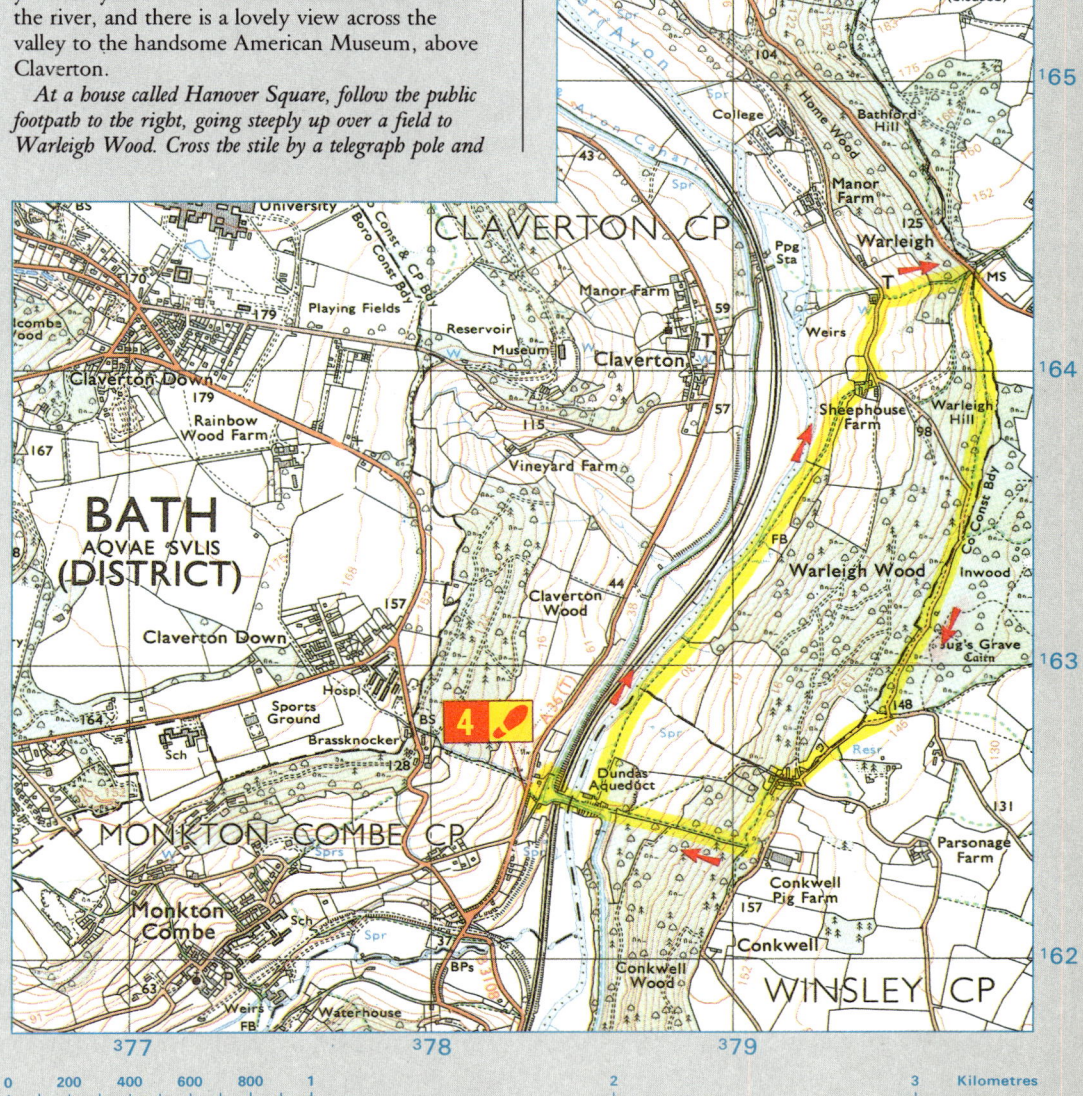

WALK 5
Downside Abbey

Allow 2½ hours

Downside Abbey is the target of this rural ramble. Short sections may be very overgrown and muddy. Please take care with children: this walk crosses a main road.

Park in the long layby on the B3139 by the 'Chilcompton' sign, approaching from the north (ST655519). Walk up the track from the layby towards Tyning House. Near the house go through a metal gate leading left into the field and follow the wall round to the right. Go over the stile and straight across the next field to another stile. Walk along the edge of the next field with the hedge to your left. Go carefully out on to the A367, cross and turn right. After 20yds go left down Manor Farm drive. Go round to the right of the green and swing right to go behind the imposing farmhouse. Left is a bell tower folly, behind the house an outhouse with Corinthian columns.

Go over the stile into the field, and walk down with the hedge on your left. At the end of the garden go left through a kissing gate, down through the avenue of handsome trees and over another stile. Go immediately left over another stile and walk with the hedge on your left along the top of the field, then go down, over the stile at the bottom of the field, and across the footbridge. This part may be muddy.

Walk up the field edge keeping the woods to your left. Shortly go over the stile on your left, into the wood. There is no obvious path through the wood, but bear right round the hill for a few yards into a clearing. Go down to the footbridge at the bottom of the clearing. This section may be overgrown with brambles.

Take the path up out of the hollow. If you detour right you will see a lake through the rhododendrons.

Follow the path out of the wood and go diagonally right to the top of the field. Cross the stile and walk with the wood on your right. Where the wood finishes, go across the fence and straight across the field to a gate. (A detour can be made left on the woodland path, down and up to Holcombe's pretty church.) Downside Abbey is ahead to your right.

Continue along the track to the road. Go left for 30yds to an iron gate on your right. You will once again see the tower of Downside Abbey. The right of way follows this line through two fields. Go across the first field (or around it, if sown) to the overgrown gate in the far right corner. Go over the gate and straight on with the hedge on your right to a farmyard. Walk to the right of the barns on to the road. Turn right at the King's Arms on to the main road. This is Stratton-on-the-Fosse, straddling the Foss Way Roman Road (here the A367).

Walk past the entrance to Downside Abbey School on your left and the war memorial on your right. Turn left up Abbey Road to visit Downside Abbey Church. Originally from Flanders, the Benedictine monks of Downside (both monastery and school) came here early in the 19th century. The magnificent Abbey Church is by Sir Giles Gilbert Scott.

Walk back towards Abbey Road but hairpin left on to the right of way. Walk up the field and on to the metalled path which goes back to Chilcompton through three kissing gates. Turn right on to the main road through the village. It is about ¾ mile to your car.

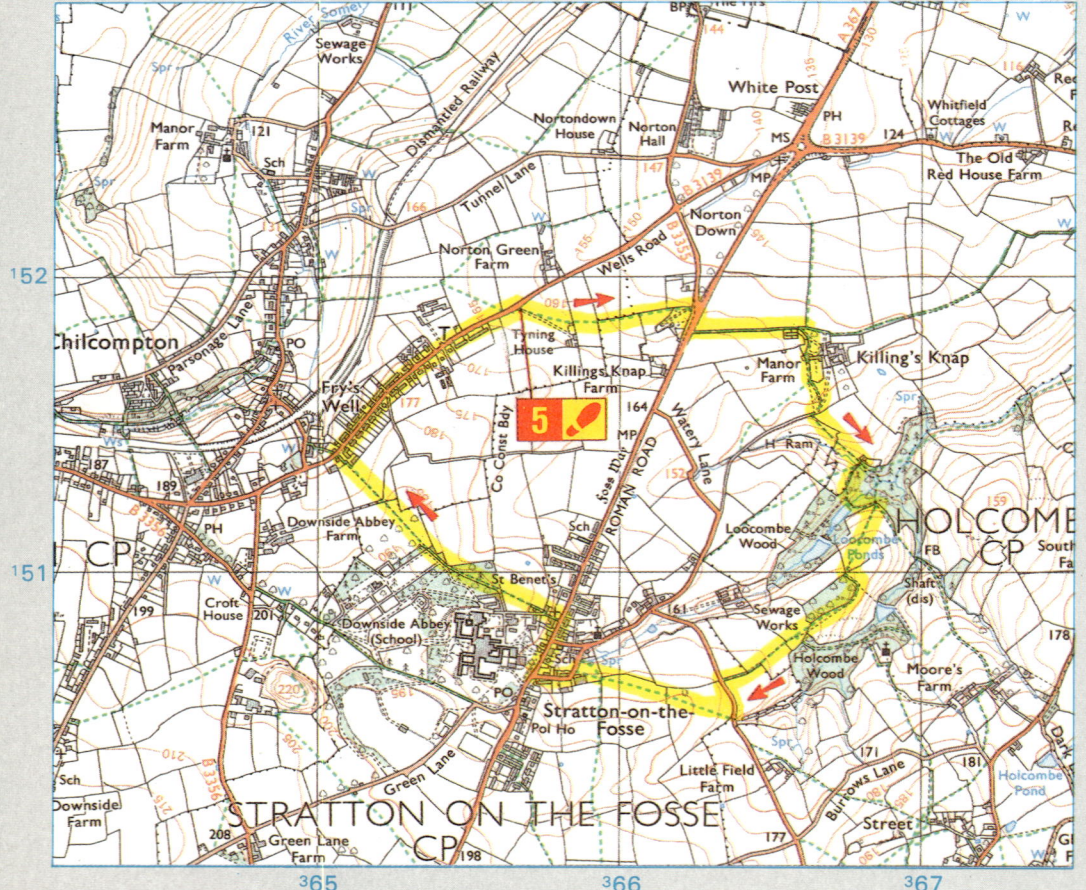

WALK 6

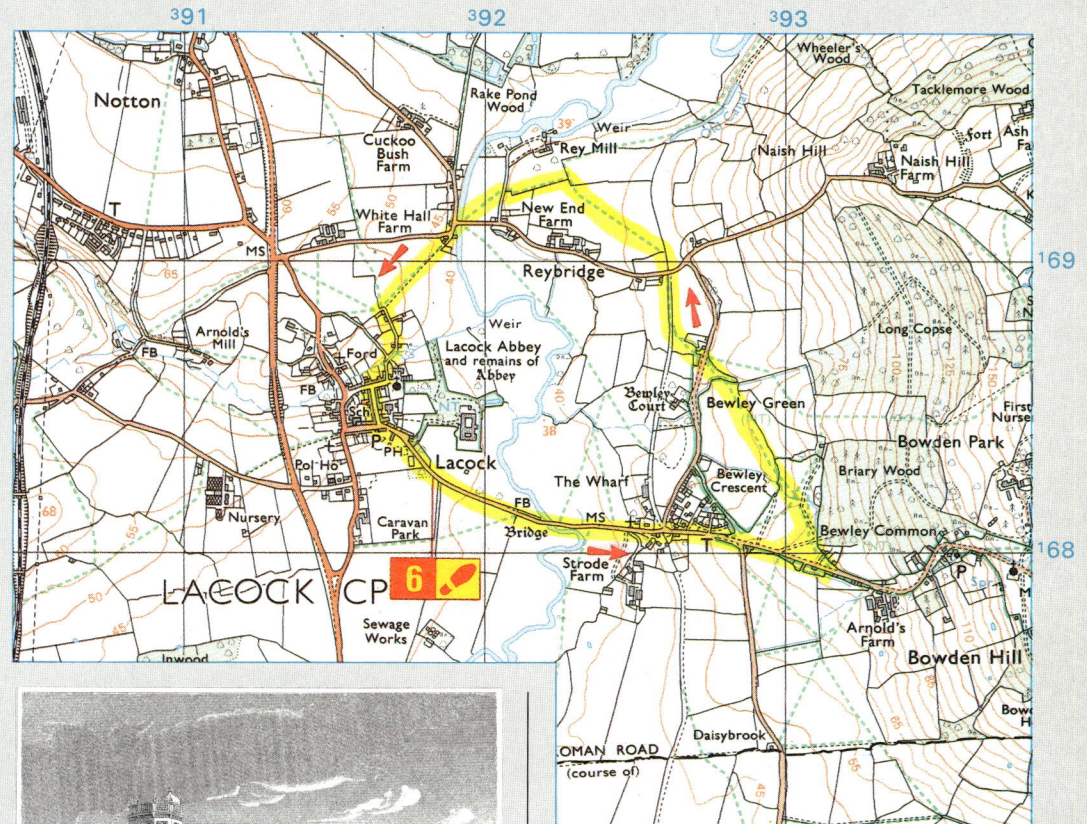

Lacock Abbey, Fox Talbot's home

Fox Talbot Territory

Allow 2 hours

A pleasant walk that begins and ends in one of the most beautiful villages in England. Sections may be very overgrown.

Park your car in the car park for Lacock Abbey (NT) (ST918683). Turn right out of the car park and right again towards the countryside with Lacock Abbey on your left. An unusual feature along this road is the elevated floodwalk.

Leave the floodwalk, cross the River Avon and walk on with care into The Wharf. A canal once ran here and there was indeed a wharf.

Walk on up through Bewley Crescent, past the Bell Inn towards Bowden Hill. Just past the NT 'Bewley Common' signpost, turn left along the track towards the gates of Bowden Park. At the gates turn left down the well-defined track. Very soon, once you have crossed the streambed go left off the track towards a house, keeping with the streambed. The footpath soon goes right alongside the hedge and you head towards the cable pole. Just before the pole go left and over a step stile, then right and along the edge of the field as it curves to the left.

Go over a step stile on the right and over a ditch. Keep the hedge to your right and walk to the road. Go past another National Trust 'Bewley Common' sign, straight across the road with the houses on your right and through a gate into a field. You may have to unhitch and replace a removable barbed wire fence to get into the field. Walk diagonally right across this field. Reybridge is clearly visible straight ahead.

When you reach the hedge turn right and walk alongside it to the road. To your right Bowden Park stands impressively on the hill.

Go across the road through a metal gate immediately opposite and continue on the left-hand side of the field. Halfway through the field there is a metal gate: go through this and head for two tall poplars in the distance. At the corner of the field, go through a gap in the fence and then through a green squeeze-belly stile on to a well-kept footpath which brings you out on to a metalled lane. As you walk along the footpath, notice the handsome Rey Mill House on the right.

Go straight across the road into the field and head diagonally left for the bridge. Go over the stile at the corner of the field and on to the road, turning right. Go over the bridge and left in front of some lovely thatched cottages. Go straight and off the road in between two houses on to a tarmac footpath. This takes you across the fields. When you reach the road cross and go immediately left down the lane and into the village of Lacock (NT). The village has many beautiful 18th-century buildings. Look for the magnificent 14th-century tithe barn and the Blind House, or gaol. St Cyriac's Church has a fine wagon roof.

From the centre of the village, make your way back to Lacock Abbey. Shortly after the Dissolution, this Augustinian nunnery came into the hands of the Talbot family, and it was here that W H Fox Talbot, pioneer of photography, worked.

Return to the car park.

SCALE 1:25 000

WALK 7

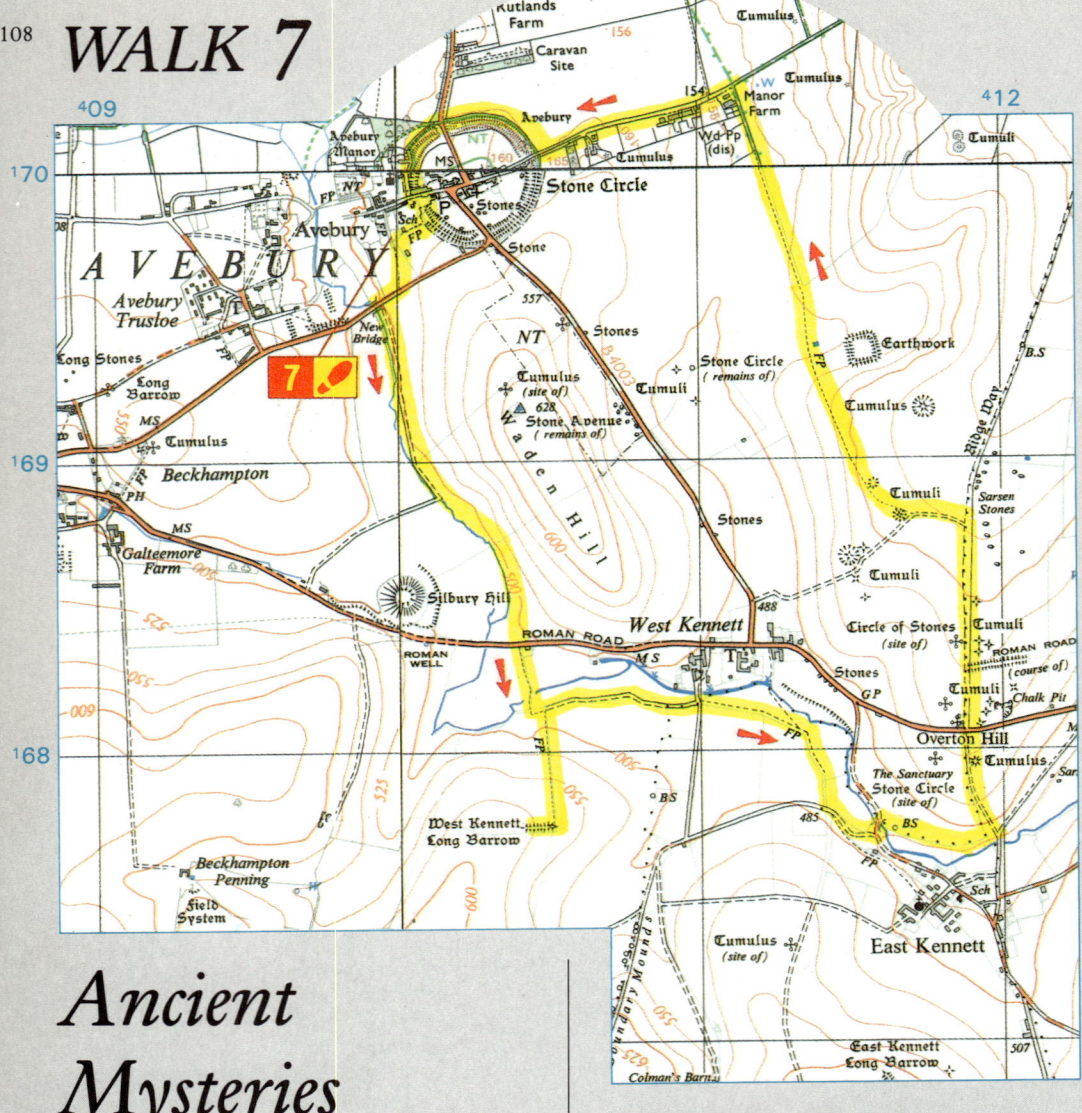

Ancient Mysteries

Allow 3½ hours, or more with visits to monuments

Some of Britain's finest ancient sites can be seen along this long walk, including mysterious Silbury Hill, a stone avenue and the remarkable stone circles of Avebury. Please take care with children: the route crosses the busy A4.

Park in the well-signed, free car park at Avebury (SU100697). Walk back to the road and turn right, then follow the sign to West Kennett Long Barrow, turning left off the road on to the bridle-way, with the stream on your right. Ahead is Silbury Hill, Europe's largest artificial prehistoric mound, probably created between 2500 and 2000BC. The great ditch surrounding it is flooded in winter, like a moat.

Go straight on, following the sign to West Kennett Long Barrow. Cross the A4 with care, and go left. After 20yds, turn right on the path signed to the barrow. After a bend left, a right turn can be taken up to the barrow. One of the largest in Britain, it can be entered. Its chambers held some 50 burials, probably made at intervals from 3500 to 2500BC.

Return to the original path and continue east over stiles. Cross the stile by a gate and go straight on to a metal road. Go straight over and cross a stile. Cross the field with the fence close to your right. Go through the gate and follow the path, veering rightwards to another stile. Cross this and the stile in the far right corner of the next field. Go left, as shown by the yellow arrow on the stile, and go down the track to the road by the pumping station. Turn left over the bridge and immediately right along the bridle-path round the bottom of the field. Go through the metal gate and turn immediately left. Walk up the hill by a line of trees, to a burial mound and the A4. Look left to see a plan of the Sanctuary, site of two vanished stone circles. The positions of the stones are marked.

Cross the A4 with great care and continue up the hill on the Ridge Way footpath. This long distance footpath is based on a route used in the Bronze Age and perhaps earlier.

Continue for nearly half a mile. Before the top, take the track to the left, to the right of a burial mound. Follow this track across four large fields for about a mile, going through a metal gate and straight on. On the left is the Avenue, a prehistoric double row of sarsen stones which once linked Avebury and the Sanctuary. Sarsens are surface boulders of sandstone, and did not need to be quarried.

Keep the fence of the fourth field close to your right, and emerge on to a track. At the T-junction, turn left, following the sign to Avebury. Go up the metal road to Avebury Ring. This magnificent embankment and ring of sarsen stones goes round the village. Within were two lesser circles. It dates from about 2600BC and the main road through Avebury (A361) may be of the same age.

Turn right on to the path round the Ring. When it stops before the road, go left to the gate, over the road and rejoin the path. Follow the line of stones round to the left. Go down the steps and turn left. Cross the road and go straight on, along the path signed to the car park.

WALK 8

Chalk Downs

Allow 3½ hours

A long walk with steep climbs, rewarded by fine views from the top of the Pewsey Downs, rich in wildflowers. Sights include an ancient earthwork and a white horse cut in the chalk.

Follow the sign 'Stanton St Bernard only' off the minor road between Alton Barnes and Devizes, and park immediately in the layby (SY094626). Go back to the Devizes road, turn right and walk to Alton Barnes. Left is the White Horse on Walker's Hill, cut in 1812 and said to be visible from Salisbury Cathedral spire.

At the junction, turn right into Alton Barnes, then go left, signed 'St Mary's Saxon Church'. After 200yds go through a turnstile on your left and diagonally across the field. The tiny church has typically Saxon long and short corner-stones and a narrow nave.

Over two footbridges and through two more turnstiles, pass Alton Priors Church. Old and simple, standing in a field, it is no longer regularly used.

Go straight on. From the field continue through another stile on the road through Alton Priors to the main road. Note the thatched barn on your left.

Go left and then immediately right following the yellow arrow. Follow the green track up the hill. At the top turn right on to the road then left into the Pewsey Downs National Nature Reserve. This is one of Britain's best chalk downlands for wildflowers. Species include chalk milkwort, horseshoe vetch, various orchids, devil's-bit scabious and early gentian. Butterflies abound, including chalkhill and common blue and Duke of Burgundy. Look back for fine views of the Vale of Pewsey.

Follow the Ridge Way path upwards, skirting Walker's Hill. When you come back to the road, go right over a stile on to the road and go on up the hill to a stile by a metal gate. Go through the stile and follow the fence, past a group of trees on your right. Close to the trees is a dewpond. In the days before water could be piped to outlying areas, dewponds were essential watering holes for sheep. The porous chalk in a natural hollow was rammed until it became watertight and filled with rain water.

Carry on up the hill, going through two metal gates, to the earthwork of Wansdyke on the brow of the hill. Wansdyke is a great earthen defence, still several miles long. Originally pallisaded, it was probably constructed by Romanised Britons in the mid-6th century to hold back the Saxons. The wide view below includes Silbury Hill and Avebury.

Immediately after Wansdyke turn left over a stile and continue in the lee of the earthworks. Go over another stile and on for about 200yds. Look out for a break in the Wansdyke bank with a fence on the other side. Climb up to this break and emerge on to a track. A small sign indicates the Tan Hill Way. *Go straight across the track and over the stile next to a yellow arrow. Go south with the fence on your left. Cross another stile, marked with a yellow arrow, and follow the track to the left and on round to the right.* The ancient earthwork on the opposite hill is Rybury Camp.

An enclosure is passed on the left. Go through the next metal gate and turn right. Walk down Milk Hill following the fence (on your right) round and down. At the bottom turn left around the base of the hill. Go over a stile and down across a field towards an old barn. Go straight on when a track crosses your path near the barn. At the road go right and then left to your car.

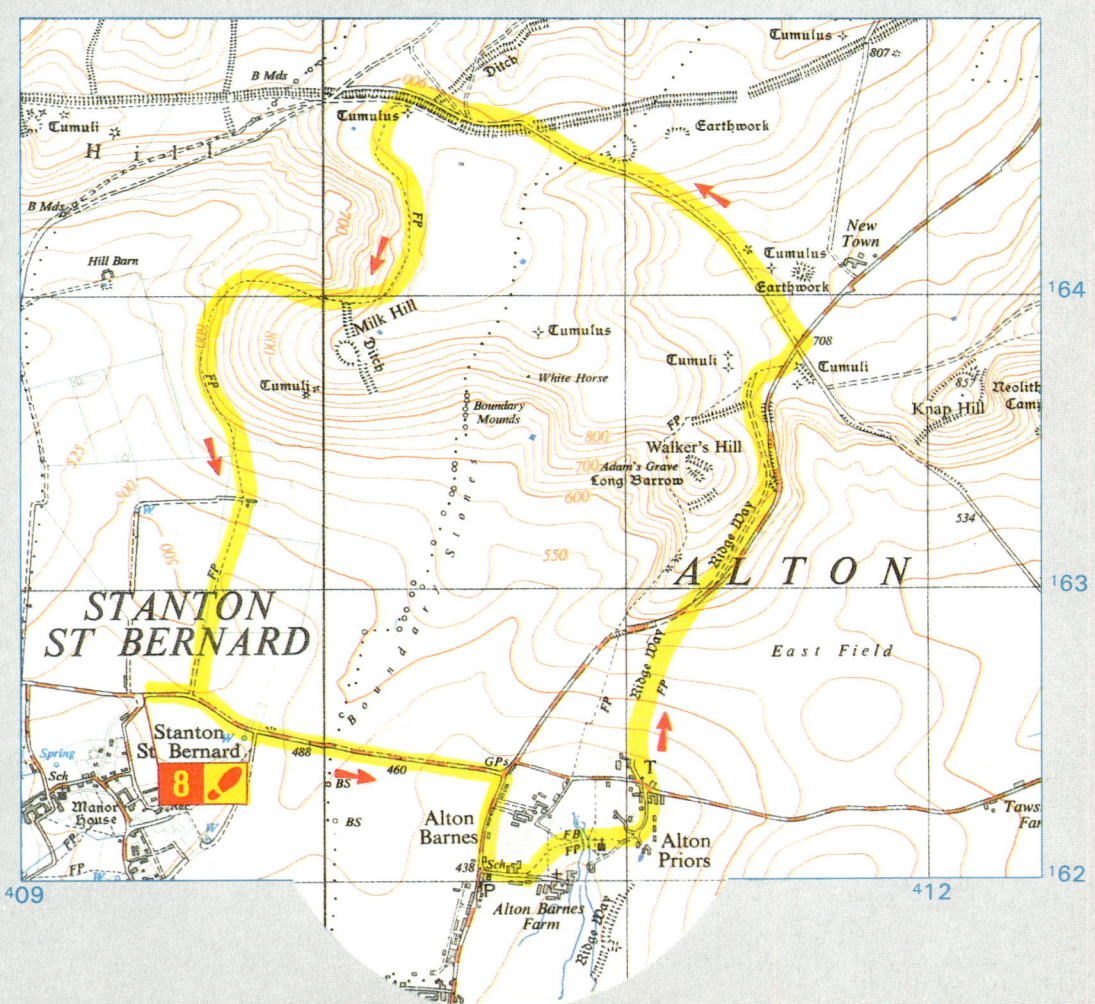

WALK 9

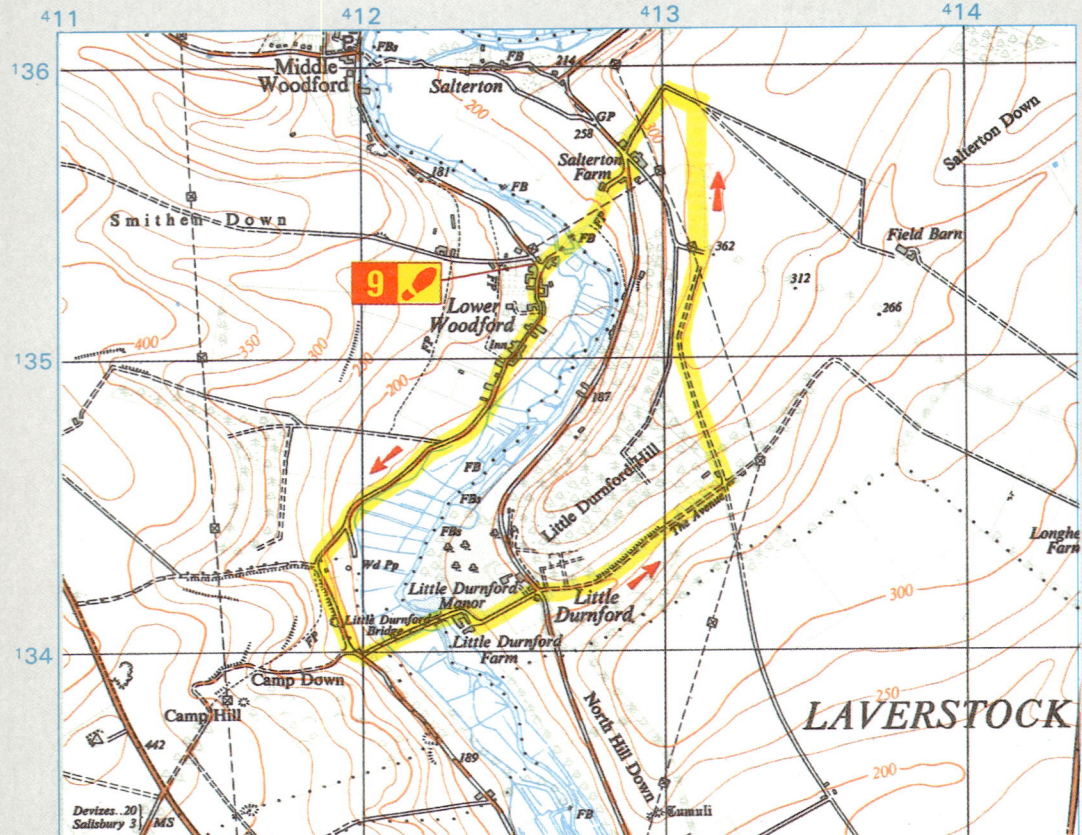

Water Meadows

Allow 1¾ hours

An easy walk past the water meadows and trout-rich waters of the River Avon, with a gentle climb up Little Durnford Hill. Military aircraft will probably be seen, and a variety of other planes from Old Sarum Airfield, home of the Optica spotter plane.

The trout, lover of chalk streams

Park at the north end or centre of Lower Woodford, off the road (SU126353). Walk south through Lower Woodford keeping to the road and up the hill to the road junction. Little Durnford Manor and Farm is on the left. Go left down the private road and through the well-maintained estate. The walk takes you alongside and across some beautiful water meadows, once important to Wessex chalkland sheep farming. These are particularly fine examples. They were made because, until recent times, March and April were difficult months to ensure that sheep had enough feed. The solution was the creation of a system of trenches and drains, leading off and eventually back into a main river. Controlled flooding protected grass from frost early in the year, without the meadows becoming swamps. The person who harnessed the water was called a 'drowner' and this was a skilled occupation.

Hatches or sluices were used to control the flow of water and examples can be seen at Lower Woodford and many other places around Salisbury, where the five rivers of South Wiltshire were extensively used to irrigate water meadows.

Your route finally emerges through a door in the wall on to the road. Go straight over the road and up the lane by the wood (marked as The Avenue on the map). Go left at the crossroads at the top by an attractive thatched cottage. The road becomes a track. Go straight up over the ridge to the end of the track. Large flints are plentiful on the ground here, and flintwork is a characteristic of local houses. There are good views north to Salisbury Plain and south to Old Sarum and Salisbury Cathedral spire.

The footpath continues through a copse (the footpath is indicated on a post by a disc). Go through the gate at the opposite edge of the copse and walk across the edge of the field keeping the fence close by your left. At the end of the field there is a barbed wire gate which can be opened, and closed again, by a wire loop around the post. Turn left and proceed down the track through the farmyard and on to the road.

Turn left and almost immediately right down a lane marked with a dead-end sign. The lane develops into a footpath which goes over two footbridges. Anglers fly-fishing for trout may be seen as well as swans, water voles and coots.

The path comes back on to the road in Lower Woodford, where you left your car.

WALK 10

Hilltop Views

Allow 3 hours

The walk is an uphill one for much of the way, but you will be rewarded with some magnificent views. A wildflower guide would be useful. The path may be muddy in places. Please take care with children: the route crosses a main road.

Park near the New Inn, Stoke Abbott (ST453008). The footpath is directly opposite the inn. Start walking up the gentle slope, and keep going up the hill with the path curving to the left. The path has been worn down through use into a 'hollow way'.

Go through the gate at the top of the path. Walk diagonally left up across the field, towards the telegraph poles. Above on the right are the ramparts of Waddon Hill Roman Fort, built during the invasion of AD43. It still stands out on the skyline despite various quarrying operations and excavations over the last 150 years.

At the top of the field, go through the metal gate between telegraph poles and turn right to climb along a high-banked lane. Pass Stoke Knapp Cottage on the left and reach the main road. Cross the road immediately, with care, and take the track next to the metal gate. After 25yds the track swings right, up to Lewesdon Hill. Before the track swings right, pause for the view on your left which includes lynchets – terraces formed by ancient ploughing.

Go straight on when a track cuts across yours diagonally. Your track may be muddy in wet weather. It enters Lewesdon Wood through an avenue of tall beech trees. A boundary stone (BS on the map) can be seen almost opposite a National Trust notice.

Carry on along the track skirting the wood. There are splendid views to the right, towards Broadwindsor. At the second NT signpost turn left into the wood. The track sweeps up, going left to the top of the hill, 890ft (297m) above sea level. In the winter the floor of the wood is carpeted in russet beech leaves. You should find the long climb worthwhile, with beautiful views to the Dorset coast. The flat top of Golden Cap is prominent, and to the east are Doghouse Hill and Thorncombe Beacon.

Continue on the path to go down out of the wood on the steep footpath leading due south. On reaching the concrete road, turn left and go on down the hill. It goes over a cattle grid and joins the main road at Buck's Head. Cross with care and turn right to walk along the verge. After 200yds, at the brow of the hill, turn left following the sign to Stoke Abbott. Keep on the road all the way back to Stoke Abbott, and walk back through the village to your car. Stoke Abbott is a village of lichen-mottled, golden stoned houses with mullioned windows. St Mary's Church has a Jacobean pulpit and a Norman font, carved with brightly expressive faces, thought perhaps to be Noah and his family. There is also a pretty well.

Primroses may be seen on this walk in spring

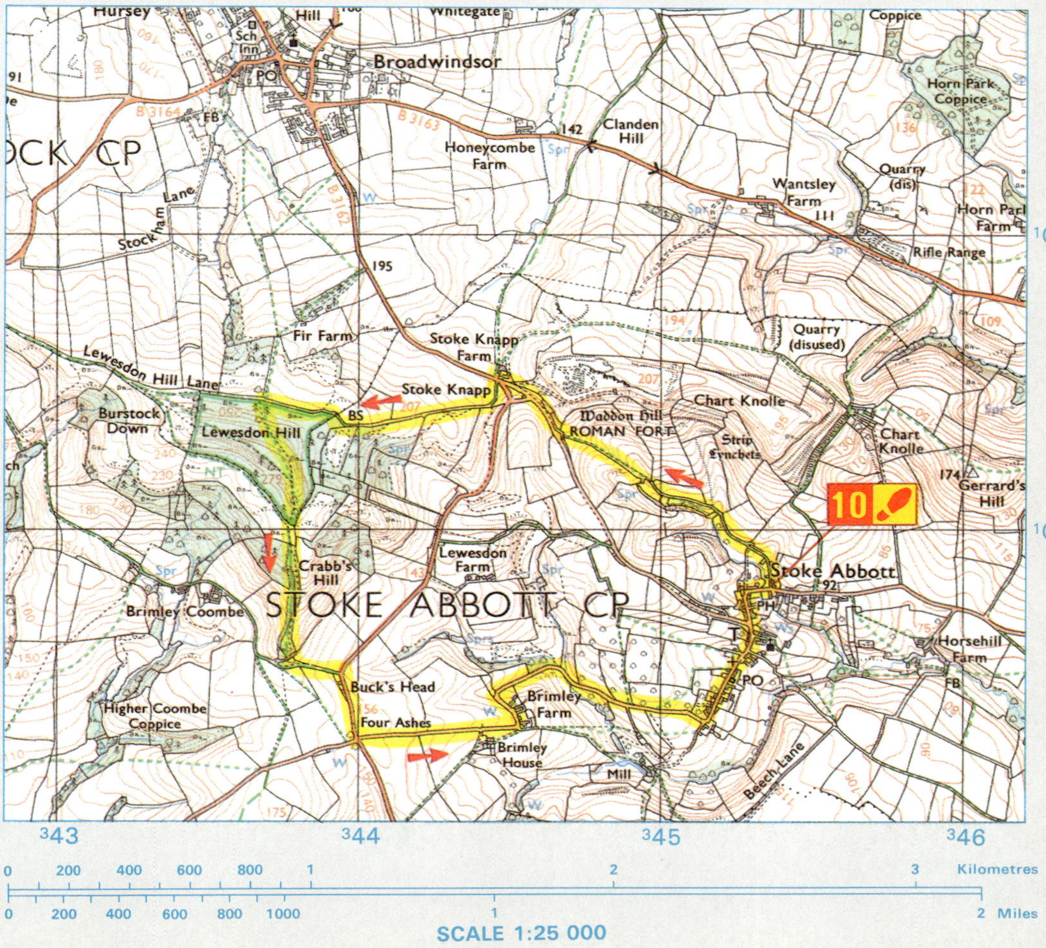

SCALE 1:25 000

WALK 11

A Cliff Walk

Allow 3 hours

On a clear day this walk offers spectacular cliff-top views from the Dorset Coast Path between Eype Mouth and Thorncombe Beacon. Take care: the walk goes close to the cliff-edge.

Park in the car park at Eype Mouth (SY448911). Follow the coastal path sign out of the car park heading west with the sea on your left, and climb over the NT stile marked 'Down House Farm'. The well-trodden path rises sharply and for the first ¾ mile keeps fairly close to the cliff-edge. Care should be taken here. The climb begins to level off. The top of Thorncombe Beacon can now be seen ahead with Eype Down and Down House Farm visible to the right.

Cross over a second stile and either continue on along the very steep but more direct route to the Beacon or follow the gentler gradient which curves inland to the right of the coastal path. The coastal route is not for the unfit. The inland route circles the rim of a huge amphitheatre-shaped hollow, over 200ft deep. Near the bottom of this hollow there is a spring which may well have provided water for the prehistoric tribesmen who once lived on these uplands. In late spring the hollow is carpeted in bluebells and red campion.

Having reached the summit by either route, admire the magnificent views to the east and west before beginning the approach to the summit of Eype Down. Head inland towards an ancient British burial mound (those who took the gentler route to the Beacon will already have gone up this path) and pass the tumulus on your left. After crossing another stile into a field (signposted Eype Down), continue alongside a hedge towards a small wood. The village of Chideock can be seen nestling down in the valley to your left.

At the end of this field, cross another stile on to Eype Common. At the summit admire the downland of west Dorset – the Vale of Marshwood lies between Quarr Hill and the smaller Colmers' Hill.

Follow the narrow path down through gorse and bracken to a wide, open, grassed plateau. Follow the sign to Eype again through gorse and out into another grassed opening. Here turn sharp left and continue for about 50yds. Follow the well-defined path down towards a road and house at the bottom of the hill. Veer right – but instead of taking up the right turn into the road continue along a path parallel with the lane but at a higher level. This path eventually rejoins the lane at 'Howe's Eype'. Turn right. Look out for the many wildflowers that grow in the banks.

Walk along the lane for 300–400yds before you can rejoin the footpath. Continue west up the lane past the first turn on the right, signed 'Down House Lane'. Take the next turn on the right (a driveway into two cottages) and enter the field on the left from the stile. Cross this field heading towards the church and transmitter. Pass through a stile shaped like a doorframe, and follow the hedge on your right towards the church. At the end of this field the path dips down to a half-hidden gate and on to the Eype road. Beware on the road.

Turn right into the lane and immediately after the church drive, cross a stile on the left-hand side, back on to the path. Turn right and go down towards the sea. The footpath finishes near the end of the second field; turn right out of the field at the cottages and left into the lane to return to the car park.

WALK 12

Woodlanders Way

Allow 2½–3 hours

A long but easy walk through woods, fields and parkland between Evershot and Melbury Osmond – scenery evocatively described by Thomas Hardy in *The Woodlanders*.

Park near the bottom of the hill in Evershot (ST575046). Evershot is the second highest village in Dorset at 700ft above sea level. The spring at St John's Well is thought to be the source of the Dorset Frome, which meets the sea at Poole. Evershot is Hardy's *Evershead*. There is a cottage near the church, to the right of the road, where Tess stops for breakfast in *Tess of the d'Urbervilles*.

Walk downhill past Back Lane and go left at the fork, following the public footpath sign on the left. Go right at the next fork and walk up the hill. Running between huge old trees, this old lane has been worn down into a 'hollow way', lined with wildflowers.

At the top of the hill the path enters a wood, passing a water tower on the left. Continue straight down. At the bottom of the hill take the left fork. On the right is the kind of mixed deciduous wood Giles Winterbourne in Hardy's *The Woodlanders* might have known; on the left a plantation.

Walk on past Lake Lucerne, visible through trees on the right. At the far end is a thatched boathouse.

Go through a wooden gate and turn right off the main track, then follow your track north through wooden gates and over the stream. Go straight on, following the public footpath notice. Walk up across the field through the metal gate and continue along the ridge of the field, passing splendid old trees. Turn left on to the metal drive, and just before the house (Chetnole Lodge) turn right. The stream is on your left. Go over a wooden stile and up the field, keeping the woods near to you on the left. Take the bridge left across the stream, go through the gate and go right and through two wooden gates on to a concrete road, leaving the farm on your left. When you come to the minor road turn left into Melbury Osmond. Melbury Osmond is a delightful place of thatched cottages, deep lanes and well-tended gardens. It was the home of Thomas Hardy's maternal ancestors and the *King's Hintock* of his novels.

Turn left to go through the churchyard of St Osmond's Church. On the north side of the church is the thatched cottage where Hardy's mother lived. Hardy's parents were married in the church, which has an unusual bell-ringing chamber above the main entrance.

Turn left out of the churchyard, going south and down through the village and across the water, coming eventually to the gates into Melbury Park. Go through the gates and follow the road to Melbury House. Melbury Park has a 16th-century manor house (not open) and the tiny 500-year-old church of Melbury Sampford. On your walk through the impeccable park you are almost certain to see a herd of deer. Beyond the park, on your left, are the woods where Hardy's Giles Winterbourne makes his home.

At the house follow the public footpath sign round to the right, keeping on the road which swings round and up and leads eventually to the bottom of the hill in Evershot, and your car.

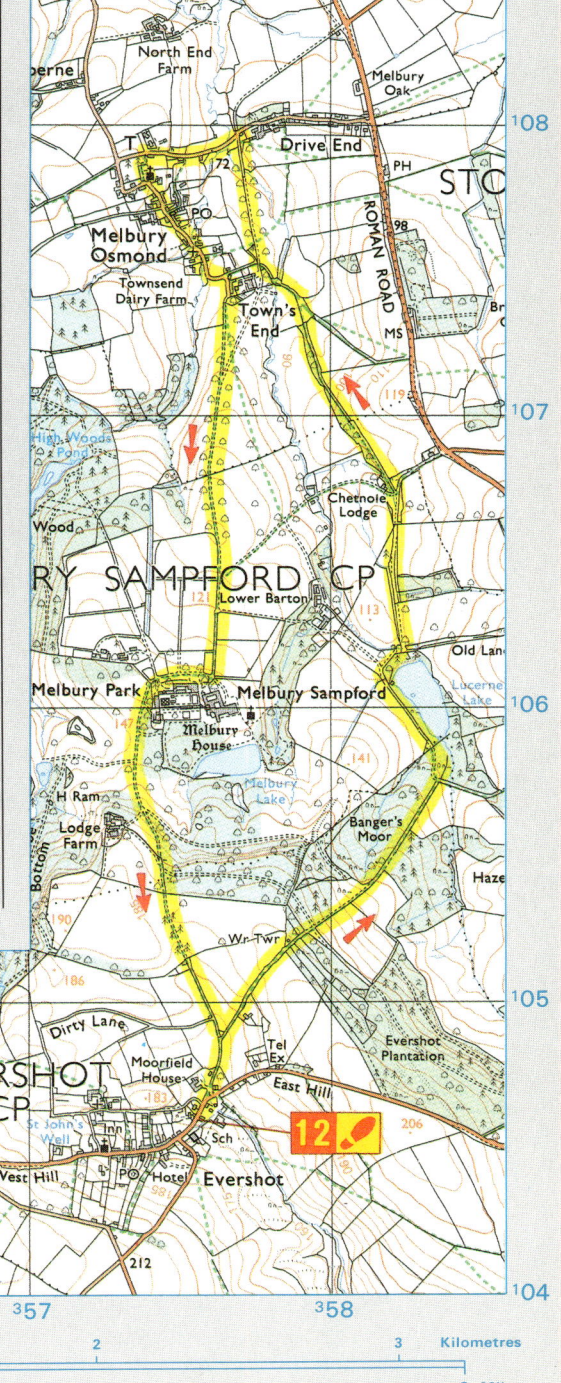

WALK 13
Two Poets

Allow 2½ hours

The homes of Dorset's most famous poets are passed on this walk through lush water meadows, Hardy's 'Valley of the Great Dairies'. Take care: the walk includes a main road.

Park off the road in front of Stinsford Church (SY711910). Stinsford is Hardy's *Mellstock*. His grandfather, father and uncle were all in the church choir, and Hardy's heart is buried here.

With the church on your right, walk down the lane. At the T-junction of paths, go left and cross the bridge. Turn immediately right to join another footpath, with the water on your right. Cross a small bridge. A drainage ditch appears, with the remains of brick arches and machinery. The regulated flooding of water meadows protected them from frost in early spring, so ensuring feed for livestock. This is described in *Tess of the d'Urbervilles*.

The path takes you over a stile and on to a track which bears left. Follow the track, going left over a red-brick bridge crossing the Frome main stream. When the track meets a minor road, turn right then first left (Eddison Avenue). Go straight on, taking the footpath ahead which leads on to a railway bridge. The footpath brings you on to the main road. Cross with care and turn left to walk along the road. On the left is Max Gate (NT but not open), designed by Thomas Hardy and his home for over 40 years.

Turn right on to the signposted path leading down and up the hill to a wood. Go through the wood and down a gradual slope with fine views to Came House. Cross the road at the bottom and follow the path to the right to visit Winterbourne Came and its church. William Barnes, the Dorset dialect poet, was rector of St Peter's Chuch and is buried in the churchyard. The 13th-century church, hidden in a small wood, lies in the peaceful park of 18th-century Came House (open by appointment).

Return to the road and turn right. This takes you out of the park to the main road (A352). Turn right along the A352 and walk with great care for about 250yds to a bridleway on the left, signposted to West Stafford. Follow this through lush fields watered by the South Winterborne, with hedges at first on the left, then on the right, and enter West Stafford under a railway bridge. Follow the track, which becomes a metalled road leading to the main road in front of the church. The small, pretty church was probably the scene of Tess's marriage to Angel Clare in Hardy's *Tess of the d'Urbervilles*.

Turn left on to the road, unless visiting the church. As you leave the village, handsome Stafford House on your right is part 17th-, part 19th-century.

At the T-junction, turn right and go over the bridge. The lane goes over several small bridges. Just before the bridge after the Lower Bockhampton sign, turn left along a well-defined footpath by the water. This pleasant causeway borders the water meadows and passes below 18th-century Kingston Maurward House, now the Dorset College of Agriculture.

After about ½ mile follow the main path as it swings right, back to the starting point.

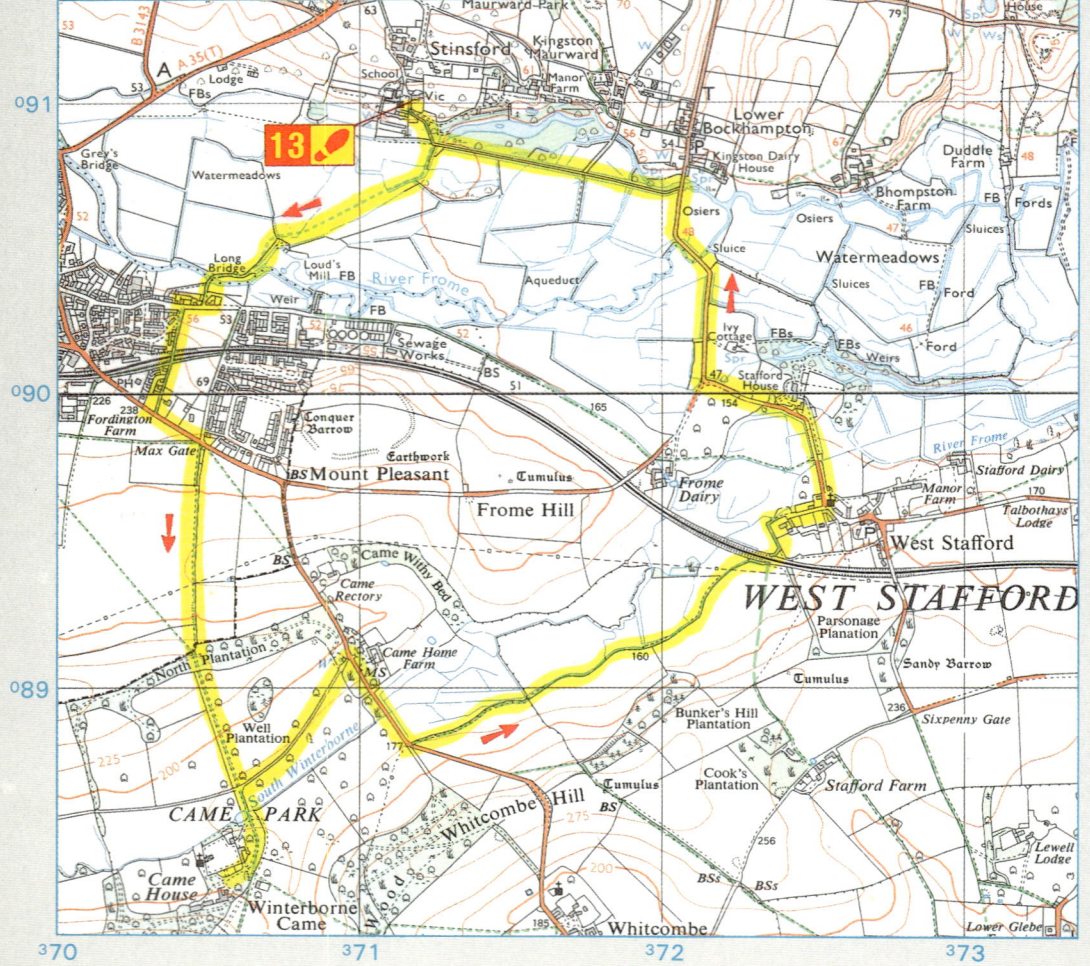

WALK 14

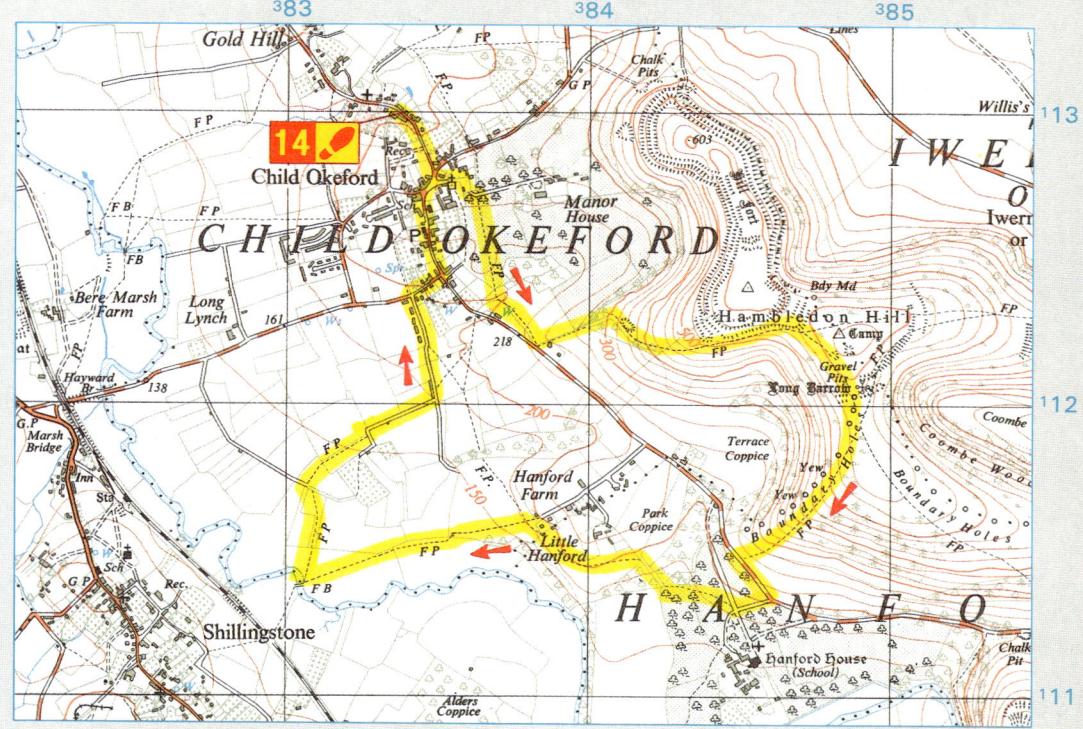

Hambledon Hill

Allow 3 hours

A magnificent Iron Age hillfort is the literal high point of the walk, parts of which are steep and strenuous. Some parts of the walk may be muddy.

Park near the village hall at Child Okeford (ST834130), which is on the main road at the north end of the village, going towards Manston. Walk back towards the village up the road, and turn left at the war memorial, to the Church of St Nicholas. The church dates back to 1250, and has lovely stained glass and an old Bible.

Continue out through the back gate of the church on to a gravel road. Cross a stile over a fence to the right, into a field. Go straight across the field, over another stile, and slightly left across the next meadow to a gate and stile. Keep the hedge near to your right. At the water butt look up towards the hillfort on Hambledon Hill, its ramparts shaping the skyline.

At the road, go over the stone stile and immediately left up a deep, rutted track signed 'Bridleway'. Continue up the hill and, at the wood, take a path right into it. At the end of the wood, climb out over the metal bar fence and continue up the hill. The way becomes a track. As the path begins to level out, you can clearly see the ramparts of Iron Age Hambledon Hill hillfort to the left. The fort may be reached by climbing up to the left, and the effort will be rewarded with superb views. The hillfort encloses over 30 acres. It has double ramparts most of the way round, with extra defences to the south-east, and is thought to have been built in three phases over a number of centuries. Depressions in the ground may show where huts once stood. Also on this dramatically placed site are the remains of a much earlier Neolithic 'causewayed camp', with two long barrows thought to date from around 3000BC.

Return to the path. Cross the field to the right and go through a metal gate. Continue by the fence for about 50yds to a low stile (on the right), then go straight down the field with the hedge on your right, through a gate and down between the hedge and fence on to the road. Go left along the road, taking care, for about 200yds. Ahead on the skyline can be glimpsed a fine yew copse and the ramparts of Hod Hill, which has an Iron Age and Roman fort.

Turn right along the road marked No Through Road and Hanford Farm. Jacobean Hanford House (now a school) is on your left.

At the crossroads of tracks, turn right. Go across to a signed footpath between houses and gardens. At the end, go over a stile and right on to a gravel track through the gate and wood beyond. Half-way up the track, Little Hanford House is ahead on your left. Turn left through the gate and cross the field below the house, turning right around its grounds and keeping to the top of the field, until you come to a footpath sign by the red brick farmhouse. Turn left, going down and across to a metal gate in the corner of the field. Go left through the gate and immediately right into the lower field, keeping the fence to your right, past two water troughs.

Through the next gateway, walk left around the field to the River Stour and then right along the river to a metal footbridge. The Stour is wide and meandering here, and the bridge makes a pleasant place to pause.

Do not cross the bridge but cut across the field to a metal gate and then go diagonally left, over a stile and into a green lane. Turn left and then right into a field. Go straight across from the gateway to another stile on the far side of the field. Turn left into the green lane. At a T-junction by farm buildings, turn left and go along the lane, past bungalows, to the road. Turn right at the T-junction then left, to walk through the village and back to your car.

WALK 15

Capital of the Chase

Allow 2½ hours

A walk on Cranborne Chase, a hunting preserve since Saxon times.

Park your car in Tollard Royal (ST944178). The fine medieval King John's House, near the 14th-century church, was a hunting lodge used by King John.

Walk south through Tollard Royal past the Grundfos Well. 50yds past the well go left through a gate and up the track which forks off the road. At the brow, veer left over the hill, keeping the fence on your left. At the top, Rushmore Park comes into view.

Go on through a metal gate and down to Tinkley Bottom. Turn right to walk along the bottom of the valley, with Tollard Farm at the top of the hill on your right. Just before the main road, at a junction of tracks, turn left across the adjacent track and go diagonally left up the field following the route marked by a yellow arrow on the gate. Go over a stile at the top left of the field, again arrow-marked, and go towards the woods. South Lodge appears to your left. At the edge of the woods, go over the stile across the road and into the wood. Shortly at a junction of tracks, go right. Keep straight on the footpath, conifers on the left. The fence on your left is the perimeter of Rushmore Park. From 1880, this was the home of General Pitt-Rivers, the archaeological pioneer (see page 58).

Follow the fence as it eventually takes a sharp righthand turn. When you come to an open field on your left go through the gate with the yellow arrow and follow the path as it veers left. The woods on your left eventually give way to estate buildings. Go on along the edge of the field, through a metal gate and straight ahead on a track, keeping the parkland and then woods to your left – your way leads into a field. Cross the stile and follow the power lines, keeping to the left of the field. Through the gate by a cottage, turn immediately left into the woods along the left fork track.

Continue along the well-defined track and pass Bridmore Lodge on your left. Walk on up to the road at the handsome lodge gate house. Turn right on the road and, within 30yds, left over a stile. Go through the trees to the edge of the field, and turn left.

Walk around the field keeping the trees on your left. Continue on the track down the hill. When the track goes left through the fence, carry straight on, down to the corner of the field, over a stile and on steeply down into the valley keeping the fence to your left.

At the bottom turn left through a gate and continue straight on down. Go through the gate next to Munday's Pond. Start walking up the hill to the fence, where the power lines cross it. Go through the metal gate and follow the power lines to join a track at the top of the hill. Go through the gate at the end of a line of beech trees. Continue straight on, a fence to your right. Tollard Royal comes into view. At the bottom of the field, go through a small gate. The path veers left downhill. Walk down on to the road through a last metal gate, under a chestnut tree. Return to your car.

WALK 16

Coastal Heritage

Allow 2½ hours

This walk includes a section of the Dorset coast protected by the Heritage Coast Scheme. There is a steep climb up some steps, with rewarding views at the top. Please take care: the path goes very close to the cliff edge in places.

Park in the Worth Matravers car park near the Square and Compass Pub (SY974776). Turn right out of the car park and walk down through Worth Matravers keeping the duck pond on your left. The cottages are built of local Purbeck limestone. Much of the church dates from 1100.

Pass the church and then the children's play area on your right and go out along the road towards a farm silo. You can now see the sea on your left. Past Weston Farm, fork left, following the signpost indicating a footpath to St Aldhelm's Head 1½ miles. Shortly go right over a stile at a signpost indicating Chapman's Pool. Soon you cross another stile at a signpost to Renscombe, ¼ mile. As you walk straight ahead across the field, Renscombe Farm appears on the right. At the track, turn left where the milestone indicates St Aldhelm's Head 1½ miles.

You are now walking due south along a wide track towards the sea. Where a track goes off to the left (you keep straight on), you will see, on the hills over to the left, a good example of strip lynchets. These are the long, terraced banks on the contours of a hill, caused by ploughing.

Turn right on to a track at a sign indicating Pier Bottom and the coast path, ½ mile. Shortly after another track joins from the right, turn right, over a stile, into the field. Turn left and walk down into the valley. On your left is St Aldhelm's Head quarry. The south Purbeck Downs have been quarried since the 17th century. The limestone has been used for kerbs, headstones, flagstones, walls and buildings, notably Salisbury Cathedral.

Eventually you arrive at a step stile near the sea. Standing on the stile you have a magnificent view of the cliffs of the Kimmeridge Ledges.

Turn left to tackle the steps of the coastal path. Pause for rest and look back at the breathtaking scenery of the Dorset coast. At the top, you will see the mast of the coastguard station. Care must be taken here: you are very close to the cliff-edge. Next to the coastguard station is St Aldhelm's Chapel, about 350ft above sea level. It is a small Norman building possibly built as a chapel dedicated to St Aldhelm.

Continue along the coastal path, heading east. In front, you can see the coastal cliffs as far as Durlston Head. On your right you will see ruins of an RAF telecommunications station.

Follow the Coast Path sign to Winspit. Eventually the path turns left and inland to skirt an old quarry. Go around the northern edge of the quarry and turn left to walk up into Winspit Bottom. Where the path divides into two, bear right and follow the path through a field, over two stiles and into Worth Matravers. Bear right to return to the car park.

Index

Page numbers in bold type indicate main entries.

A

Abbotsbury **28**, 76, 79, 98
Alfred, King 6, 7, **29**, 73
Alton Barnes 109
American Museum in Britain **31**, 78, 105
Amesbury **28**
angling 75
archaeology **6-13**, 79
Arnolfini Gallery 78
Arthur, King **44**, 45, 60, 73
Assembly Rooms, Bath 78
Athelhampton **58**, 77, 98
Athelney **29**
Avebury 11, **29**, 57, 78, 79, 108
Avon Walkway 79
Avonmouth **29**
Axbridge 30

B

Badbury Rings **44**, 47, 79
Badminton **30**
Barbury Castle 79
Barnes, William 21, 43, 62, 114
barns 57
Barnton Farm 79
Barrington Court **46**, 77
basket making 25
Bath 13, **30**, 75, 78, 94
Bathampton 31
Battlesbury Camp 68
Beaminster **32**, 75, 77
Bere Regis **32**
Big Four Railways Museum 78
Blaise Hamlet **32**
Blandford Forum **32**
Blandford St Mary **32**
Bournemouth **33**, 75, 78
Bovington Camp and Tank Museum 67, 74, 78
Bowood House **37**, 77
Bradford-on-Avon **34**, 57, 77
Bratton Camp 79
Bridgwater **34**
Bridport **35**
Bristol **36**, 75, 78, 79, 94
British Encampment 79
Broad Chalke 100
Broadleas 77
Brown, Lancelot (Capability) **37**, 41, 49, 53
Brownsea Island 55
Brunel, Isambard Kingdom 63
Bruton **37**
Brympton d'Evercy 74, 77
Burnham-on-Sea **37**
Burrington Combe 103
Burrow Mump **29**, 96
Burrowbridge **29**

C

Cadbury Camp 102
Calne **37**, 77
Castle Cary **38**, 76
Castle Combe **38**
castles 76
caves 76
Cerne Abbas **38**, 57, 76, 79
Chard **38**
Cheddar 23, **39**, 76, 94
Cheddon Fitzpaine 76
cheese 23
Chesil Beach 28, 35, 56
Chewton Mendip 76
Child Okeford 115
Chippenham **40**, 77
Chipping Sodbury **40**, 77
Christchurch **40**
Cider 26, 76
Clapton Court Gardens 77
Clark, Cyrus and James 62
Claverton Manor 31, 78, 105
Clevedon **41**, 77
cloth industry **23**
Clouds Hill 67, 98
Coate Agricultural Museum 78
Corfe Castle **41**, 76, 98
Corsham **41**
Cotswold Water Park 79
country parks 79
crafts **22-26**, 75
Cranborne Chase 100, 116
Crewkerne **42**, 77
Cricket St Thomas **42**, 79
Crispin Hall 62
cycling 75

D

Desperate Remedies 21
Devizes **42**, 77
Dinosaur Museum 78
Dolebury Warren 79
Dorchester 19, **43**, 78, 79, 98
Dorset Coast Path 63, 112, 117
Dorset County Museum 78
Doulting 57
Dowlish Lake 76
Downside Abbey **52**, 106
Duke of Edinburgh's Royal Regiment Museum 78
Durleston 79
Dynasts, The 20
Dyrham Park **40**, 77

E

Easton 56
English Heritage 75
events 80
Evershot 21, 113
Eype 112

F

Far From the Madding Crowd 19, 21
Farleigh Hungerford 53, 76
Fleet Air Arm Museum **46**, 78
food and drink 76
Fortuneswell 56
fossils 48
Fovant 100
Fox Talbot Gallery of Photography 47, 78, 107
Fox Talbot, William Henry 47, 107
French Lieutenant's Woman, The 49
Frome **44**

G

gardens 76
Gillingham **44**
Glastonbury **44**, 45, 57, 78, 96
golf 75
Great Barn Museum of Wiltshire Folk Life 78
Great Chalfield Manor **34**
Great Hall of Winchester Castle 78
Great Western Railway 30, 63, 78
Great Western Railway Museum 78

H

Hadspen House Gardens 76
Hambledon Hill 115
Ham Hill Camp 79
Hand of Ethelberta, The 21
Hardy, Thomas **18-22**, 32, 43, 51, 74, 113, 114
Hardy's Cottage 77
Hestercombe House 65, 76
Higher Bockhampton **18**, 77
historic houses 77
Holbourne of Menstrie Museum 78
Holt **34**
Horton Court 77

I

Ilchester **46**
Ilminster **46**, 77
Industrial Museum, Bristol 78
information centres 75

J

Jude the Obscure 20, 21

K

Keiller, Alexander and museum 29, 78
Kennet and Avon Canal **31**, 54, 79, 105
Kimmeridge 41, 98
Kingston Lacy **46**, 77
Kingston Russell Stone Circle 79

L

Lacock **47**, 77, 78, 107
landscape gardens **53**
Langport **47**
Lawrence, T E (Lawrence of Arabia) 66, 67
Little Badminton **30**
Littlecote House 77
Lodmoor 71
Longleat **48**, 77, 79
Lower Woodford 110
Lulworth **49**, 98
Lyme Regis **49**
Lytes Cary **61**, 77

M

Madame Tussaud's, Wookey Hole 74, 76